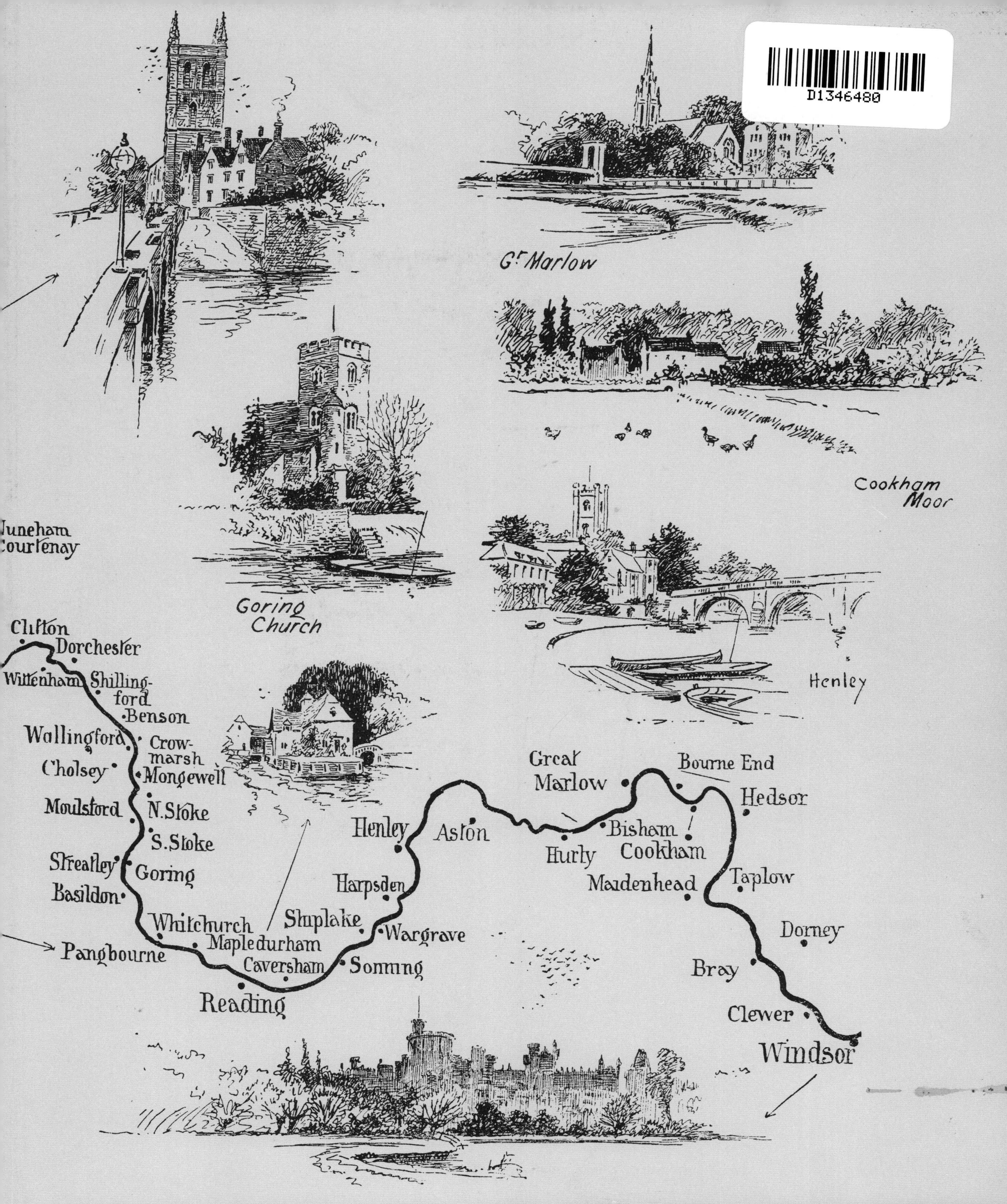

Gt Marlow
Cookham Moor
uneham
ourtenay
Goring Church
Henley
Clifton
Dorchester
Wittenham
Shilling-ford
Benson
Wallingford
Crow-marsh
Cholsey
Mongewell
Moulsford
N. Stoke
S. Stoke
Streatley
Goring
Basildon
Whitchurch
Pangbourne
Mapledurham
Caversham
Reading
Sonning
Shiplake
Wargrave
Harpsden
Henley
Aston
Hurly
Great Marlow
Bisham
Cookham
Bourne End
Hedsor
Maidenhead
Taplow
Dorney
Bray
Clewer
Windsor

FRANCES LINCOLN LIMITED
PUBLISHERS
www.franceslincoln.com

Contents

Foreword

Title page: Moorings by Swinford Bridge near Oxford at sunset.

Contents: A fog-shrouded sunrise at Newbridge.

The Thames is England's longest river, although the United Kingdom accolade goes to the Severn, which, at 220 miles from its source in Wales to the Bristol Channel, measures just 5 miles longer. If only the seemingly arbitrary lines traced across both estuaries could be manipulated slightly, one of Europe's most iconic waterways could be elevated to the top of the list.

I have encountered the River Thames countless times during decades spent travelling the length and breadth of England, but never really focused my camera on the river itself. I have crossed it countless times, photographed and written about places that happened to be in close proximity to it, but now feel that the balance should be redressed. Such a historic waterway deserves a book to itself, rather than simply featuring as a 'non-speaking, walk-on extra' in another production.

Many of the world's longest and most famous rivers have appropriately spectacular sources set high up amid mountains and glaciers but, in a typically English understated and almost apologetic fashion, the Thames starts its journey from a slightly damp patch in the middle of a Gloucestershire field. However, although its origin may be comparatively low-key and humble, the Thames gradually asserts itself upon the landscape, transforming from stream to fully fledged river by the many tributaries joining its course *en route* to the North Sea.

Although the narrative of my book flows in the same direction as the Thames, it is not necessarily intended as a detailed guide to the river, but rather as

a personal account of the landscape, towns and villages through which it flows. As such, I know full well that I will have omitted places deemed essential by some readers and included some locations that are not. The Thames now has its own officially designated National Trail long-distance footpath (The Thames Path), and there are guides and maps aplenty for those who wish to accompany the river along every one of its 184 miles to the Trail's ending at the Thames Barrier in Woolwich. However, my journey does not end abruptly in Woolwich but continues on until the river has become an estuary and the horizon filled by only sea and sky.

I have tried to compile a celebration of the Thames's imprint upon the landscape, and the historical and architectural legacies that linger in the hamlets, villages, towns and cities that grew up alongside its meandering course across southern England. Although this book will fit in neither pocket nor rucksack, I have still tried to retain an element of 'guide book' to help orientate both walkers and motorists. First-time visitors to an area will naturally be unfamiliar with the local road network so I have tried to offer some guidance that might be later cross referenced on the reader's own maps or navigation system. By unashamedly leapfrogging the inevitable bland and dreary stretches, I have attempted to distil the river's very essence into a portfolio of photographs and accompanying text that do full justice to one of the world's most iconic rivers.

Derry Brabbs (Spring 2010)

Swinford Bridge, Eynsham.

CHAPTER ONE

A River is Born
From the Source to Lechlade

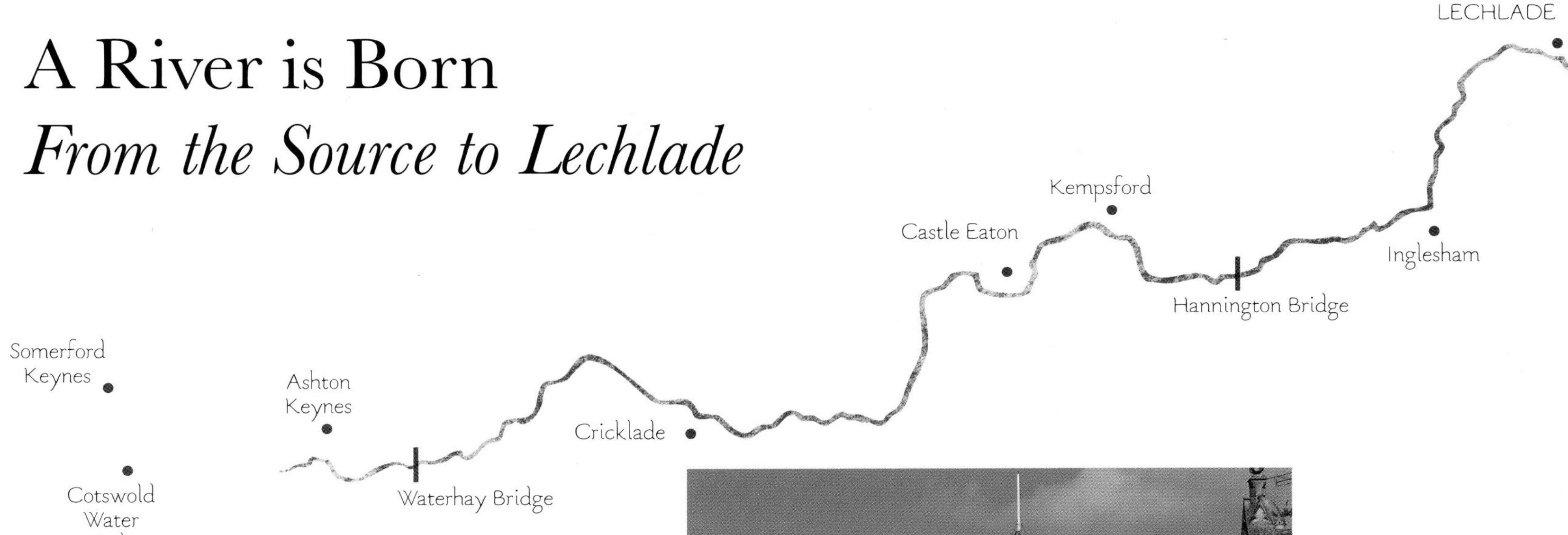

Intrepid explorers seeking the source of the River Thames will patently have no need to emulate their Victorian predecessors by traversing hostile mountain ranges or hacking through vast tracts of dense, malarial jungle. However, tracking down the birthplace of England's longest river is not without a slight element of risk, as one has to survive a brief, but potentially hazardous encounter with the Fosse Way, one of the most famous Roman Roads in Britain. The river's source lies just a few miles to the south-west of Cirencester, established originally by the Romans as Corinium and regarded as one of the most important settlements within the Empire's island outpost of Britannia.

The course of the Fosse Way is now occupied by the A433, which, in typical Roman fashion, runs straight as an arrow past the fields leading to the source of the Thames. As there are no dedicated roadside footpaths at this point, pedestrians do need to keep a wary eye upon the fast-moving traffic, as twenty-first-century cars and lorries move considerably faster than a horse-drawn chariot. A clearly marked footpath passes through a couple of fields before petering out in the vicinity of a shallow depression shaded by an ancient ash tree. Prior to 1974, anyone seeking the river's source would have been left in no doubt that their objective had been achieved, as the site was graced by a large, 3-ton stone statue of 'Old Father Thames' surrounded by protective iron railings. Sadly, even those metal barriers offered scant protection against the mindless morons who delight in defacing and vandalizing such artworks, and so he was relocated to the safer haven of St John's lock, just a few hundred metres downstream from Lechlade. The old boy will therefore feature in the next stage of the journey, rather than in his rightful place at the river's source.

When one considers the history, art, literature and architectural grandeur associated with the Thames, its emergence into the world is a disappointingly low-key affair. Thames Head lies within Trewsbury Mead, a network of cattle-grazed pastures flanked on either side by man-made embankments; one carrying the First Great Western railway and the other marking the course of the now defunct Thames & Severn Canal. In fact, the river's birthplace is so unremarkable that for much of the year, its life-giving subterranean spring seems incapable of generating sufficient power to propel its waters up to ground level. Indeed, were it not for an inscribed marker stone set alongside the ash tree, whose bark has also been inscribed with the letters T.H. for 'Thames Head', the majority of visitors would be none the wiser.

During my most recent trip to the site, I observed a quartet of foreign tourists clutching guidebooks and maps, but patently nonplussed by the total absence of water.

Opposite: The infant Thames swirls gently into Ashton Keynes alongside the mellow stone cottages lining Church Walk.

Above: Cirencester is the nearest town to the source of the Thames, its market place dominated by the imposing Perpendicular tower and elaborately decorated south porch of St John the Baptist.

Maps were turned upside down and rechecked, the immediate vicinity scoured for additional proof, all accompanied by much gesticulation and shoulder shrugging. However, having finally accepted that the faded stone was undoubtedly the source of the Thames, photographs were duly taken and the somewhat disgruntled party shuffled back to their rental car. It was sad to see them drive off, because had they persevered across the other side of the Fosse Way, significantly more tangible evidence of a fledgling river would have been encountered. A roadside stile and signpost bearing the distinctive acorn symbol of a National Trail indicate that the Thames Path continues through a large meadow, across which snakes the distinctive outline of a watercourse.

Although quite obviously a water-carrying channel marked by long, verdant grass, the Thames still makes only occasional post-English-monsoon appearances here, and it is not until after another 200 metres or so that the river becomes a reality near an ancient spring known as Lyd Well. Clear water bubbles through rectangular culverts at the base of a retaining stone wall, and although the stream becomes almost immediately enveloped by dense weeds and grasses, its banks trampled into a muddy morass by thirsty livestock, the embryo Thames is finally born and on its way to the North Sea. There can actually be no definitive word on where and when the river's water actually breaks the surface, as that is entirely dependent on the season and general level of the water table beneath ground, but the area around the Lyd Spring wall is a reasonably consistent yardstick.

Having emerged from those wooded and claustrophobic environs, the stream flows briefly through a stretch of open meadow, a scene that evokes distant memories of childhood. Long, summer days when you were packed off down to the local stream with a packet of sandwiches, a bottle of fizzy dandelion and burdock, a bamboo-cane fishing net and string-tied jam jar. Dense beds of brightly flowered river water-crowfoot provided perfect hiding places for tiny river fishes such as minnows and sticklebacks, but any hapless specimens that ventured out into open water quickly found themselves ensnared in a pink nylon envelope and plopped into the gleaming jar. The basic instinct of hunter-gathering was obviously already lodged in our young psyches but the concept of animal cruelty had not yet been instilled, so the day's wriggling catch were proudly transported home and having been politely declined as potential supper ingredients, were usually placed on a window ledge to await repatriation the following day.

The path here is doubly trod, due to the fact that the majority of those intent on completing the National Trail footpath from the river's source to the Thames Barrier will most likely have arrived by train at nearby Kemble

The official source of the Tiver Thames is marked by a commemorative stone erected by the Thames Conservators, an ancient ash tree and a spring that seldom generates water above ground.

Left: A swathe of luxuriant grass and the slight indentation of a channel mark the course of the Thames near its source, although it remains largely below ground at this point unless there has been a very wet spell.

Overleaf: Just a few metres downstream from Lyd Well, the Thames has already carved out a significant course through the meadows near Kemble.

Right: The river finally emerges as a tangible water course near Lyd Well.

Below: Narrow country lanes mirror the twisting course of the Thames as it weaves around the villages of Ewen and Kemble.

station, and although it would be the easiest thing in the world simply to pick up the path at the nearest point, it would rather defeat the object of the entire expedition.

The riverside path actually bypasses Kemble and while the village with its Early English church is the kind of place one could happily potter around for a while, it is just far too early in the journey to be distracted by minor diversions. A similar comment could also apply to the next rural community of Ewen, although it might be slightly more difficult to force oneself past The Wild Duck Inn should the door just happen to be slightly ajar. One of the more noteworthy features of the river's first few miles is just how many mills there were operating here at one time. Of course, they are largely now remembered in name only, but it is surprising to realize that even this far upstream, sufficient water power could be harnessed to power the heavy millstones. From Ewen *en route* to the next settlement of Somerford Keynes, the river flows past three such examples – Upper and Lower Mill Farm and Kemble Mill – although curiously, the latter is actually the furthest away from the village with which it is associated.

The landscape around Kemble Mill marks the start of a quite surreal segment of the journey where the Thames and its attendant footpath become almost literally swamped by the watery expanses of the Cotswold Water Park. This network of around 140 lakes is the result of protracted gravel extraction within an area extending to more than 40 square miles. However, what could have been a desolate industrial wasteland has been transformed into centres for water-based sport and leisure activities, fishing lakes, wildlife reserves and general recreational areas. Although the regeneration of this vast site is to be welcomed, one cannot help thinking that it might have been better if such mass desecration of the landscape had not occurred in the first place.

Unfortunately, roads and other building projects constructed with concrete need gravel, and so mineral extraction companies will need to keep scooping out tracts of irreplaceable land. In fairness, it has to be said that the industry is obliged to pay a levy to the government, the funds from which are then made available as monetary

Because the Thames at Ashton Keynes flows parallel to High Road, many houses have their own stone pedestrian bridges.

grants for specific restoration and community-based projects within extraction areas such as the Cotswolds Water Park. Despite my personal misgivings about the plundering of unspoilt countryside in pursuit of raw materials, one does have to be reluctantly pragmatic about such matters. It comes down to the good old omelette-and-egg scenario – you can't have one without breaking the other. During the production of this book, I made numerous trips from North Yorkshire to the River Thames, driving along roads that could well have been laid using Cotswold gravel.

Of course it is good that people have access to sport and leisure centres, and that comparatively rare flora and fauna now have the opportunity to thrive in ideal habitats, but I can't help wondering that if we actually really cared that much, appropriate sites would have been created anyway.

It is quite remarkable that the infant river retains its identity amid so many sheets of placid water, but the Thames resolutely gurgles its way between the old gravel workings in search of a green, tree-lined meadow. A clue that an oasis of solid ground may not be too far away is provided by occasional glimpses of Ashton Keynes' church tower. The parish church, dedicated to the Holy Cross, is one of the most westerly buildings in the village and consequently almost the first to be encountered by walkers on the Thames Path. This approach along Church Walk to the village centre is one of the most enchanting along the Thames, the river at this point being just a few feet wide and passing directly in front of elegant Cotswold stone houses. The river temporarily divides here, with the larger stream veering right to run parallel with High Road, the main thoroughfare in Ashton Keynes.

The village is actually graced by four ancient crosses, an indication that this was perhaps once a place of greater commercial activity and stature than the more tranquil twenty-first-century community that exists today. That same conclusion was drawn during the 1820s by writer and radical political commentator, William Cobbett, while touring the country collecting material for a commentary on the state of early-nineteenth-century England, published under the title of *Rural Rides*. He wrote:

> It is now a straggling village; but, to a certainty, it has been a large market town. There is a market-cross still standing in an open place in it; and there are such numerous lanes, crossing each other, and cutting the land up into such little bits, that it must, at one time, have been a large town. It is a very curious place.

One of the many flooded gravel pits that now comprise the Cotswold Water Park, a vast area providing outdoor leisure activities and important wildlife habitats.

That writer's reference to Ashton Keynes being 'curious' should probably be more accurately replaced by the word 'intriguing', as it is different from most villages: numerous houses along the main street are separated from the road by the Thames and consequently, each has its own small access bridge. The scene may look timelessly enchanting to the casual visitor, but past occupants of those riverside dwellings have had more than their fair share of unwanted Thames water flowing unfettered through their ground-floor rooms. Modern flood management schemes have obviously reduced such risk significantly, but in the current state of climate and weather deviations from the norm, people living by rivers (no matter how small), should perhaps have to learn to expect the unexpected.

Upon departure from Ashton Keynes, walkers will find that there are some places where the river and National Trail path chart slightly different courses around another series of flooded gravel pits and, after prolonged spells of rain, the path-bearing strips of land can become almost enveloped by rising water and tricky to negotiate without getting extremely soggy feet.

The Cotswold Water Park is the generic name for the whole area, but within that umbrella title are numerous smaller parks and nature reserves with dedicated parking and information boards for visitors. One such site is located at Waterhay Bridge, an unremarkable river crossing over the Thames close to the farm settlement that gave its name to the bridge. Here the customary marked paths around flooded workings can be found, each of which varies slightly in terms of surrounding vegetation and therefore the species of wildlife that flourish in such varied habitats. However, the most engaging sight in this location has neither fur nor feathers and is set amid low-lying pastures a little to the south of the river. Just a little way past the Waterhay Farm complex, a roadside 'church' sign points down a bridle track leading to the truncated, but perfectly preserved segment of a medieval church.

All Saints' Old Chancel is the remaining part of a medieval parish church that was dismantled in 1896 and relocated closer to the community of Leigh it had served for centuries. In that exciting era of discovery, exploration and innovation, few logistical problems

Below: The curiously truncated and heavily buttressed All Saints' Old Chancel stands isolated in fields near Waterhay Bridge, with just a scattering of gravestones for company.

Opposite: The movingly simple interior of the chancel is enriched by eighteenth-century texts from Genesis, Isaiah and St Matthew painted on the walls. Leigh Chancel stands as an enduring testament to the priceless work of the Churches Conservation Trust.

seemed to particularly daunt or faze the Victorians, and so the nave, tower and south porch of that dilapidated and largely abandoned place of worship were taken down and rebuilt with a larger chancel on a roadside site next to the village school. The surviving chancel was consolidated into a viable building and was apparently still used for occasional worship.

However, the chancel church was eventually declared redundant, but rather than being left to crumble into ruin, it was placed into the care of the Churches Conservation Trust in 1978. The Trust is a national charity caring for over 340 of England's finest historic churches no longer required or viable for regular parish worship, and without its invaluable but largely unsung works of conservation, many priceless parts of our architectural and religious heritage would now be reduced to little more than atmospheric piles of rubble. The small collection of furnishings left in the chancel are either surviving items from the original nave, or have been reconstituted from discarded panelling and other timber fragments from the dismantling. It really is incongruous but endearing to see the original, delicate chancel shored up by a solid gable end and flanking buttresses set amid a random scattering of headstones.

As a visit to Leigh Chancel represents a minor detour for anyone following the river, steps must be retraced back in the direction of Waterhay Bridge and the car park. Motorists have an easy run along a couple of minor roads through to Cricklade; Thames Path walkers are directed back to another gravel pit complex, of which Manorbrook Lake is the largest. This is just one of several fishing lakes controlled by a local angling club and, through a combination of nutrient-rich waters and careful management, the lake has established a reputation as being a prime location where fishermen can do battle with carp and pike, some of which can weigh up to 30 pounds. Most anglers still appear to record (and boast about) their catches in imperial weights rather than the metric equivalent; possibly because the above-mentioned fish would register as a less impressive-sounding 13 kilograms.

Although Ordnance Survey maps are usually regarded as being an essential item in a walker's kit, my experience is that they can also enrich the exploration of new territory, whether used for route finding or not. The ancient Saxon word *burh* (fortified town) of Cricklade is a

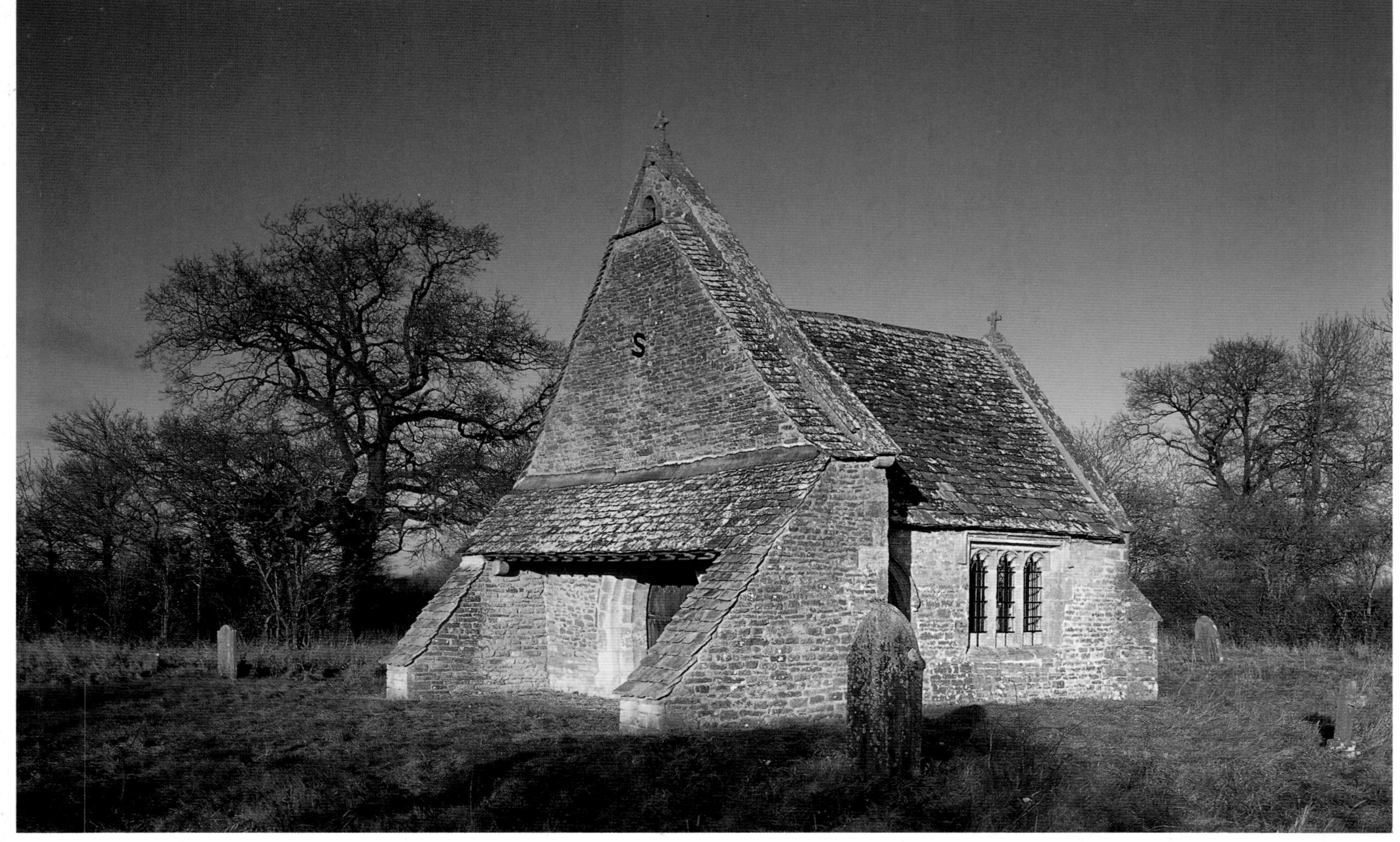

Left: Cricklade's ornate clock tower was erected to celebrate Queen Victoria's Diamond Jubilee in 1897. It stands outside The Vale Hotel on the site originally occupied by the town's fourteenth-century cross.

Below and opposite:
The imposing tower of St Sampson's, Cricklade, is remarkable in both size and design. The distinctive pinnacles and blind arcading on the upper tower and its turrets adds another dimension to the lexicon of church construction. The tower's interior is no less impressive and one can only marvel at the artistry, skill and bravery of the masons who built it.

good example; the detailed aerial perspective provided by an Ordnance Survey clearly shows the course and scope of the original pre-Conquest town walls established by King Alfred the Great. Some of the place names one sees on such a map will never feature on a road signpost, but form an integral part of a particular place's identity and evolution. Horsey Hill, Weavers Bridge, Forty Acre, Common Hill and the bleak-sounding Hailstone Hill are just some of the landmarks with a foot in the past on the present-day landscape.

Prior to its arrival at the foot of Cricklade's long, sloping High Street, the Thames Path passes through North Meadow, a vast ancient hay meadow extending to over 100 acres and one of the region's most important nature reserves. It is home to around 80 per cent of the nation's population of snakeshead fritillary, an increasingly rare flower whose habitats are predominately concentrated around the floodplains and riverside meadows of Oxfordshire. The approach to Cricklade also coincides with the line of the original Saxon *burh's* north wall, commemorated by a local street of the same name that carries the final few metres of the path along its tarmac surface to join the High Street near Town Bridge. The retrospective view up the town's main thoroughfare is one replicated in many similar small market towns up the length and breadth of England, comprising an aesthetically pleasing blend of seventeenth- and eighteenth-century buildings set against the backdrop of a church spire or tower.

Cricklade has been particularly well endowed in that respect, as the massive, richly pinnacled Tudor tower of St Sampson's Church dominates the town and surrounding countryside. The tower was completed around 1553, its construction being attributed to John Dudley, the 1st Duke of Northumberland, but it seems unlikely that he lived long enough to witness the outcome of such altruism due to an unfortunate encounter with an executioner's axe at the Tower of London in that same year, having been found guilty of High Treason. The church itself has details of every century from the twelfth to the sixteenth, but perhaps the most intriguing thing is its dedication to a little-known sixth-century Celtic saint of Welsh origin who went on to become one of the seven missionaries responsible for the Christianization of Brittany.

When the Roman legions spread westwards along the Thames, they would have found a settlement of the ancient Dobunni tribe already established at a crossing point of the river. As the Romans advanced and consolidated their newly gained territory within the province of their empire, named Britannia, they laid

down an extensive network of roads to connect major military and trading centres. Cricklade stood on Ermin Street – an important road that ran from Gloucester via Cirencester to Silchester (a Roman town located between modern-day Reading and Basingstoke) and whose arrow-straight course is now occupied along some of its length by the A419 trunk road. This Ermin Street (without an 'e') is easily and frequently confused with the even more famous Ermine Street, the latter being the great highway linking London with York.

Cricklade achieved greater importance in Saxon times as one of the main fortified frontier towns of Wessex, a status reflected in the fact that it once housed its own mint. So much of our knowledge of English and World history relies on contemporary printed accounts of personalities and events, but how much accuracy and detail has been 'lost in translation'? The famous Anglo Saxon Chronicles are an invaluable source of information about life in Britain from the late-ninth century onwards, but even the best scholars know that taking every passage at face value is potentially risky in terms of historical accuracy.

The entry covering 1016 states that 'King Knute [Canute] came with a marine force of one hundred and sixty ships over the Thames into Mercia at Cricklade'. Anyone standing on Town Bridge looking down at the shallow trickling stream might raise a questioning eyebrow at its ability to have ever carried a sailing ship, as even flat-bottomed craft such as punts or kayaks barely have sufficient draught to negotiate this stretch of the Thames. A flotilla of poohsticks could perhaps safely navigate their way downstream, but certainly not vessels of the size necessary to have previously crossed the North Sea!

On the eastern outskirts of Cricklade, the Thames becomes a little more clearly defined when its waters are swollen by the Churn, the river whose source at Seven Springs was once advocated as the official source of the Thames, rather than of one of its tributaries. For the rest of its journey through to Lechlade, the river charts a twisting and meandering course of pastoral isolation through a series of expansive meadows. This is pure farmland with few existing public rights of way, and a riverside path has been specially constructed to facilitate the progress of the Thames Footpath towards the settlement of Castle Eaton. The name Eaton is derived from the Saxon *ea-tun*, meaning riverside homestead, and although the village now comprises quite a few 'homesteads', there are absolutely no remnants of a castle.

The Thames in winter from Castle Eaton Bridge.

Right: The church of St Mary, Castle Eaton, is memorable for its unusual bell turret, but opinion is divided as to whether it was added by the Victorian restorer, William Butterfield, or is of greater antiquity. However, the church does possess two fine Norman doors and exquisitely carved wood panelling around the Elizabethan pulpit.

Opposite: Kempsford's church tower is as impressive in close-up as when first glimpsed from the Thames Path. The lierne-vaulted roof beneath the tower is fifteenth-century and adorned with coats of arms and a circle of Lancastrian red roses in celebration of John of Gaunt, 1st Duke of Lancaster.

The only two buildings worthy of particular note in Castle Eaton are unsurprisingly The Red Lion pub and St Mary's Church. The former is a substantial Georgian house that will be a welcome sight to walkers in need of a pit stop, the latter offering refreshment of a less tangible nature, which may not have the immediacy of a pint and a pie. St Mary's has Norman origins and a late-thirteenth-century chancel, but its more prominent features of a spire and small, corbelled bell-turret were added by William Butterfield (1814–1900) during his 'restoration' of 1860.

For much of the remainder of this first stage, the Thames and its attendant footpath are barely on speaking terms until a welcome reconciliation on the final approach to Lechlade. It is a pity that the Thames Path does not accompany the river to Kempsford but, as a place steeped in history, it is certainly worth a detour for walkers with time to spare and strength in their legs. However, its magnificent church tower can still be admired from afar without the need for excessive calorie burning; motorists have no such dilemmas to face, as the road onwards from Cricklade to Lechlade passes through the village centre anyway.

As its name suggests, Kempsford was an important strategic crossing point on a stretch of river that marks the boundary between Gloucestershire and Wiltshire. There was certainly a ford based upon a solid bed of gravel, but even using that was potentially fraught with danger, as the solid footing did not go in a straight line from bank to bank. It required special local knowledge to navigate a safe passage, a fact discovered all too late by many individuals or warring parties intent on sacking the castle that once guarded Kempsford and the river crossing. The recently expanded village may now be the domain of commuters, but it will be forever associated with the legendary fourteenth-century figure, John of Gaunt.

John of Gaunt (1340–99) was the third surviving son of Edward III, one of medieval England's most influential and successful rulers. His marriage to Philippa of Hainault produced an astounding twelve offspring, of whom nine survived through to adulthood. The dynasties subsequently created by four of his male heirs had a profound effect on the nation's history, with events such as the Wars of the Roses being fought between different factions of his descendants. John of Gaunt's own contribution to England's historical jigsaw was significant, not only during his own lifetime through his influence on the English throne during the minority reign of his nephew, Richard II, but particularly through his male heirs from three marriages.

Gaunt's association with Kempsford stems from his marriage in 1359 to Blanche of Lancaster, the daughter of Henry of Grosmont, 1st Duke of Lancaster, whose father had earlier acquired the manor of Kempsford. As Blanche's father had died without issue, John of Gaunt inherited the Earldom of Lancaster, other titles and vast estates through marriage, thereby rendering him one of the wealthiest and most powerful men in the land. Their only son to survive past infancy was Henry, who subsequently headed the House of Lancaster and was crowned Henry IV after a series of complex plotlines that any current television soap writer would have given his right arm to have created. (In fact, the plot did indeed thicken considerably later in Gaunt's life, when producing four children by his mistress, later wife, Kathryn Swinford. They were given the family name of Beaufort and, through their son John, became ancestral founders of the mighty Tudor dynasty. He was the grandfather of Margaret Beaufort, whose son, Henry Tudor, won the English crown from Richard III at the Battle of Bosworth in 1485.)

Blanche tragically succumbed to bubonic plague and died in 1369 after just ten years of marriage, and the magnificent tower of Kempsford's church was built by John of Gaunt to honour her memory. Parish records appear to indicate that at least one family in the village is directly descended from the masons who worked on the

tower during the last decade of the fourteenth century. It is somewhat disappointing that St Mary the Virgin's interior does not quite match up to its exterior splendour, largely due to the lofty space being darkened by rather overbearing, Victorian stained-glass windows and tessellated tiles. Nevertheless, it is extraordinary to think that the church tower of an ostensibly unremarkable rural village can be considered an integral part of England's royal heritage.

However, the church was not the only tangible tribute to Blanche of Lancaster created after her death; she had been patroness to the poet and writer Geoffrey Chaucer, and one of his most notable early works, *The Book of the Duchess*, was considered to be an elegy to Blanche, although historians are not entirely sure whether it was written of his own volition as a personal tribute or directly commissioned by John of Gaunt.

Hopefully not too overburdened by the sheer weight of centuries of history, walkers must retrace their steps to Hannington Bridge and, having crossed the river towards Bridge Farm, temporarily bid farewell to the Thames in favour of a long-established bridle path leading to Inglesham. The track's surface is sufficiently well surfaced to enable you to stride out at a good pace, and the rich array of flowers, foliage and bird life inhabiting the accompanying hedgerow considerably enhances the pleasure of the walk. There can be a faint but irritatingly persistent drone of traffic borne on the breeze to intrude upon the silence as the track progresses, but certainly no sound of running water, as the Thames is two fields or more away and will not be encountered again until the Thames Path and river are united past Inglesham. From that point onwards to the National Trail's conclusion at the Thames Barrier, there are comparatively few instances when the footpath deviates away from whichever side of the riverbank it happens to be following at any given time.

The bridle path comes to an abrupt and definitely unwelcome end at Upper Inglesham because there follows a section along a busy main road, the A361 linking Lechlade and Swindon. Fortunately, provision has been made for walkers along one of the grass verges, which is just as well, for drivers here 'take no prisoners'. Calm and sanity is soon restored via a narrow lane leading back to the river and one of the journey's most unexpected treasures – the church of St John the Baptist at Inglesham. A small cluster of buildings surround the diminutive church of golden grey Cotswold stone, whose exterior comprises a hotchpotch of styles and repairs from several centuries. But it is the interior that really commands attention.

The hedgerows and verges of the footpaths and bridle tracks that comprise the Thames Path are transformed into a palette of vibrant colours in springtime. Although far too many English hedgerows have been lost to agriculture, those *en route* to Inglesham are still laden with wild flowers such as wild comfrey (above) and various shades of hawthorn (below).

Left: The tiny church of St John the Baptist at Inglesham may no longer have a congregation but it is still lovingly maintained by volunteers under the auspices of the Churches Conservation Trust.

Below: Inglesham was one of the first projects undertaken by William Morris's Society for the Preservation of Ancient Buildings, and although there appear to be few surviving right angles or vertical lines present, had it not been for SPAB's intervention, it would have simply crumbled to rubble.

Inglesham's interior has probably changed little since Cromwell's time and is therefore a most unusual survivor. Some of the wood screens date from the late-fifteenth or early-sixteenth century and the floors are equally old and uneven.

Inglesham is now in the care of the Churches Conservation Trust, but fortuitously had originally come to the attention of a much older conservation body, the Society for the Protection of Ancient Buildings (SPAB), founded in 1877 by William Morris who by then was living at nearby Kelmscott Manor (see page 70). In founding the society, Morris was belatedly attempting to arrest what he perceived as the architectural vandalism inflicted on churches and other medieval building by over-zealous and insensitive Victorian architects. It may sound like a cliché, but walking though the door on Inglesham church really is akin to stepping back in time. Despite a wall display of the Hanovarian Arms and some nineteenth-century texts, the pulpit and many of the pews are from the Jacobean era, but the wooden fittings of greatest antiquity are the late-fifteenth-century aisle screens.

The quantity of wall paintings is substantial, and upon closer inspection of some examples, it can be clearly seen that considerable over-painting has occurred on the original medieval versions. It seems somehow illogical that an artist should attempt his own work on a wall without first obliterating that which already existed but

Above: Many of the medieval wall paintings have been stabilized using modern techniques, their decay arrested and where possible have been gradually revealed.

Left: A Saxon relief carving of the Virgin and Child blessed by the hand of God was rescued from the exterior south wall in 1910 where it had served as a sundial.

that certainly seems to be the case. Precise interpretation of each tableau is consequently quite difficult but there are individual portraits of angels, a clearly discernable 'doom' painting and other less obvious subjects.

Inglesham is an interesting, if perhaps extreme, example of the conundrum facing those charged with the restoration or ongoing preservation of ancient buildings. Morris's opinion was that medieval buildings should be stabilized via effective roof repairs using materials appropriate to that particular structure and their interiors repaired where necessary, but with such a light touch that the presence of the restorer would be barely discernible. In many cases, that would mean buildings such as churches, not necessarily being viable for ongoing use, and if such cases arose, he suggested that it would be better to raise a new one 'fit for purpose' while retaining the original as a monument to a bygone age. The society still plays a vital and active role in the conservation of ancient buildings: advising, educating and campaigning to ensure that our priceless built heritage survives intact for the pleasure and enlightenment of future generations.

It is just a short stroll across a meadow to rejoin the narrow, shallow Thames and its reed-lined banks, and although the elegant spire of Lechlade's parish church of St Lawrence appears as an increasingly prominent landmark ahead, the intervening stretch of river is still laden with considerable interest. Although much overgrown with foliage and a dense curtain of weeping willows obscuring much of the detail, the far bank is the location for the confluence of the River Coln and the final (or first) lock of the long-abandoned Thames & Severn Canal. Tangible evidence of the latter's presence is marked by a curious round building that originally served as the lock keeper's dwelling. Round houses such as this were quite commonplace on the nation's canal network, their external appearance resembling a cross between a truncated lighthouse and a fortified tower with lancet windows. The majority of the round houses were built with inverted roofs to act as a rain trap and to provide fresh drinking water for the occupants. William Cobbet's seemingly circuitous ride around the region during the early nineteenth century brought him in a roundabout kind of way from Ashton Keynes to the canal at Inglesham, and its presence elicited a fairly pithy comment on the incursion of the Industrial Revolution into the countryside in his essay. 'Is this an "improvement"? Is a nation richer for the carrying away of the food from those who raise it, and giving it to bayonet men and others, who are assembled in great masses? . . . It is eaten, for the main part, by those who do not work.' Based upon those heartfelt comments, one

Left: The distinctive outline of Inglesham Roundhouse once stood alone like a fortified tower but is now flanked by later additions and a dense growth of trees. These buildings were once commonplace on England's canal network and served as dwellings for the lengthsmen (workers responsible for the maintenance of a section of canal).

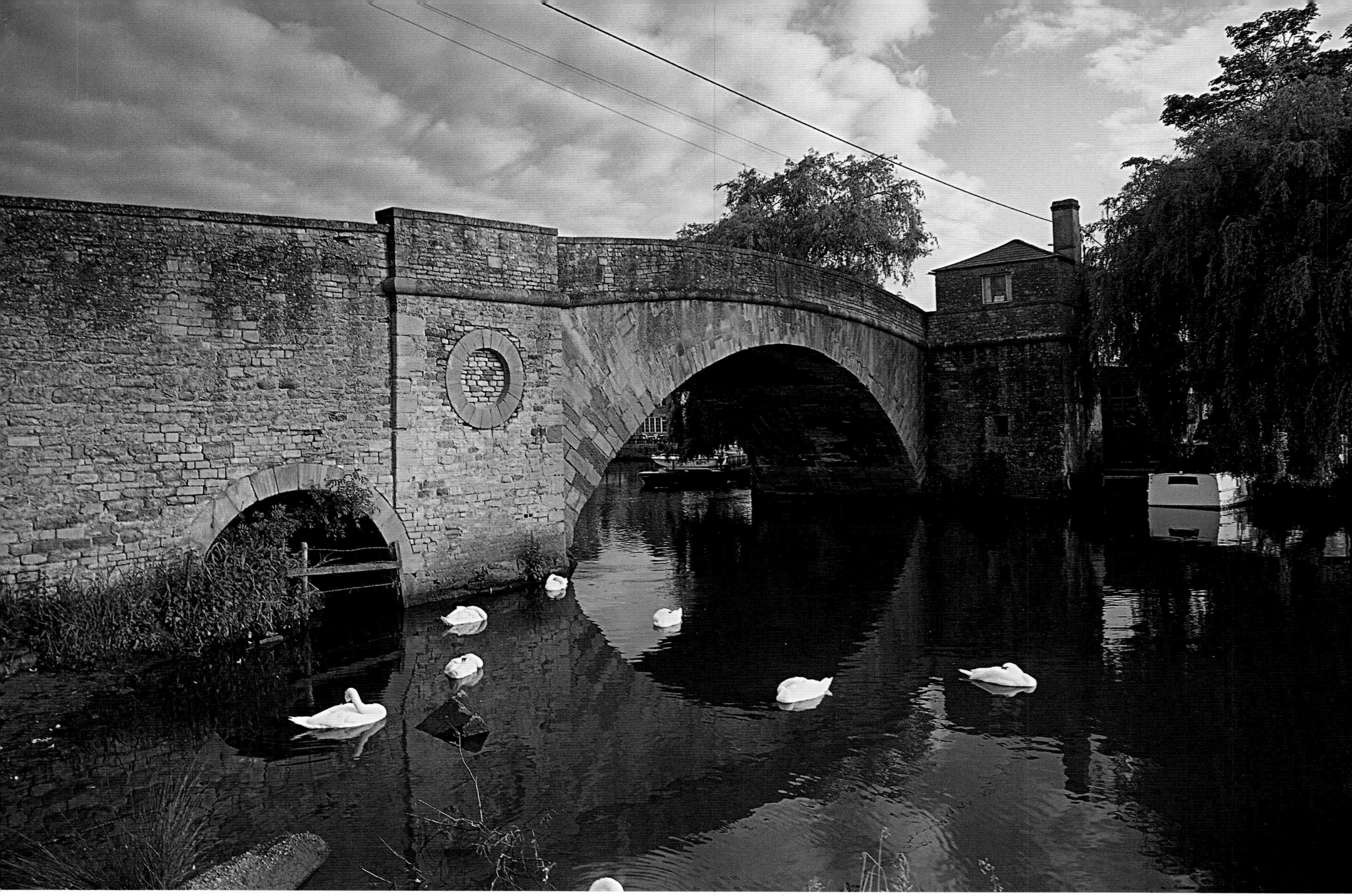

The distinctive bow-backed outline of the late-eigheenth-century Halfpenny Bridge at Lechlade marks the start of the navigable Thames. The toll-keeper's cottage has been a private dwelling since rendered redundant 1839 when all tolls were abolished.

suspects that Mr Cobbett might have an apoplectic fit if he were to discover how the global distribution of food works in the twenty-first century.

A wooden footbridge allows access to the place where the Coln enters the Thames, but there is no public right of way to the now privately owned Round House. While crossing the final few fields *en route* to Lechlade, the first of countless motor launches may be seen moored along the river bank. Despite navigation rights actually beginning at Cricklade, and the river's volume noticeably increased by the Coln's contribution, this is the furthest upstream that even the smallest powered craft can tentatively venture without the risk of mishap. However, that situation changes markedly as one draws even nearer to Lechlade, where a fully equipped marina of up to 100 berths can be seen tucked away behind the opposite bank. What is now a flourishing leisure facility utilizes the wharves that made the town into an important trading and commercial centre.

Lechlade originally thrived on the wool trade due to its close proximity to the renowned sheep-rearing hills and valleys of the Cotswolds and also having a direct river link to London via the Thames. As with so many other 'wool' towns in rural England, the wealth generated by that trade is manifested in the opulence of the parish churches, built with earthly profits in the hope of a sound investment for a secure heavenly future. Cotswold limestone has always been a highly prized building material and that too would have been one of Lechlade's more lucrative cargoes. Although St Paul's Cathedral in London was constructed predominately with gleaming white Portland stone, the accounts tendered by its architect, Sir Christopher Wren show that 25,000 tonnes of other stone was used and a sizeable proportion of that quantity would have been shipped down river on heavily laden barges.

The digging and inauguration of the Thames & Severn Canal in 1789 was expected to open a new chapter in Lechlade's prosperity, but although appearing as a sound proposition on paper, the great economic boom never really materialized. Those approaching Lechlade by road from the south will cross the Thames via Halfpenny Bridge, a sturdy humpback stone bridge with a toll house at one end. The bridge replaced an existing ferry and was completed in 1792 to accommodate the voluminous traffic expected as a result of the canal's presence. The bridge is so named because a halfpenny was the toll charged for each person, but anyone driving cattle across would expect to pay one penny per head. Modern-day motorists can rest easy at their wheels without fumbling for loose change, as the toll ceased operation in 1839.

Lechlade was also an important staging post for coaches on the road to Bristol and the West, and that era is reflected in some of the Georgian houses grouped around the market place. Old coaching inns such as The New Inn and The Crown Inn still provide hospitality for travellers and for those who like English beer at its traditional best. The latter has now established its own micro-brewery, the Halfpenny Brewery. Although the town makes an excellent base from which to explore the southern Cotswolds, those intent on following the Thames would be well advised not to get too comfortably settled as there are many miles still to travel.

Lechlade's position on the Thames enabled it to thrive for centuries as an inland port, prospering initially from the medieval Cotswold wool trade. Many of the town's older buildings flank its large market place where the historic coaching inns now cater for tourists rather than merchants and bargees.

Substantial Georgian houses of Cotswold stone clustered around the east end of Lechlade's market place near the parish church of St Lawrence, reflect the town's past commercial stature.

CHAPTER TWO

Rivers, Streams & Canals
Tributaries of the Thames

In common with most major rivers, the Thames would probably be little more than a paltry stream if it had to rely solely on the output of Lyd Well and the other springs comprising its source. So it depends on the many tributaries that sacrifice their own identities to its swell as it flows eastwards to London and the sea. When the Thames's catchment area is viewed on a map stripped of all other detail except the courses of streams and rivers, it resembles the skeletal veins of a back-lit leaf whose stalk is represented by the estuary.

Although water's chemical balance varies according to the kind of rock or terrain it emanates from or flows over, as a pure entity it has no real character of its own, relying instead on its immediate surroundings to endow it with different characteristics. Some tributaries are just streams, performing no other function than draining the land; others are larger rivers and watercourses that have played their own significant roles in the settlement, economy and history of the region. Canals deliver no water and therefore do not contribute to the physical stature of the Thames, but as man-made arteries of trade, commerce and communication, they are as much the river's lifeblood as the natural streams and rivers that combine to create one of Europe's most iconic rivers.

The tributaries of the Thames are sufficiently numerous to fill a book in their own right and so I have tried to include a representative selection that encompasses both idyllic rural streams and those of greater strategic importance that have themselves given rise to the development of historic towns and villages along their own banks, many of which derived their names from the rivers upon which they were founded. The tributaries I have selected are listed in the order in which they join the Thames from the source eastwards.

The **River Churn** rises some 3 miles to the south-west of Cheltenham at Seven Springs, flows down through the Roman town of Cirencester to join the Thames at Cricklade and was once cited by many 'experts' as actually being the source of the Thames. After all, a clearly visible outpouring of water represents a far more tangible and satisfactory start to England's longest river than an occasionally damp patch in a field. On my most recent visit, the site was rather overgrown and difficult to access but the springs are set beneath a lay-by near the junction of the A436 from Cheltenham and the A435 that roughly follows the course of the Churn down to Cirencester. The site is marked by a stone bearing an unnecessarily superior Latin inscription: 'Hic Tuus O Tamesine Pater Septemgeminus Fons' but it is probably best left that way, as the translation sounds even more academically pompous: 'Here, O Father Thames is Thy Sevenfold Source'!

It is extraordinary to note that back in 1937, at a time when the Spanish Civil War was raging and the rise of Nazi Germany continued apace, a gentlemanly altercation over the river's source took place in the House of Commons between Mr Robert Perkins, the MP for Stroud in Gloucestershire and Mr W.S. Morrison, the Minister of Agriculture and MP for Cirencester.

Most of the Thames's significant tributaries joining the river upstream from Oxford emanate from the Cotswolds, appearing as little more than shallow streams through picturesque villages of mellow golden limestone. This is the River Coln running through the small town of Fairford prior to joining the Thames by the Inglesham Roundhouse near Lechlade.

Mr Perkins enquired of the Minister whether the next revision of the Ordnance Survey would indicate that Seven Springs was the true source of the Thames. Morrison responded by suggesting that it was 'not an invariable rule in geographical practice to regard as the source of a large river the source of the tributary furthest from its estuary'. The distance from the Churn's source to Cricklade is undoubtedly further than from Cricklade to the that of the Thames, but most scientists, geographers and geologists agree that the Churn is not the Thames masquerading under another name and the dispute no longer appears on any Parliamentary agendas!

The Churn valley that runs down to Cirencester is a tranquil, untroubled place and despite the presence of the main road, settlements are surprisingly few and far between. Such limited human presence around the vicinity of the river has allowed some of England's rarer species of wildlife to flourish. Included among them is the shy, retiring water vole, whose survival is threatened by loss or fragmentation of habitats or predation by hunters such as the American mink, imported during the 1920s for commercial fur farming but now living and breeding in the wild. It was actually a vole that featured as the 'water rat' in Kenneth Grahame's immortal tale of the

riverbank, *The Wind in the Willows*, but maybe it had to be 'Ratty' because one could not really have had 'Moley' and 'Voley' in the same sentence!

The feral mink now roaming our river banks are not the only imported threat to our native species because the American signal crayfish also escaped from captivity in the 1970s and is now running amok in many of our inland waterways. The 6-inch long killing machine is a voracious predator and has decimated stocks of the smaller native white claw crayfish and eats anything in its path such as snails, invertebrates, small fish and fish eggs. Its habit of digging burrows up to 3 feet long into the riverbank to lay eggs is causing accelerated erosion and collapse of many banks when large numbers of breeding crayfish have colonized one particular stretch of river.

The road up through the valley from Cirencester was part of the old coaching network, for which the spa town of Cheltenham was not only an important destination in its own right, but also a staging post for the routes onwards to Worcester and the Midlands. That era is remembered in old coaching halts such as the Colesbourne Inn, set midway between Cirencester and Cheltenham. Although the advent of the railways sounded the death knell for coach travel, many parts of rural England relied on horse-drawn transport significantly longer than their urban neighbours.

The Churn has given its name to villages along the valley such as North Cerney, renowned for its beautiful Norman church with a distinctive and unusual saddleback tower and Cirencester too might have been named after the river, especially when taking account of its Roman name Corinium. The town's full Roman name Corinium Dobunnorum shows that when the Roman invaders built a fort and subsequent town there, it was already a settlement of the Celtic Dobunni tribe. Cirencester's location at a junction of three important roads resulted in it temporarily becoming the second most important town in the Roman Empire's most northern province, after London (Londinium). The grassy remains of the old amphitheatre survive to the west and the local Corinium Museum has a wealth of exhibits dating from that era.

Cirencester's prosperity continued through into the medieval period, flourishing on the proceeds of the wool trade. The Cotswolds have always been associated with sheep farming and Cirencester grew into England's largest wool market during the Middle Ages. As with other English towns that grew rich from sheep, that affluence was reflected in the lavish architecture and decoration bestowed upon their churches. St John the Baptist is acknowledged as the largest and most splendid of the region's 'wool churches', and arguably one of the most beautiful Perpendicular style churches in England. The church's most familiar feature is its unusual three-storey porch built in 1490, referred to locally as the town hall, although it never performed that precise civic function.

After Cirencester, the Churn passes through South Cerney before having to negotiate a safe passage through the network of flooded gravel pits of the Cotswold Water Park. It thereafter flows parallel to the Thames and the nearby Roman road of Ermin Street, passing alongside the great expanse of Cricklade's North Meadow Nature reserve before merging into the Thames near the town's High Bridge.

Another significant contributor to the infant Thames is the **River Coln**, a crystal-clear stream rising in the limestone hills of the Cotswolds to the east of Cheltenham and thereafter flowing south-east to join the Thames a little way upstream from Lechlade in the shadow of the Round House at Inglesham. The Coln apparently enjoys a high reputation among the angling fraternity, who regard it as one of the best rivers in England for brown trout and grayling, not least because the clarity of the water gives a clear sighting of the fish. Being able to see them is one thing but persuading them that there really is such a thing as a free lunch is a different matter.

Two clusters of tiny villages with the prefix Coln (Coln St Dennis, Coln St Aldwyn, etc.) sit either side of Bibury, one of the Cotswolds' picture perfect villages that have made the region such a popular tourist destination, although now often too crowded for comfort. Just a little further downstream lies the far less congested and equally rewarding small town of Fairford. The name will be familiar to many because of the nearby airbase, renowned for having the longest runway in Europe, designated as the European emergency landing site for the US Space Shuttle and for hosting spectacular shows that make grown men go weak at the knees at the sight of so much jet powered hardware and weaponry in one place. However, this particular set of knees experiences a similar effect when confronted by the most complete set of late-medieval glass extant in Britain that is set in the windows of Fairford's late-fifteenth-century Perpendicular parish church of St Mary.

The glass windows portray key elements of both Old and New Testaments of the Bible, beginning with Adam and Eve and ending with a most sublime portrayal of the Last Judgment. England's medieval churches were once awash with colourful wall paintings, some telling allegorical stories but most designed to convey

Opposite: The River Churn's source at Seven Springs was long thought by many to be that of the Thames, but in reality it is just a tributary stream, passing anonymously through a pastoral landscape. As the infant Churn is crossed by few roads or tracks, it is a rich haven for wildlife.

Left: Coaching inns are an integral part of the English landscape, and although many are located on minor roads, they were once important halts on major routes. The Colesbourne Inn provided hospitality to those travelling along the Churn valley between Cirencester, Cheltenham and Gloucester.

Right and opposite: Set high above Fairford's main street and the River Coln is the complete and perfect Perpendicular church of St Mary the Virgin, built of warm, mellow-toned Cotswold limestone. It may be smaller in physical stature than many other 'wool' churches, but is unique in that it contains the best fifteenth- and sixteenth-century glass in England. Some windows have aged better than others but the great west window's portrayal of the Last Judgement is a complex masterpiece of design and colour that reveals some new facet with every viewing.

the message of impending doom laced with just a fragment of hope to a largely illiterate population. The lower part of Fairford's Last Judgment window depicts the weighing of souls, and those passing the test of the scales join the swathe of the Blessed all dressed in gold; those found wanting are clearly seen being shovelled unceremoniously into the fires of Hell.

The upper segment features Christ in Majesty, flanked by Mary and John the Baptist and surrounded by martyrs and a host of angels. Many of the windows can be attributed to Henry VII's Flemish master glazier Barnard Flowers, and in those windows featuring any buildings, they tend to show Dutch gables and other architectural traits from the Low Countries rather than contemporary English architecture. The Last Judgment windows all suffered storm damage in the eighteenth century and needed restoration, but every window was removed to a place of safety during the Second World War to avert the threat from bombs.

On a quiet midsummer's day, the Coln seems innocuous enough as it drifts slowly past the reed beds below Fairford's main street, but in 2007, a protracted period of torrential rain caused the river to overflow its banks and cause extensive flooding within the town. It does seem to be an increasingly common and worrying occurrence for those living on the floodplains of the nation's rivers and a stark reminder of nature's awesome and all-too-destructive power. In much the way that the afterlife portrayed in the Last Judgment window ranged from angelic gold to hellish red, our watercourses can change from gently gurgling stream to an angry raging torrent in a matter of hours.

The River Windrush winds around the foot of Burford's busy High Street, and because this ancient market town was established at an important crossing point of the Windrush, it is consequently now at the junction of several main roads and seldom free from traffic. I always try and photograph such places with minimal intrusion from motor vehicles, but in Burford's case, by the time the sun had risen high enough to light the buildings, rush hour was well under way.

After leaving Fairford, the Coln touches the edge of only one further village prior to joining the Thames at a confluence draped with a curtain of willows. Despite the help of the Coln, Churn and another significant tributary, the Swill Brook, the Thames arrives at the ancient river port of Lechlade with a barely navigable depth of water. That situation improves slightly when the **River Leach** joins in just a little downstream from St John's Lock. The upstream villages of East and Northleach are clearly set directly on the Leach and it is after that river that Lechlade itself was named. Unfortunately, the Leach itself cannot quite match the stature of the town, being reduced in places to a seasonal bourn, resurfacing only after an extended period of rain has raised the water levels sufficiently high enough.

Although the countryside through which the Thames flows after Lechlade is laced with small streams, brooks and man-made cuts, it is another 16 miles before the next major tributary joins the river at Newbridge. The delightfully named **River Windrush** is another Thames feeder whose source lies up in the limestone watershed of the Cotswolds and whose meandering 40-mile journey encompasses villages of golden limestone, hidden valleys, ruined castles and the major town of Witney. For centuries that name was synonymous with the best quality woollen blankets, but the introduction of bed linen made from artificial fibres and the ubiquitous duvet resulted in a rapid decline and the last blanket mill closed in 2002.

However, in terms of history, landscape and architecture, one of the more rewarding sections of the Windrush valley lies a little further upstream from Witney in the direction of Burford. It was once a strategically important crossing point on the river, whose name is an amalgamation of the Saxon '*burh*' (fortified town) and ford. Burford's handsome sloping High Street was originally built as a market place, with narrow plots on which the traders erected their stalls extending back from the broad street. Shops have now replaced the market pitches and the High Street is lined with elegant houses, many of which date back to the seventeenth century and earlier. The markets were administered by the local Guild of Merchants from the Tolsey, a building where market sellers and merchants had to pay their dues before each day's trading could begin. It survives today as a small museum.

Burford's parish church, dedicated to St John the Baptist, lies at the foot of the hill and it was the unsympathetic treatment of the church's interior by restorers that persuaded William Morris of the pressing need to form his Society for the Protection of Ancient

Buildings. The Society was also affectionately referred to as the 'Anti-Scrape Movement' because its aims were to try and regulate Victorian architects and builders from wilfully scraping away layers of accumulated history within an ancient building, simply to produce a sanitized version of the original.

The main A40 road from Oxford to Gloucester and the west bypasses the edge of Burford, but the town's old coaching inns attest to its importance as a major halt during the coaching era. Few of those travelling along the old coach road and its tarmac successor will even be aware of the Windrush valley lying secreted away to the north of the highway. Set amid the meanders of the Windrush and out of earshot from the speeding traffic lies the village of Swinbrook, a place noted for its associations with two prominent families set centuries apart – the Fettiplaces and the Mitfords. It was at Asthall Manor in Swinbrooke that the famous Mitford sisters spent part of their childhood. The youngest of the six, Deborah, was born there in 1920 and is now of course the Dowager Duchess of Devonshire, chatelaine of Chatsworth House in Derbyshire for over fifty years following her marriage in 1941 to Andrew Cavendish, the 11th Duke of Devonshire. That family link with Swinbrooke has been maintained to the present day, as the Dowager Duchess now owns the award-winning Swan Inn in the village, whose rooms are adorned with snapshots from the Mitford family album.

A more poignant reminder of the family's association with Swinbrooke lies in the churchyard of St Mary, final resting place of Nancy Mitford and two of her sisters, Unity and Pamela, but Swinbrooke's greatest treasure, the Fettiplace family monument, lies within the church itself. The Fettiplaces were one of the region's greatest and

Below: The Fettiplace monuments in St Mary the Blessed Virgin, Swinbrooke, comprise two niches of three figures, dating from the early and latter decades of the seventeenth century. Such family memorials can be found in parish churches throughout the country and it is often the case that the more grandiose pieces of funerary sculpture are set within the humblest of churches.

most influential families. Their seat, Swinbrook Manor, was regarded as one of the finest Tudor mansions in Oxfordshire but was demolished in 1806. Fortunately, the Fettiplaces survive in stone rather than merely in spirit, although one cannot help wondering whether, if given the opportunity, they might have considered redesigning those lasting memorials. Eternity is a long time to be squashed into an alcove propped on one elbow, despite having two other family members in the same alcove for company. There are two separate arched niches each containing a trio of almost identical recumbent effigies dating from the early and later parts of the seventeenth century. The oldest collection is located just outside the sanctuary and was commissioned by Sir Edmund Fettiplace (d.1613) to carry his own effigy and those of his father and grandfather. Their pose is very stiff and regimented, but at least the sculptor has given them all a shallow cushion on which to rest their elbows. The later memorial set on the other side of the sanctuary rail was ordered by another member of the family, also named Edmund, who died in 1686. The occupants of that second niche, Sir Edmund, his father and uncle convey an altogether more relaxed style in both dress and posture, seemingly quite content with their lot.

According to legend, another past resident of the valley who lived downstream from Swinbrook at Minster Lovell Hall faced his own demise in a chillingly less ordered and celebrated manner. The hall was built during the mid-fifteenth century by Lord William Lovell, 7th Baron Tichmarsh, but the story centres around his grandson, Francis Lovell, a lifelong friend of Richard III and staunch supporter of the Yorkist cause both during and after the Wars of the Roses. Francis fled into exile having been declared a traitor by the newly crowned Lancastrian king, Henry VII after the Battle of Bosworth in 1485 at which Richard was slain.

Lovell returned two years later to support the campaign of the pretender to the throne Lambert Simnel, and was allegedly killed at the Battle of Stoke in 1487, at which the rebel army was crushed. However, the legend suggests that he escaped the field of conflict, returned to Minster Lovell Hall and took refuge in a secret chamber known only to one loyal servant who rather inconveniently died suddenly and without warning. It must have been a rather too secret and definitely too secure place because, when workmen opened up that part of the hall during building work some 200 years later, they discovered a man's skeleton sitting bolt

Opposite below: The River Windrush charts a long, meandering course around the village of Minster Lovell and the extensive ruins and dovecote of Minster Lovell Hall.

Above: Minster Lovell Hall was built by Lord William Lovell, 7th Baron Tichmarsh, during the fifteenth century, and although most of the buildings are reduced to foundation level, substantial remains of the Great Hall, entrance porch and the tower from the south wing have survived. The Hall and adjacent dovecote are now in the care of English Heritage.

upright at a table with paper and writing implements set out before him. Unfortunately, everything disintegrated when the room was opened to the atmosphere and so we shall never know what literary masterpiece was written by the doomed occupant.

Strangely enough, there is no suggestion that Francis Lovell still haunts the ruins that were dismantled during the eighteenth century by the Earl of Leicester prior to his relocation to Holkham Hall in Norfolk, although the atmospheric site could not be more perfect for a bit of ghostly wandering. The ruins themselves sit at the base of a hill flanked on two sides by dark woodland and accessed through Lord William's church dedicated to St Kenelm (the seven-year-old son of a Saxon King of Mercia who was murdered by his sister). It may just all be suggestive, but the River Windrush does seem to slither its way through Minster Lovell rather than gently flow in the manner of an untroubled stream.

As the Thames arches round its most northerly point and then swings south towards Oxford, it flows almost parallel to the **River Cherwell**, a significant tributary whose confluence with the Thames is by Christ Church Meadow. The Cherwell has its origins over 70 miles to the north in a small watershed set amid the ironstone hills of Hellidon near Daventry, thereafter weaving its way across largely unremarkable arable landscape towards Banbury, the only town of significance on its journey to the Thames. Prior to arriving in Banbury the Cherwell flows through the village of Cropredy, whose ancient bridge was the focal point of a Civil War battle in 1644. It was a typically protracted skirmish extending for several miles and although there was no decisive outcome, Parliamentary losses totalled around 700 through death or desertion but King Charles' army suffered few casualties.

It is impossible to guess how many toddlers have been bounced on parental knees in time to the rhythmical beat of the old nursery rhyme 'Ride a cock horse to Banbury Cross, to see a fine Lady upon a white horse.' Unfortunately, it is just one of countless similar traditional songs or verses with no clear-cut historical origins and the identity of the 'lady' varies between Queen Elizabeth I, Lady Godiva or even Lady Fiennes from nearby Broughton Castle. Several eighteenth-century songbooks contain rhymes beginning with the same first line but a different story.

The Cherwell enters Oxford alongside the University Parks, a public space extending to around 70 acres comprising an arboretum, genetic gardens and open parkland. Some maps of the park still identify an area near its south-east corner, close to the weir and boat

Right: Immediately prior to joining the Thames, the River Cherwell passes alongside Christ Church Meadow in the heart of Oxford. The bench seats set along its banks afford magnificent views back across the meadow to Oxford's historic skyline and although the Cherwell can be a place for quiet contemplation, it is also renowned as Oxford's punting river and on busy summer afternoons can be anything but tranquil.

Above: The River Cherwell at Magdalene Bridge, Oxford.

Below: Either the first or final lock on the Oxford Canal, depending on one's direction of travel. The single lock gate appears very basic in contrast to the more sophisticated hydraulic double-gated Thames locks.

rollers, as being Parson's Pleasure – a name that conjures up innumerable fanciful images. The name actually refers to a secluded spot originally set aside for male-only nude bathing, and of course has since been adopted into University folklore. The tales usually centred around accounts of how sunbathing dons preserved their modesty by using devices ranging from straw boaters to copies of *The Times* when passing boats contained female passengers. Equality of the sexes was maintained because there was also an equivalent provision made for female bathers near by, named Dame's Delight.

Bathing is still commonplace on the Cherwell but the unwilling participants these days are more likely to be students or tourists left forlornly hanging on to a punting pole as their boat drifts away. The Cherwell is Oxford's punting centre (see pages 158–9) and can occasionally be noisy around Magdalene Bridge, but the environs of the Botanic Gardens, through an extended bower of trees and overhanging foliage, are contrastingly tranquil. Oxford's Botanic Garden is the oldest in Britain, predating Chelsea's Physic Garden of 1673 (see page 218) by several decades.

In between the Thames and Cherwell rivers lies a third watercourse, the **Oxford Canal**, which, although man-made is no less significant in terms of its impact on the city's landscape, environment and economic development. The canal was one of the earliest to be dug during the frantic outburst of 'canal mania' that took place during the latter two decades of the eighteenth century. It was largely the work of the prolific canal building pioneer, James Brindley (1716–72) who had engineered approximately 365 miles of canals in a period spanning thirteen years, although his death meant that the Oxford Canal was completed by his assistant (and brother-in-law) Samuel Simcock. Throughout much of its length from Oxford up towards the Midlands, the canal mirrors the course of the River Cherwell, in places charting what seems like an unnecessarily tortuous route for a pre-planned, artificially dug channel. The reason behind those extra miles was simply that, whenever possible, Brindley built 'contour canals' that twisted around hills to minimize vertical deviation and thereby avoided the expense of extra locks, embankments or tunnels.

The canal was designed as an integral part of the network linking the developing industrial centres of the Midlands and northern England to the four main navigable rivers of the Trent, Mersey, Severn and Thames. The requisite Act of Parliament sanctioning its building was passed in 1769 and work began shortly thereafter at the canal's northern junction near Coventry. Financial difficulties for the company resulted in constant delays to the planned construction schedule, and the final stretch into Oxford was not begun until 1786 and officially opened four years later. Those final few miles were constructed as cheaply as possible using cost-cutting devices such as wooden swing bridges instead of expensive brick arches and the customary double-gated locks were replaced by deeper versions using only single gates at either end.

The canal company and local business thrived for fifteen years, shipping coal from Warwickshire to London and stone from local quarries, commodities that were impossible to transport by road in any meaningful quantities. Unfortunately, the Oxford Canal became blighted through its reliance on the Thames for shipping goods to the heart of London because the upper reaches of the river were in such poor condition, suffered from stretches of shallow water and still relied on flash locks (see pages 97–101) in some places. Consequently, a new route was surveyed between Brentford near London and the canal junction at Braunston on the upper segment of the Oxford waterway. That led to the creation of the Grand Junction Canal, and by 1805 a faster, more efficient route from London to the Midlands took trade away from the Oxford Canal.

Despite that significant setback and advent of rail transport from the 1830s, the canal remained profitable and continued to pay dividends to shareholders right up until nationalization in 1948. Coal remained one of the canal's most consistent sources of income and in spite of the weight of those barges, horse traction remained the favoured form of power by many Oxford bargees long after their contemporaries on other routes had made the transition to diesel engines. The last horse-drawn coal barge in Britain was actually recorded on the Oxford Canal as recently as 1958, a vessel that is now preserved in the Ellesmere Port Boat Museum in Merseyside. Despite the canal's apparent longevity, its southern section in particular joined many others in near terminal decline but was rescued from the brink of closure by the rise in popularity of boating holidays. Whether you are sauntering along the towpath on foot or gently chugging along in a brightly painted narrowboat, the Oxford Canal is blessed with some outstanding waterside pubs and is a joy to explore as it winds out into the open countryside.

The **River Thame** may be a river by name but is more of a stream by nature and unless in spate, it trickles rather than flows into the Thames by Dorchester. Some guides do suggest that is might be navigable some way upstream in a very small boat with minimal draught. The Thame is obviously one of the key factors in the

Above: The confluence of the Oxford Canal and River Thames is set amid a landscape of railway girder bridges and allotments; a stark contrast to the University college quadrangles and towers located a little further downstream.

question regarding how the Thames (with an 's') came to be so named. However, as that subject has been debated for so long and gone round in so many circles, there is really nothing new to add, and people must do as they always have: pick the version they feel most comfortable with and accept that as fact. To summarize the choices: The Thames is in fact the Isis until Dorchester, at which point the Thame and Isis amalgamate into 'Thames'. Or: the Thames was known as Tamesis by the Romans and that name has evolved linguistically over time. Or: the Romans got their version of the name from an existing Celt word '*Tems*', meaning 'dark', or its ancient Sanskrit equivalent '*tamas*'. If one studies how many English rivers there are with basic derivatives of those words – Tamar, Tame, Teme, Team, etc. – there is perhaps merit in that argument, but if so, how does the name of an Egyptian goddess sensibly apply to half a river in rural England? Perhaps we had better progress back to the River Thame!

The river rises in the Vale of Aylesbury, to the north of the Chiltern Hills, and flows roughly south-west for approximately 40 miles. The historic market town of Thame has retained many impressive fifteenth- to seventeenth-century buildings, including the grouping of the old grammar school and almshouses. The imposing church of St Mary the Virgin is set apart from the main body of the town with only the restored Prebendal House and river for company. Although the original Saxon town developed close to the river, it was 'planted' (deliberately planned) on neighbouring virgin land and the town's current 'boat shaped' layout of the market place with narrow, easily monitored entrances at both ends is typical of many medieval 'new towns'. The current church was also begun around this time and is noted for its collection of brasses and the magnificent tomb of local benefactor, Lord Williams and his wife Elizabeth.

St Mary's choir stalls contain some particularly fine linenfold wood panelling, saved from the nearby Cistercian monastery at the Dissolution. The twelfth-century monastic foundation had been established at Thame following a grant of land made by the lord of the manor, Alexander de Blois, Bishop of Lincoln. The lavishly endowed monastery subsequently came into the ownership of Lord Williams of Thames at the Dissolution and passed through his daughter into the Wenman family, who fashioned a grand country mansion from the monastic buildings during the eighteenth century.

The older parts of Thame have been rescued from the worst excesses of modern traffic by the introduction of a bypass and the road that once led past the church and over the Thames bridge is now a public footpath whose tranquillity is secured by bollards set into the tarmac. A reminder of the significant part played by England's rivers in marking many of our county boundaries can

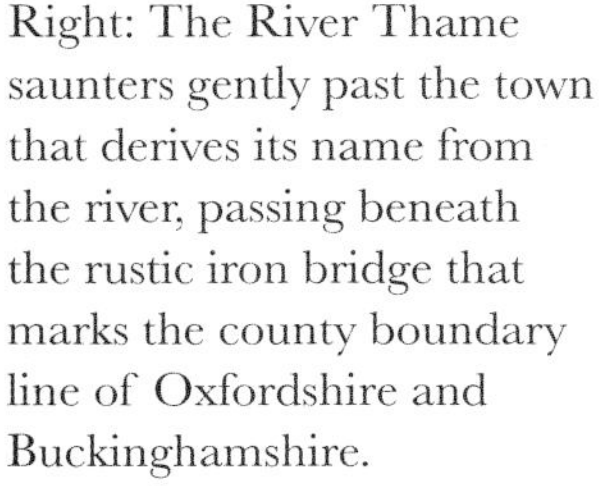

Right: The River Thame saunters gently past the town that derives its name from the river, passing beneath the rustic iron bridge that marks the county boundary line of Oxfordshire and Buckinghamshire.

Opposite, above and below: the cruciform church of St Mary the Virgin has evolved from its Norman origins into a fine building that reflects the later prosperity of Thame. The wealth associated with the church is also manifested in the massive tithe barn that stands nearby. The interior of St Mary's is richly endowed with both furnishing and monuments, the latter varying from lavish sculptures of wealthy patrons to intricately crafted brasses set in the chancel walls and floor.

be found engraved onto the wrought-iron balustrade of the bridge. A vertical line is flanked on either side by arrows indicating that Oxfordshire lies on one bank and Buckinghamshire on the other. The Thame actually changes little in terms of both its physical stature and the characteristics of the landscape through which its passes *en route* to the Thames, ending its journey as the same rural stream it has been throughout.

The finest building passed by the Thame is appropriately its 'swan song': the magnificent Dorchester Abbey set close by the river just a few hundred metres from it confluence. However, as the abbey church has been described in the main narrative (see pages 123–7) it is time to continue downstream in pursuit of the next major tributary, the **River Kennet**.

The Kennet is the Thames's largest tributary and during the summer months contributes up to half its flow. The Kennet can be confusing to follow as it also forms a substantial part of the Kennet and Avon Canal, a title that has evolved into something of generic term for the both the Kennet itself and the two river navigations and interconnecting stretch of canal that link the Thames at Reading with the River Severn near Bristol. The contrast between the Kennet's source at Swallowhead Springs and its confluence with the Thames at Reading some 45 miles later could not be more extreme. The river rises on the Marlborough Downs in the immediate vicinity of some of our most important prehistoric monuments – most notably Silbury Hill, the Avebury complex of stone circles and avenues and the West Kennet Long Barrow. After such an auspicious and inspirational birth, one of England's most important chalk streams spends its final moments muddily swirling past gas holders and beneath red-brick railway bridges.

The Kennet was made navigable to Newbury in 1723 and its western counterpart, the Avon along to Bath four years later. The river navigations were finally connected by a canal in 1810: a waterway particularly renowned for the accomplished and innovative feats of engineering required of Scottish canal builder, John Rennie (1761–1821), to overcome sections of difficult terrain. The Caen Hill locks flight near Devizes in Wiltshire comprises

twenty-nine locks with a central flight of sixteen set close together. The total rise over 2 miles is around 72 metres and a passage through the central section alone can take up to five hours to complete. A smaller and maybe less extreme flight closer to Reading are the nine Crofton locks, rising just 19 metres, but their summit pound does mark the canal's highest point, clearly marked from afar by the tall chimneys of Crofton Pumping Station. Gravity and canal locks are not perfect partners and so the massive beam engine powered pumps were necessary to keep a constant supply of water in the locks.

Many canal companies experienced varying degrees of hardship when the railway network became established; the Kennet and Avon suffering more than most at the hands of Isambard Kingdom Brunel's Great Western Railway. There is one particular stretch of canal near Crofton where the railway tracks actually run parallel to the towpath and, although simply following the easiest stretch of terrain already claimed by the canal, the prospect of fully laden speeding trains passing single, lumbering cargo barges must have brought a sense of foreboding to the canal company's owners. Their worst fears were realized with the opening of the GWR in 1841, and just eleven years later in 1852 the railway had bought the Kennet and Avon and proceeded to drive barge traffic away through high tolls and a policy of zero maintenance.

As the twentieth century progressed, the canal fell into almost total dereliction and probably would have formally closed had it not been for the superhuman efforts of the Kennet and Avon Canal Trust, a registered charity whose volunteer members worked tirelessly to restore the doomed canal back to the thriving waterway opened by the Queen in 1990. The local authorities and other volunteer groups have also done a great deal to clean up the Kennet's confluence and it is arguably easier and more interesting to walk into the town from the Thames than from the west. One passes initially either over or under the old horseshoe bridge, a legacy of when horses towing vessels along the Thames were led over the Kennet. The towpath then goes under two rail bridges that really do epitomize that great burgeoning era of railway development.

Blake's Lock is the final barrier on the Kennet and lies midway between the Thames and Reading's town centre, a place whose skyline has changed dramatically over the years. Riverside office and housing developments have replaced most traces of a more industrial past and the vast new Oracle shopping and entertainment complex actually makes a feature of the Kennet, neatly sanitized and harnessed as a permanently flowing water feature through the heart of the mall. Set amid soaring blocks of concrete, glass and steel, lie a few forlorn fragments of Reading Abbey, founded by Henry I in 1121 and who also elected to be buried there upon his death in 1135. It was rumoured that the abbey was founded specifically to house a holy relic: the hand of St James the Apostle, and indeed the bones of a human hand were discovered in the abbey ruins in 1786. However, if that had been the apostle's it can only have been there as a result of some monastic skulduggery because St James (both hands included) was supposed to be safely interred at his great pilgrimage shrine of Santiago de Compostela in northern Spain.

The abbey suffered the same fate as all monastic foundations at the Dissolution, but few abbots had the courage exhibited by Reading's Hugh Faringdon when resisting Henry VIII's edict. The brave abbot and two of his monks paid dearly for their principles and were hung, drawn and quartered in 1539. More extensive and substantial remains of the massive flint and rubble abbey walls are located in nearby Forbury Park but, despite their impressive bulk, they are nevertheless dominated by the grim presence of Reading's Victorian prison, built in 1844 as the Berkshire County Gaol. The institution's most famous inmate was Oscar Wilde (1854–1900), sentenced in 1895 to two years' hard labour after having been convicted on a charge of gross indecency. Although Wilde will always be lauded as a writer and playwright for his acerbic wit, one of his most enduring works is the epic and very moving poem, *The Ballad of Reading Gaol*, which, although ostensibly written about the fate of a fellow convict, Charles Wooleridge, who was sentenced to death for murder in 1896, clearly represented many of Wilde's own bleak impressions of prison life.

Another river navigation emanating to the south of the Thames but joining it in a more gentle environment is, the **River Wey**, rising in the Hampshire and Surry uplands and flowing north-east and north through Godalming and Guildford prior to its confluence with the Thames a short distance downstream from Weybridge at Shepperton Lock and weir basin. The Wey was a strong flowing stream that once powered over fifty mills along its route from the hills to the Thames, but its lower reaches were subsequently tamed and transformed from a river to a navigation in 1653, making it one of the first British rivers to be made navigable and open to barge traffic. That 15-mile waterway linked Weybridge and the Thames with Guildford and a 4-mile extension created in 1764 allowed barges to work further upstream to Godalming.

Opposite: An arch of Reading Abbey's mill has survived both the ravages of time and the relentless advance of modern development. It is to the great credit of local councils, planners and other conservation bodies that even such comparatively small fragments of our architectural heritage are valued and conserved.

Above: The Wey Navigation at Thames Lock near Shepperton. Despite having been converted into waterside dwellings, the wharves and warehouses have retained much of their original infrastructure.

Below: Between Thames and Town locks in Weybridge, the curtain of foliage on the right hand bank affords a degree of privacy to the exclusive houses whose gardens run right down to the water's edge.

The construction project was instigated by Sir Richard Weston (1591–1652), who had been influenced by the canal and lock systems already widely used in the Netherlands. His own stretch of navigation included twelve locks and necessitated the digging of some 10 miles of artificial channels, although he sadly died shortly before his scheme came to fruition. Coal, timber, grain and flour were the canal's staple products but one commodity particularly suited to being gently transported on water by a horse-drawn barge was gunpowder. The Chilworth Gunpowder Works near Guildford was first established by the East India Company in 1625 and grew into one of Britain's most prestigious powder mills, flourishing until its closure after the Great War ended in 1918.

Trade inevitably declined when the railways began carrying goods faster and in greater bulk but the Wey Canal managed to keep trading successfully until well after the Second World War. The navigation's last private owners, Stevens and Sons, donated the canal to the National Trust in 1964 and it is now one of the most popular stretches of water for boating on England's waterway network. Anyone walking the Thames Path can easily get a flavour of the Wey Navigation by simply taking the small passenger ferry across the Thames by Shepperton Lock. A path follows the Wey past a couple of boatyards and onwards through a small park to the first lock, overlooked by canalside warehouses converted into residential units. The towpath thereafter follows the navigation past the gardens of some eminently

desirable riverside houses to Weybridge's Town Lock and road bridge, but despite living in such a privileged location, their owners still cannot sit outside and enjoy the view without being overlooked themselves.

Although there are some natural additions to the waters of the Thames in between Weybridge and the heart of London, the next significant waterway encountered is the **Grand Union Canal**, whose main entrance lock is at Brentford, set almost directly across from Kew Gardens and adjacent to the historic parkland of Syon House. The name Brentford implies a river crossing and there is indeed a River Brent, an 18-mile-long tributary rising in low hills around the north London Borough of Barnet. The Brent loses its identity on the final approaches to Brentford, canalized and transformed into the Grand Union Canal. If the Thames was London's main trade artery with the outside world, the Grand Union was of no lesser importance as the most important national arterial waterway in an increasingly industrialized late-eighteenth- and early-nineteenth-century England.

The Grand Union was precisely that – an early-twentieth-century amalgamation of several independently owned canals to create an interconnecting network extending to over 300 miles that included branches to Leicester and industrial Nottinghamshire. However, the backbone of the specially created Canal Company remained the Grand Junction, the link between Brentford and Birmingham that had dealt such a killer blow to the future prospects of the already struggling Oxford Canal. Being able to avoid the pitfalls of poor navigation and infrastructure suffered by the Oxford enabled the custom-built Grand Junction to become the canal network's 'motorway' to and from the nation's capital. It was a busy route throughout its commercial life, although the struggle to compete with the railways from the mid-nineteenth century onwards posed a constant problem for the owners.

The merger of several canal companies was sanctioned by an Act of Parliament in 1928 and the Grand Union Canal Company emerged thereafter. The company worked hard to negate the obvious advantages held by the railways, modernizing the canal and boats to maximize efficiency. Locks were rebuilt to take wider beamed barges and there were even government grants made available to enable some of the vast numbers of unemployed to be given work and a fragment of hope during the Great Depression of the 1930s.

One of London's most famous landmarks, and now a leisure facility enjoyed by many, whether afloat, on foot or bicycle, is the **Regent's Canal**. It was created

The Regent's Canal at Little Venice in the Maida Vale district of London, a much sought-after address both on or adjacent to the canal. The residential narrowboats are double parked in places, necessitating a high level of consideration for one's neighbours – especially when returning home to the outer-berthed vessel late at night after a good party.

Above: Elegant Georgian villas line both banks of the Regent's Canal around Little Venice, and as the canal then marked the northern boundary of London, their windows would have looked out onto open countryside

Opposite: Monuments in Kensal Green Cemetery vary from elegant simplicity to Egyptian and Greek extravagance, graphically illustrated in the mausoleum of circus impresario, Andrew Ducrow (1793–1842).

during the second decade of the nineteenth century to connect the Grand Junction's Paddington Arm (opened in 1801) with the River Thames at Limehouse. The canal curves around north London like a bow, and at the time of its construction actually did mark the extent of the capital's northern suburbs. Parts of the canal were dug out of green fields, but as soon as the waterway opened, building materials became easier to transport enabling further development to take place. That spurt in building explains the band of late-Georgian and early-Victorian terraces and squares alongside the canal in Hackney, Islington, Camden and Paddington, although not all have managed to retain the elegance they were no doubt endowed with originally

One of the Regent's Canal Company's major shareholders and promoters of the scheme was John Nash, chief architect to the Prince Regent, later George IV. At the same time that the canal project was becoming reality, Nash was in the process of laying out Marylebone Park (to become Regent's Park), and it obviously seemed logical to physically combine the two in both name and dedication and a segment of the canal follows the park's northern perimeter. A little further west from Regent's Park lies an area known as Little Venice, a phrase coined by Robert Browning to describe the junction of the Paddington basin, Grand Junction (now Union) and Regent's canals. It is a great place for wandering along and sampling the outdoor restaurants, bars and cafés but property prices in the area reflect its desirability and appear to have far too many noughts attached.

Further west towards Brentford lies Kensal Green, where the canal passes by the walls of one of London's great Victorian cemeteries. Kensal Green was established in 1833 and, although perhaps not able to match Highgate in respect of the number of celebrity graves from the worlds of the arts, literature, and politics, Kensal Green was established six years earlier than its north London rival and has more than its fair share or architectural gems. By the beginning of the nineteenth century, some of London's parish burial grounds and churchyards were full. Some churches purchased land outside the city's boundary to create additional space, but continuing high mortality rates,

The River Lea Navigation near Waltham Abbey, which, although canalized, still manages to retain some vestiges of a rural river.

coupled with outbreaks of disease such as cholera, led to the establishment of privately run cemeteries after a bill was passed in Parliament n 1832.

Kensal Green, the first to be consecrated, had initial difficulty attracting clients until two of George III's children, Augustus Frederick, Duke of Sussex, and Princess Sophia were interred there in front of the Anglican chapel. Kensal Green promptly became a fashionable burial place and competition for the best sites suddenly became intense. The topography of the cemetery was a microcosm of society, with royalty and nobility at the centre in the most architecturally exotic tombs, the affluent middle classes radiating outwards and the poorer graves marked by simple crosses on the outside.

Limehouse was an obvious place to end the canal as its original dock basin was then set amid 4 acres of quays and wharfs close to London's main docks, where sea-faring vessels loaded cargo for export or unshipped goods for internal distribution. Although initially a commercial failure and not attracting the anticipated amount of trade, the canal came into its own during the mid-nineteenth century and flourished as a vital conduit for the transportation of coal to the numerous gasworks and, latterly, electricity generating stations. The Regent's Canal was not the only commercial waterway to use the Limehouse Basin as a dead straight artificial channel; the Limehouse Cut was sanctioned by the River Lea Act of 1766 to connect the Thames with the River Lea Navigation.

The **River Lea** rises in the Chilterns, thereafter flowing gently south-east to join the Thames to the east of Millwall and the Isle of Dogs. It combines with the River Stort to the south of Hertford and, in terms of medieval trade in particular, both rivers were important trade routes, especially for the shipment of grain from the eastern Home Counties, Essex and Cambridgeshire. The River Lea's final stage prior to joining the Thames is a tortuously winding tidal waterway known as Bow Creek and was totally unsuitable for the unwieldy sailing barges that used the river. Limehouse Cut also saved them from having to wait for the tide before being able to sail around the long southward loop of the Isle of Dogs. Bow Creek is an ugly duckling of a waterway that will probably never achieve swan status, although the arrival of the London Olympics in 2012 will significantly enhance its plumage and the lower Lea valley is now the recipient of some long overdue regeneration.

The contrast between the rural upper and more industrialized lower sections of the Lea (often also spelled Lee) could scarcely be more pronounced, although the buffer zone created by the 26-mile green corridor of the Lea Valley Regional Park is an invaluable blend of nature reserves, riverside trails and sporting facilities within easy reach of London.

The **River Medway** just manages to sneak onto the list of tributaries, because although its discharge is into the Thames estuary rather then the river itself, the Medway still falls within the both the current and historical seaward lines marking the end of the Thames. Although the Medway's confluence with the Thames is amid the creeks, mudflats and bleak landscape of the Isle of Sheppey, the river's upper reaches emanate from the pastoral and wooded surroundings of the Kentish Weald.

Above: Bow Locks provide access to and from the tidal Bow Creek and River Thames into the Lea Navigation and the Limehouse Cut. A little further 'upstream' lies Three Mills Island, the site of some of London's most important tidal mills, one of which has now been fully restored.

Below: Moorings on the River Medway at Rochester reflect its popularity with owners of leisure craft, but it was once an important naval base and the historic Chatham Dockyards lie just a little further downstream.

The Medway has played a significant role in both Kentish and English history. For centuries it carried timber and then later, both iron and guns from the Weald downstream to the towns of the Thames estuary. Looking across the green expanses of the Weald today, it is difficult to imagine that such a rural scene was once a prosperous industrial area bustling with ironworks. The south-east's rich ore deposits had been identified and exploited both by Celts and Romans but the most productive period occurred during the fifteenth and sixteenth centuries, a period when Henry VII and his successors were starting to build an English navy. A fortified port was built at Portsmouth on the Channel coast, but one of the navy's most important dockyards was later developed by Elizabeth I at Chatham. The Medway was deemed a safe haven for shipping because not only was its estuary littered with potentially treacherous islands and sandbanks to trap the unwary, but Chatham and the neighbouring city of Rochester were further protected by a readily defended sharp bend at the estuary's neck.

That strategic point was where Elizabeth sited the artillery fortress of Upnor Castle, but it actually saw little action during that period. However, it singularly failed to perform its designated task a century later during the second Anglo-Dutch War in 1667 when the Dutch fleet sailed past the fort and into Chatham, destroyed several

Opposite, top left and below: Rochester's castle and present cathedral were both begun under the direction of Norman bishop, Gundulf, although one of his successors, William de Corbell, was responsible for the massive early-twelfth-century keep built of Kentish ragstone.

Opposite right: The cathedral's west front is the finest Romanesque façade in England. Its tympanum depicts Christ in Majesty.

Left and below: Rochester Cathedral is England's second oldest, having been founded by Bishop Justus in AD 604. The mid-fourteenth-century door leading into the chapter house, created at the behest of Bishop Hamo de Hythe. It was sculpted during the Decorated period of the gothic, of which this example surely represents the apogee.

ships and added insult to injury by towing away the English flagship *Royal Charles*. The river at Rochester is dominated by the twin landmarks of the vast castle keep and cathedral, the latter begun under the direction of Gundulf, the second of William the Conqueror's newly appointed bishops, the first having been Lanfranc at Canterbury. Gundulf's work can still be appreciated in the cathedral's crypt, but his original church was substantially added to during a twelfth-century rebuilding programme and much typical Norman stonework remains in evidence. Two outstanding examples of the stonemason's art are represented by the exterior tympanum over the west door and the chapter house doorway, produced during the Decorated period of the fourteenth century. It exhibits a most exquisite touch from the artist and one would have to visit many churches to find a more rewarding piece of work.

The River Thames obviously has more tributaries than I have been able to feature in this chapter but my personal selection will hopefully have provided an additional insight into how the river functions and where all its water actually comes from. The next chapter will resume the narrative of our journey down the Thames, picking up the route where we left it in Lechlade.

CHAPTER THREE

Pastoral Tranquillity
From Lechlade to Oxford

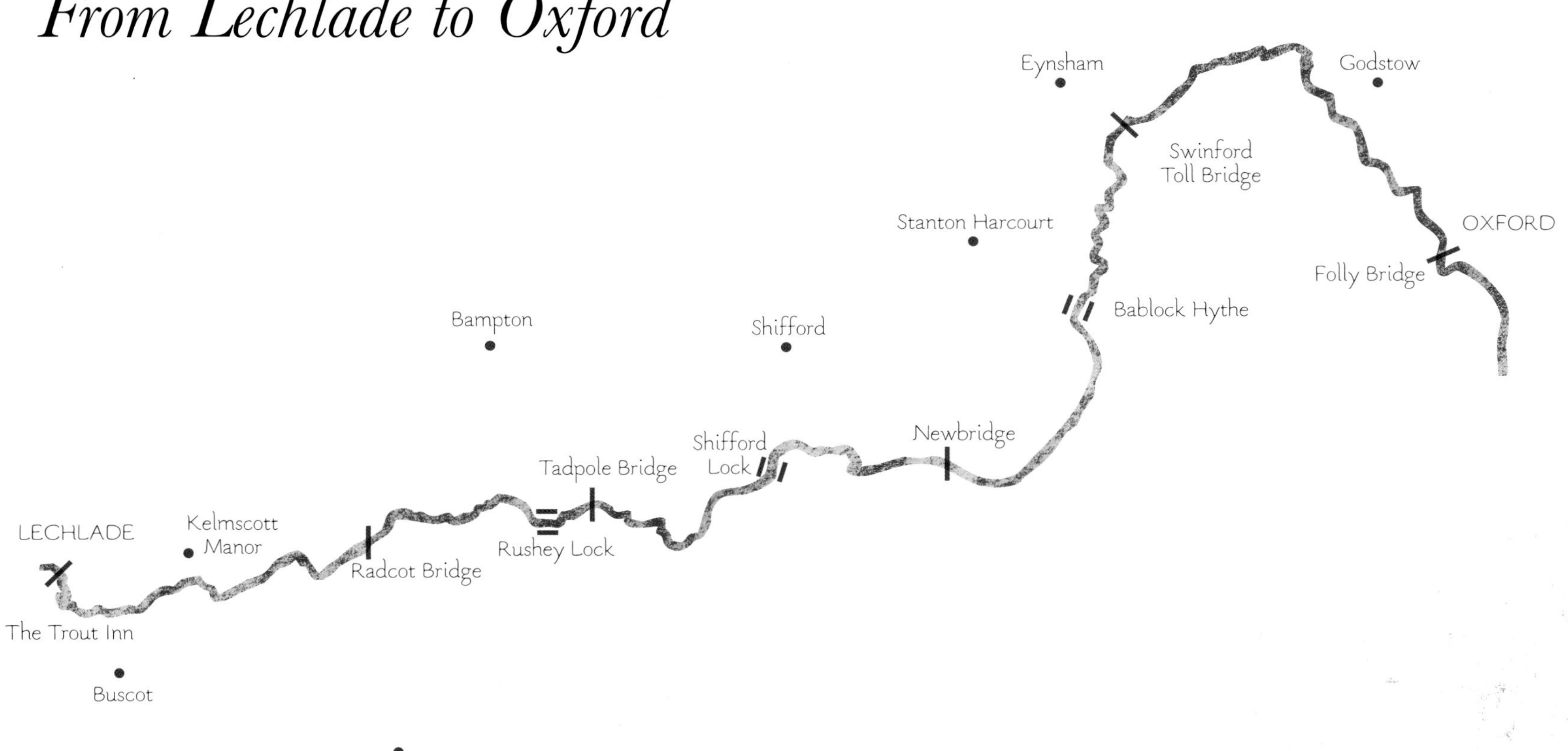

The stretch of the Thames between Lechlade and Oxford features some of the loneliest, most isolated stretches encountered along its entire length, with medieval bridges that have witnessed bloody battles fought over those priceless crossing points, a toll bridge that still levies a charge on all vehicles and, it goes without saying, some of the river's best-loved waterside pubs!

The Thames Path continues onwards from Lechlade along the river's south bank, accessed from Halfpenny Bridge via steps leading down onto the towpath. St John's is the first lock on the River Thames, located just a few hundred metres ahead across flat grazing land with its keeper's cottage clearly visible beyond a couple of lazy serpentine loops. As one draws closer to the lock, the retrospective view to Lechlade is utterly mesmerizing. It is one of those sights that invariably results in a near fatal overdose of the 'picturesque' type adjectives but, in the case of Lechlade from St John's Lock and bridge, any such hyperbole is more than warranted. I had the rare good fortune to be photographing there on a tranquil Friday evening as the sun was setting behind the octagonal spire of St Lawrence's Church. Friday night is bell ringing practice and the sound of peal after peal rolling out across the river meadows as the sun disappeared below the horizon added a totally unexpected dimension to the scene.

The only blot upon that almost idyllic composition is the completely intact concrete World War II pillbox lurking menacingly on the opposite bank midway between town and lock, the first of several that will be encountered further downstream. They offer a chilling reminder of the fear and uncertainty that pervaded the nation after the declaration of war in 1939 and the shocking, morale-sapping evacuation of Dunkirk the following year. That string of modest fortifications was a secondary line of defence should those along the south coast fail in the event of an invasion.

St John's Lock and adjacent bridge were named after the medieval Augustinian priory located near by and whose lands and rights extended down to the river. The bridge was first built from stone during the early part of the thirteenth century, replacing an earlier wooden structure that had been washed away during severe flooding. Despite this allegedly more durable version, it was neglected to such an extent by the monks charged with its upkeep that one risked life and limb to cross the Thames at this particular point. Matters got so out of

Opposite: The Thames at dawn from Halfpenny Bridge, Lechlade.

Above left: Concrete pillboxes set at strategic intervals along the banks of the Thames stand as stark reminders of the dark days of the Second World War and the Battle of Britain, when the threat of invasion was very real.

Above right: The Portland cement statue of Old Father Thames at St John's Lock, Lechlade, is weathering nicely with age but the old boy's image is not well served by the grey wooden paddle now gripped in his right hand

hand that both Edward III and later Richard II were obliged to make financial grants towards ensuring that the bridge remained viable for both civilian and potential military use.

The lock is also renowned as the home of Old Father Thames. The massive sculpture by Raffaelle Monti (1818–81) had originally been created for the fountains of Crystal Palace Park when the vast glass pavilion from the Great Exhibition of 1851 held in Hyde Park was dismantled and relocated to the south London suburb of Sydenham. When one considers that Monti was renowned for his illusionary, veiled figures carved from white marble, it was a radical departure to carve the old man from a block of Portland cement.

A disastrous fire razed the Crystal Palace to the ground in 1936 and all the surviving statuary was sold off to private bidders. 'Thames' eventually came into the possession of Mr H. Scott Freeman, a philanthropic member of the Thames Conservancy who suggested his sculpture would be a fitting memorial to celebrate the Conservancy's centenary year of 1958. Consequently, Old Father Thames was transported up to the source of the Thames, and left to the mercies of the vandals. His torment endured for sixteen years until relocated to the safety of St John's Lock, from where he now monitors the cruisers and canal boats progressing up and down his river and the old boy wears the resigned expression of someone in a dead-end job with few prospects of advancement.

It will perhaps come as no surprise to learn that the well-known riverside pub on St John's bridge is named The Trout Inn, the first of several encountered *en route* to London. The site of the current inn has probably always been in the hospitality business, as the medieval priory's hospital was thought to have occupied the same location. Being named after a beautiful river fish is particularly appropriate for a riverside establishment accustomed to feeding travellers and sending them contentedly on their way. However, one wonders with what relish earlier diners might have tucked into their rare steaks had the inn retained an earlier name (wisely abandoned in the early eighteenth century): 'John the Baptist's Head' – a hearty platter indeed.

Although starting off from St John's Lock on the south bank, the Thames Path soon transfers to the opposite side via a substantial footbridge and hugs the river's edge through a series of sinuous curves towards Buscot, a traditional English country estate now vested into the care of the National Trust. The estate comprises a late-eighteenth-century mansion set amid extensive parkland, formal and water gardens, a small village and over 3,500 acres of farmland. Buscot is typical of similar holdings extant throughout England, many of which are still owned and managed by families whose ancestors can be traced back for centuries. Buscot has slightly more recent origins, the house and parkland having been created towards the end of the eighteenth century for the somewhat confusingly named Edward

Loveden Loveden, although the estate had actually been in the family since 1557.

Prior to inheriting the estate from his great-uncle, Loveden's surname was actually Townsend but, in the idiosyncratic manner exhibited by wealthy landowners of that era, the bequest stipulated that he change his name to Loveden. The practice did not stop there, as Loveden Loveden's son inherited Buscot as Pryse Pryse, his grandson as Pryse Loveden and his great-grandson as Sir Pryse Pryse! Loveden was a prominent public figure and politician and co-founder of the organization that would eventually become the Royal Agricultural Society. However, his most notable achievement as a parliamentarian was to head a committee formed in

Above: The Trout Inn by St John's Bridge, Lechlade, is one of several of that name encountered along the length of the Thames Path, offering hospitality to both walkers and boaters.

Left: The main street of Buscot village comprises houses and cottages in differing architectural styles, a tearoom and ornate village hall with clock tower.

Left: A little upstream from Buscot Lock and village is a section of river bank that was once occupied the Cheese Wharf, dedicated to just one of the many commodities shipped to Oxford and London.

Below: The serpentine loops of the Thames between St John's and Buscot locks highlight just how difficult it must have been to navigate the river in a heavily laden barge.

Opposite left: Buscot's church of St Mary has retained its Norman chancel arch from around 1200, but much of the building has been remodelled over the centuries; the additions included a Perpendicular tower with west doorway and window.

Opposite right: St Mary's interior contains a superb seventeenth-century Spanish carved wood lectern and monuments to the Loveden family of Buscot Park, but its greatest asset is the 1891 east window by Sir Edward Burne-Jones entitled *The Good Shepherd*.

1793, whose task was improve navigation along the Thames from Staines to Lechlade – a role that earned him the affectionate nickname of 'Old Father Thames'.

Loveden's work on improving the state of the river was perhaps not entirely altruistic; his own lock at Buscot not only charged high tolls but he was also heavily involved financially in the Thames & Severn Canal. It was most certainly in his interests to ensure the smooth passage of cargo-laden barges from the canal's junction with the Thames at Lechlade and then on to London and vice versa for shipping goods and materials away from the capital. The Industrial Revolution was gathering pace and the canal 'fever' of construction reached a peak in 1792, when as many as forty-two new canals were proposed and speculation in shares was rife. Despite accruing wealth from his business interests and three prudent marriages to wealthy heiresses, the building of Buscot and considerable land acquisition resulted in the estate being passed on with a considerable burden of debt attached.

'Doing' Buscot is far from straightforward, as the village, church and parsonage are located quite close to the river but the house is located some distance away to the south. In this respect, motorists might appear to have the upper hand over pedestrians, not least because the Thames Path is on the north bank. The swings and roundabouts of fortune regarding the benefits of exploring on foot or by car just about even themselves out over the journey from source to sea. Drivers can obviously access more of the towns and villages set some distance away from the riverbank path, but will be denied the privilege of walking long stretches of the Thames Path amid the solitude of nature. There is also an element of 'tortoise and hare' between cars and walkers along this section of the river, due largely to the absence of road bridges. Those walking the Thames Path need do little than point their feet eastwards at Buscot Lock and continue their march onwards towards the next objective of Kelsmscott Manor. Motorists are obliged to retrace the route back to St John's bridge at Lechlade, cross the river and thereafter follow a narrow country lane to the village of Kelmscott, leave their vehicles in the designated car park and continue on foot for a further ten minutes!

Right: Buscot Park.

Above: The entrance to William Morris's Kelmscott Manor.

Below: The Old Kitchen of Kelmscott Manor has been recently renovated to reflect the Elizabethan simplicity of the building that so appealed to Morris.

Opposite above: St George's Kelmscott has a small medieval glass portrayal of the dragon slaying set into the east window.

Opposite below: William Morris fabrics and wall coverings adorn part of the chancel and there is a monument to him in the churchyard.

Although slightly irksome during inclement weather, the exclusion of most vehicles from the site (disabled 'blue badge' holders excepted) ensures that visitors can more fully appreciate the tranquillity of the Elizabethan mansion's riverside setting. It is not difficult to understand why William Morris (1834–96) fell in love with this place and made it his home for some twenty-five years and during that period, it served as the inspirational hub for the Arts and Crafts movement he spearheaded. The house originated as a Tudor farmhouse in the 1500s and was later extended by the addition of a wing to the north-east corner during the mid-seventeenth century. Morris chose it as his summer home, signing a joint lease with the pre-Raphaelite painter Dante Gabriel Rossetti in 1871. The house contains a collection of the possessions and works of Morris and his associates, including furniture, textiles, carpets and ceramics.

The river lies but a few metres from the manor's entrance and having perhaps spent a leisurely hour amid the quietly inspirational environs of Kelmscott, it seems somehow appropriate that walkers on the Thames Path should spend the next couple of miles travelling solely among the sights and sounds of nature. Nonetheless, the river and its immediate surroundings on the north bank footpath are devoid of notable (or indeed, any) landmarks and, with the exception of Grafton Lock, there are no man-made structures between Kelsmcott and Radcot Bridge. This is the first of several similar stretches on the way to Oxford punctuated only by locks, bridges and the welcome sight of riverside inns located by those river crossings, several of which have been established for centuries, catering for both water-borne travellers and those using the turnpike coach roads.

The Thames saunters through this unremarkable slice of English countryside with no great urgency and even customarily shy herons seem barely able to raise sufficient energy to fly away from advancing walkers. However, any collective apathy is soon dispersed by initial sightings of Radcot Bridge, thought to be the oldest stone bridge over the Thames and vying with Newbridge (next but one downstream) to be considered the most elegant. The bridge at Radcot was built from a particularly high-quality Cotswold limestone quarried at Taynton, a village lying 2 miles to the north-west of Burford. The quarry was still in operation until fairly recently and certainly boasts an impressive architectural *curriculum vitae*, its stone having been used in the construction of such notable buildings as St Paul's Cathedral, Windsor Castle and, in Oxford, the New Bodleian Library, Merton College and Christ Church.

That original bridge now straddles a backwater of the river as the main channel now flows under the single-arch Canal Bridge built by the Thames Commissioners and named after the navigation cut dug out in 1787. This was to facilitate the heavier traffic anticipated by the imminent completion of the Thames & Severn Canal, whose junction with the Thames was at Lechlade, some 10 miles further upriver.

A river crossing existed at this point long before the Norman Conquest, carrying the main north–south road linking the Saxons kingdoms of Mercia and Wessex, and although the earliest structures would have been of timber, there is brief reference to a stone bridge in a tenth-century document relating to a grant of land in the vicinity of the river. Consequently, the date of 1225 generally attributed to its construction by Cistercian monks was most probably the time when they actually dismantled and rebuilt that more rudimentary structure.

Radcot exhibits the features typical of most medieval bridges, most notably the triangular buttresses incorporated into the upstream facing piers. Their purpose was to minimize the potentially damaging effect of strong currents during times of flooding and divert

Pollarded willow trees line the banks of the River Thames near Radcot Bridge on a tranquil, frosty morning in the depths of winter.

Above: This view of Radcot Bridge under flood conditions clearly shows how the upstream-facing buttresses used by its medieval builders successfully divert any debris through the arches. This practice alleviated the risk of flooding by not allowing a log jam to build up and create a dam across the arches.

Opposite: Faringdon's market place is quintessentially English and the coffee shop and delicatessen housed within a seventeenth-century building that was once a saddler's shop boasts the town's oldest shop frontage, having remained unaltered for a century. The interior is as endearingly topsy-turvy as the curiously angled window frames suggest it might be.

fallen trees and other floating debris through the arches on either side. Medieval bridges are also noted for their humpback appearance, created by the natural upward flow of pointed gothic arches and even though the gradient of the central arch has obviously been reduced, the tarmac surface of the road is well and truly gauged by modern vehicles unable to negotiate such an abrupt contour at speed.

As a strategically located river crossing, war and turmoil have inevitably featured in the bridge's history, although perhaps surprisingly Radcot has witnessed few really notable events. However, there was one battle in English history of sufficient significance to actually have been named after the bridge. The Battle of Radcot Bridge was fought on 20 December 1387 between supporters of the young king Richard II (led by Robert de Vere) and the Lords Appellant, a powerful group of barons including Henry Bolingbroke, Earl of Derby (the future Henry IV), who sought better stewardship of the nation's affairs from the monarch and his closest advisers. The King's adversaries won the day, but de Vere did manage to escape by swimming upstream under cover of darkness, thereafter fleeing to France and remaining in permanent exile. A substantial part of the bridge was sabotaged in advance of the engagement and further damage inflicted during fighting and so the majority of that which survives today is a late-fourteenth-century restoration of the earlier version.

The Swan Inn stands right by the banks of the main navigation channel and single arched bridge, its riverside garden offering a perfect vantage point from which to observe the varied assortment of passing cruisers and longboats. Radcot is not the easiest of the Thames bridges to negotiate, due to the narrowness of the arch, a sharp blind bend on the upstream side of the bridge and the fact that downstream traffic has right of way. That combination can make for interesting and frequently amusing viewing, especially during the summer months when many boats have inexperienced helmsmen at the wheel.

The A4095 road over the Radcot bridges heads south towards the historic market town of Faringdon, set on high ground less than 3 miles from the river. For motorists following the Thames it is a really worthwhile detour but for walkers on the Thames Path, such a deviation is less straightforward due to the paucity of public transport around Radcot. The views back across the floodplain from Faringdon are quite breathtaking and one can readily appreciate why it was perceived as a coveted strategic position. Because it suffered considerable damage during the Civil War, Faringdon's buildings are generally not as old as might be expected from a place which was granted a market charter in 1218 and whose history extends back to long before the Conquest. One exception is the richly endowed parish church of All Saints, parts of which date back to the twelfth century,

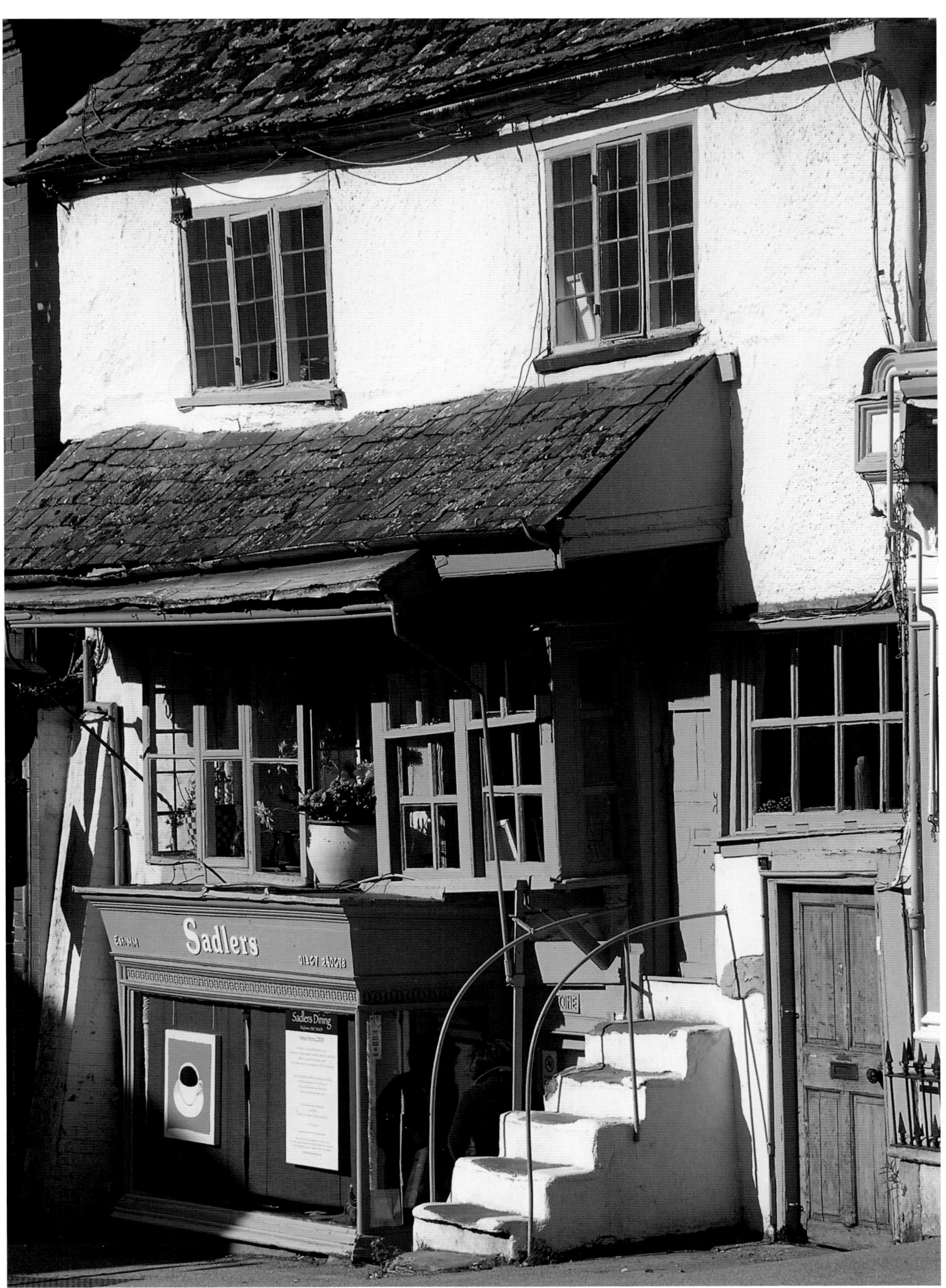
Sadlers
Sadlers Dining

Below and bottom: All Saints' Church looks down on Faringdon's market place but its air of superiority is somewhat diminished by a truncated tower, damaged during the English Civil War. The church ranges from the twelfth to the nineteenth century but, is predominately thirteenth-century Transitional and includes impressive details such as the wrought-iron dragon's head design on the south door.

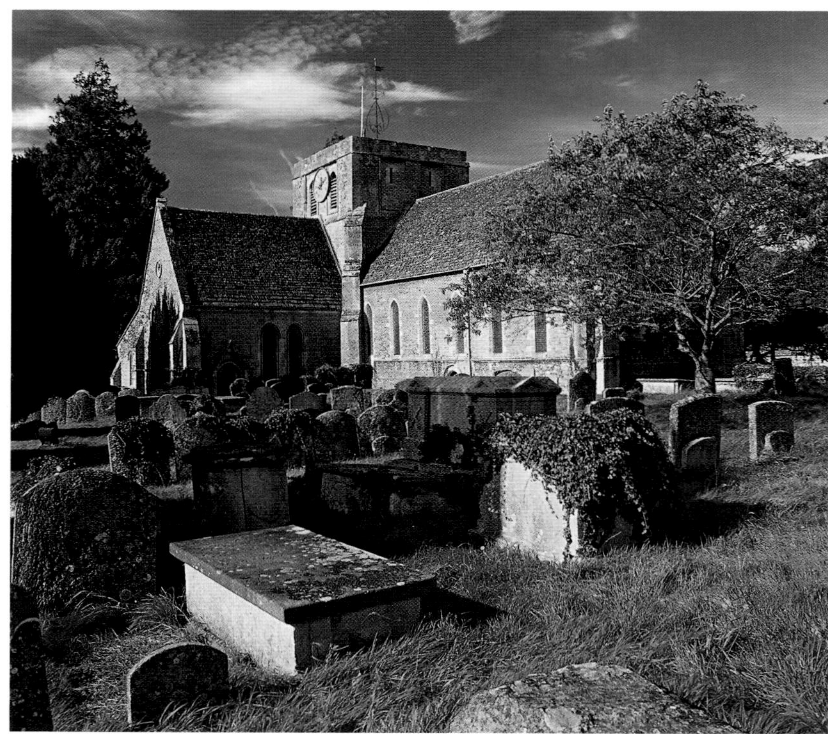

but the building's most arresting physical attribute is the rather squat tower that once carried a steeple until it fell foul of a cannonball during the 1645 fighting. The visual proportions of All Saints' would be aesthetically enhanced if the spire had been rebuilt, but whether for reasons of finance or technical considerations, the tower remains in its truncated state.

The church is entered through a door bearing some incredibly accomplished examples of wrought iron, most aptly described by Sir Nikolaus Pevsner as 'splendid agitated scrollwork'. However, it is to the monuments dedicated to prominent local families, the Pyes of Faringdon House and the Untons from Wadley House, that one's attention is unerringly drawn. The Pyes have their own chapel near the chancel but the star of the monumental show in the north aisle is the kneeling figure of Dorothy, Lady Unton. It is carved in the most intricate detail from the finest quality alabaster, endowing every fold and stitch of fabric on her clothes with an almost lifelike texture. The most extraordinary feature is the vast mourning hood that surely could only have been worn indoors as it looks incapable of surviving anything more that a gentle breeze. Lady Unton kneels in front of an elaborate wall mounted plaque to her first husband, Sir Henry Unton (1557–96), ambassador to France for Elizabeth I.

The Thames Path eastwards from Radcot to Tadpole Bridge transfers to the south bank, passes Radcot Lock and just a few hundred metres further on, arrives at Old Man's Bridge, an arched wooden footbridge on the site of a weir known as Old Man's or Harper's weir, dismantled during the 1860s. A footbridge stood next to the weir as this point on the river was an important crossing point linking communities on either side, so even though the weir was dispensed with, the bridge remained in service. That original bridge became unstable, was replaced with another but that too was deemed unsafe and so a new version was finally put in place around 1894.

In much the same way that pubs are frequently located on road crossings of the Thames, this pedestrian route is reputed to have once boasted a riverside inn named The Spotted Cow. Its isolated location away from the prying eyes of the local constabulary ensured that it attracted an infamous clientèle and was used for cock fighting, gambling and other dubious activities. Sadly, for those walking the Thames Path, there is now but a sturdy

Left: Old Man's Bridge stands on the site of a former weir and adjacent footbridge but although the weir has long since disappeared, the continuity of a public right of way has been maintained.

Below: Rushey Lock may be one the more isolated on this deeply rural section of the Thames but is also renowned for its immaculately kept gardens, a tradition maintained with pride by all lock keepers along the non-tidal river.

wooden bridge and any cows in the immediate vicinity are most likely to be very much alive and of the black and white variety, rather than spotted and swinging back and forth on a pub sign.

Cartographers mapping the section between Radcot and Tadpole bridges will have had little opportunity to reach for the brown contour pen, the landscape on either side of the Thames being untroubled by much in the way of undulation. However, despite the flatness of its immediate environs, the river is really quite fascinating here, as it performs a seemingly never-ending series of meanders. Some of those loops are so pronounced that one senses that in the not too distant future (geologically speaking, rather than next year), there could well be the formation of one or more oxbow lakes. As the river cuts on the outside edge of a meander, it deposits soil and material on the inside. Over thousands of years, the river will actually double back and draw sufficiently close enough in certain areas that when a flood occurs, a new channel cuts across the exaggerated loop to create an oxbow lake. The river's course is then straightened, the oxbow lake becomes isolated and the whole process can start all over again.

The footpath sensibly cuts across some of the loops until they relent in the vicinity of Rushey Lock. Rushey is notable for possessing one of the most perfectly preserved 'paddle and rymer' weirs on the river (see pages 102–3). Rushey was one of six new stone pound locks built by the Thames Commissioners towards the end of the eighteenth century, most located in exactly the same place as former flash weirs. The lock on this section of the Thames might have been created a mile further upstream at the site of another flow control point, Nan's Weir, but surveys revealed that the structure and condition of the riverbed in that location was less favourable than at Rushey.

The Rushey Lock that visitors see today is a rebuilt version created in 1896 and although lock keepers along

Above and left: Despite appearing as diminutive as its namesake, Tadpole Bridge is nevertheless a much-frequented crossing, although deep gauges in the tarmac of its hump show that it was never intended to carry modern motor vehicles. Its single arch may not match the gothic of its upstream and downstream neighbours of Radcot and Newbridge respectively; it is nevertheless built from a particularly mellow Cotswold limestone that positively glows in the soft light of sunrise or sunset.

the length of the non-tidal Thames are renowned for their impeccably presented gardens and lock surroundings, Rushey is well above average. The keeper's cottage, with its charming, pyramid-style roof with protruding dormer-type windows, was reputed to have once been a guesthouse. It was not only patronized by those who sought the peace and tranquillity of nature, but also by certain celebrities who sought privacy away from the public gaze. Movie icons such as Douglas Fairbanks and Errol Flynn were known to have relaxed around Rushey. Imagine the mayhem and ensuing kerfuffle from the paparazzi if a present-day celebrity were to hide out in a Thames lock keeper's cottage!

The Thames Path once again transfers walkers from one bank to another at Rushey, a throwback to when the river towpath was continually forced to keep swapping sides at locks, weirs or bridges due ancient landowning rights. However, it is hardly an arduous task and, during the course of a day's hike, the different perspectives created by the change in angle and direction of the sun (when shining) as one transfers from south to north bank, or vice versa, can be quite rewarding.

Most of the remaining distance between Rushey Lock and Tadpole Bridge is along the gravel track used as an access road to the lock, so good progress can be made towards the riverside oasis of The Trout Inn. The inn's public bar once displayed a stuffed freak trout with teeth in its tongue, and although The Trout still functions as a traditional pub, its elegant bedrooms and good food could probably tempt all but the most resolute Thames Path walkers to linger longer than they might have originally intended. Still, expecting the unexpected has always been one of the joys of travelling and it seems a shame that the constraints placed upon so many people's time means that daily schedules have to be rigorously adhered to in the style of a military operation.

Tadpole Bridge itself is a single-arched structure dating from the end of the eighteenth century, and although it lacks the architectural and historical pedigree of neighbouring Thames crossings, there is an elegant simplicity about it. The road links the villages of Buckland and Bampton – the former probably having already been encountered by motorists heading towards Tadpole Bridge and the latter deserving significantly more than a cursory glance while driving through. Pedestrians may have to contemplate the clock, their maps and the state of their legs before deciding whether to include Bampton in the day's itinerary, as the next segment of the walk is one of the longest and loneliest of the entire journey. However, it is for such occasions that comfortable riverside inns were created, and the ancient market town is but a gentle stroll up the road.

Although archaeologists can trace Bampton's existence back to Roman times and beyond into the Iron Age, its name is pure Saxon in origin, *beam-tun* meaning 'tree enclosure'. People often get confused between the Bampton in Oxfordshire and its namesake in Devon, a mistake readily compounded by the fact that for centuries both held famous annual horse fairs that attracted buyers and sellers from far and wide. In common with many other towns and villages granted similar ancient rights, those dates on the calendar are now more likely to be marked by the arrival of a traditional funfair rather than an influx of horses.

Bampton's two most distinctive buildings are the church of St Mary the Virgin, whose tall spire is a landmark for miles around, and the rather grand Italianate town hall of 1838. The latter building was originally designed as a dual-purpose building, whose open ground floor would be a covered market and the upper storey act as the town hall. Unfortunately it failed to live up to expectations as a boost to market trade and the open arches were subsequently filled in. After late-twentieth-century restoration work it has now taken on a new lease of life as a valuable public resource and well used by the local community, even if there is just a hint

Below and bottom: Bampton lies to the north of Tadpole Bridge, and the architectural style of its town hall suggests that provincial Italy has been relocated to deepest Oxfordshire. However, the rest of the village is unquestionably rural England, not least the attractive houses grouped around the broad expanse of St Mary's churchyard.

Right: As the Thames flows past the isolated communities of Duxford and Chimney, the wooded sections on either bank alternate between natural copses and the more structured, geometric lines of man-made plantations.

Opposite: A vivid sunset photographed through one of Newbridge's gothic arches.

of 'white elephant' about it. Bampton's church is tucked away behind the busy main street, set amid narrow lanes lined with traditional cottages and flanked by Georgian and earlier period houses, including a fourteenth-century deanery (with later additions) built by the See of Exeter as a summer residence.

The next river crossing is at Newbridge, easily accessed by road from Bampton via Aston and Standlake on the B4449 and thereafter the A415 main road from Witney to Abingdon. The Thames Path departs from Tadpole Bridge to follow the north bank as far as Shifford Lock, transferring to the opposite side of the river for the remainder of the journey to Newbridge. The walk from bridge to bridge is 6½ miles along yet another section of either deep rural tranquillity or disconcerting isolation, depending on one's mood on that particular day.

A few hundred metres to the east of Tadpole Bridge, the Thames executes a couple of tight hairpins, and at the apex of one of these loops sits another wartime concrete pillbox, exposed and starkly ugly during winter, but more modestly cloaked by nettles and other greenery during the summer months. This particular one is worthy of note because it has been adapted for use as a hibernaculum, although sad to note that despite signs clearly stating its 'change of use', those responsible for its conversion have been obliged to post a further notice advising people that it is neither a rubbish dump nor a public toilet.

The path emerges from the shade of a deeply wooded section out into the vast open expanses of the Chimney Meadows Nature Reserve, comprising some 600 acres of flower- and wildlife-rich floodplain, waterways, hedgerows and wet woodland. Public accessibility to this priceless resource is being increased year on year, but the Thames Path remains a separate entity, skirting the reserve's south-eastern boundary. Another slice of river history is encountered just a little further downstream, when the wooden-arched frame of Tenfoot Bridge comes into view. This marks the site of another of the river's many old flash weirs, but rather than indicating the available headroom beneath its arch, the bridge's title refers to the actual width of the old weir. In common with several other similar pedestrian-only crossings over the Thames, Tenfoot Bridge was built to maintain a public right of way established over the now long dismantled weirs.

The public footpaths leading away from the south bank lead to either Buckland Marsh or to Duxford, the latter being a small farming community set just below a winding loop of what was the original course of the Thames and, as the name implies, a recognized crossing place where humans or livestock could negotiate the ford when conditions were favourable. The right of way does continue past Duxford alongside the river, rejoining the main channel at Shifford Lock and weir complex. If that course is followed, walkers must be sure to take an extra half-hour to walk back along the lock cut to where a footbridge carries the Thames Path from north to south banks. This is a few hundred yards of dense tree cover, and during the height of summer, when the foliage is at its densest, the silence on a still day is absolute, and even birds seem reluctant to open their beaks in song for fear of breaking the spell.

Shifford Lock is one of the youngest on the river, built in 1897 a little upstream from the site of an old flash weir. This lock is slightly unusual in that it was dug and constructed on dry land and only when completed was the lock cut excavated and the Thames allowed to flow along the straight course rather than the impossible meanders in the vicinity of Duxford. This is also the loneliest, most isolated lock on the river, and even though the current keeper has access to the outside world courtesy of a gravel track and a car, Bampton is still a long to go for a pint of milk and a newspaper. In the days before individual car ownership was commonplace, a posting to Shifford would not have been for the unfit or fainthearted. It is a lifestyle set in a rural retreat that some now crave and would pay a small fortune to achieve, but one wonders how quickly the enthusiasm would pall.

The village of Shifford (its name meaning 'sheep ford') is visible but inaccessible from the Thames, but motorists on the Bampton to Newbridge route will be able to wend their way down narrow lanes to get there. It seems quite incomprehensible, but legend has it that King Alfred held an important gathering of lords and nobles at Shifford in AD 890, some sources even going so far as to suggest that it was a parliamentary assembly. That alleged meeting was apparently mentioned in seventeenth-century documents, suggesting that the information came from the Anglo Saxon Chronicles or similar manuscripts of that era. Unfortunately for the romantics, linguists and historians are united in their opinion that any such references to Shifford were erroneously translated.

As the outline of buildings disappears from view across the northern bank, the Thames Path disappears into another wooded section that can be rather damp and slippery underfoot, but any difficulty is short-lived and the final few hundred metres to Newbridge are across a series of fields with easily manipulated gates. Newbridge is a sight for sore eyes and parched mouths, but even before thirsts are quenched at either of the two riverside pubs, The Maybush or The Rose Revived, one should really pause to admire the sublime architecture of the bridge itself.

Comparisons with Radcot are inevitable, not least because they were both constructed using golden Cotswold limestone from the same quarries at Taynton, and although both have been substantially repaired over time, both still retain the elegance of their original gothic arches. Newbridge was built in 1250, some two and half decades later than Radcot, hence the title 'new bridge'. Much of that which survives today dates from a substantial late-fifteenth-century 'facelift' following vociferous complaints from communities living either side of the river. The River Windrush enters the Thames just a few metres upstream from the bridge, its waters making a noticeable difference to the stature of the river. During times of heavy rain, when both are in full spate, the area around Newbridge is prone to widespread flooding, although additional smaller bridges alleviate this problem by creating an extended causeway across the Thames and Windrush floodplain.

Overleaf: Despite its traffic lights and a pub on either side (The Rose Revived left and The Maybush right), Newbridge still retains a timeless quality particularly accentuated in the depths of winter.

The bedroom windows recessed into the thatched roof of cottages in Stanton Harcourt may not let in much daylight, but the thickness of the thatch suggests that the occupants are significantly better insulated against cold and rain than many who live in more modern dwellings.

However, despite the introduction of traffic lights to create a single-file flow of vehicles over the more vulnerable stretches, asking a medieval bridge and surrounding infrastructure to cope with the demands of twenty-first-century traffic is not a viable option. It is acknowledged that the ancient monument cannot cope with much more stress and, despite weight restrictions being in force, an alternative river crossing is the most likely long-term solution and the design and consultation process is now under way. Of course it will inevitably impose a degree of visual blight upon that stretch of river but better that than a collapsed bridge. With every passing year, the problems facing those charged with conserving our medieval heritage are increasing at an alarming rate and regardless of whether one is talking about house, churches, cathedrals or bridges, the conundrum of whether to repair, replace or simply stabilize is an ongoing one that has no easy solution.

Newbridge's two waterside inns afford visitors the opportunity to sit in serene comfort and observe the extraordinary craftsmanship of those who built the arched structure. The willow-shaded gardens of The Rose Revived are perfect for morning viewing, or if you arrive at Newbridge during the late afternoon or early evening, the sixteenth-century Maybush is an ideal vantage point from which to enjoy the sight of the stonework bathed in the soft, mellow light of sunset. There are no real major sites of architectural or landscpe interest worthy of a detour in the immediate vicinity of Newbridge and so the next objectives for both pedestrians and motorists are Bablock Hythe and Stanton Harcourt – the former lying on the north bank of the river and the latter just a short distance away to the north-west.

For those heading towards Bablock Hythe along the Thames Path, there may be a sense of eager anticipation about arriving at a place famous for its centuries-old ferry and a traditional pub called The Ferryman Inn. Sadly, the modern reality does not quite match the romantic impression given by old photographs or paintings of the place, mostly depicting an appropriately clad ferrymen aboard his flat bottomed rope-hauled ferry, a heavily laden farm cart awaiting his arrival on the opposite bank. This has been an important crossing point since the Romans forded the Thames at Bablock Hythe; an altar from that period was discovered in the river and Roman coinage has also been unearthed from nearby fields.

A vehicle ferry operated here until being discontinued during the 1980s but since that time, there appears to have been only an intermittent, seasonal pedestrian-only service run by landlords of The Ferryman Inn. The reliability of that ferry tended to fluctuate, but the current incumbent of The Ferryman Inn appears determined to revive that ancient tradition. If that were the case, it would offer Thames Path walkers a useful alternative route along the towpath on the opposite bank as the official route temporarily deserts the river at Bablock Hythe, rejoining it later opposite the vast expanse of Farnmoor Reservoir and the final few meanders leading to Pinkhill Lock. The path's diversion 'inland' is due to the unsightly presence of a seemingly never-ending caravan park on the river's edge and, as one walks away from the Thames, the scene is further blighted a large development of prefabricated bungalows, euphemistically described as 'park homes'.

However, notwithstanding the inconvenience of having to leave the Thames temporarily, it actually could not have happened at a better place, because the diverted route partially follows the road to Stanton Harcourt. It is a village of pastel-hued thatched cottages and grey stone, with a church, parsonage and medieval manor house that for centuries was home to the ancient Harcourt dynasty. The family originated in Normandy, and both English and French branches have played significant roles in the histories of their respective nations. They relocated to Nuneham Courtenay (see pages 112–13) during the eighteenth century, returning to Stanton Harcourt around 1950. A Victorian restoration of the extensive original gatehouse range now forms the basis of the property, but several elements of the old manor survive, including a medieval kitchen and a tower from the same period, always referred to as Pope's Tower. The poet Alexander Pope (1688–1744) was a friend of Sir Simon Harcourt (later 1st Viscount Harcourt) and spent the summers of 1717 and 1718 in a room in the tower, working on his translation of the fifth book of Homer's *Iliad*.

The adjacent parish church of St Michael perfectly combines with the manor house and surrounding buildings to create a most agreeable grouping. Even though the large, cruciform church is noteworthy as a building in its own right, it is the collection of Harcourt monuments housed within that really take the eye. Lying in both the

Below: The parish church of St Michael, Stanton Harcourt, is richly endowed with Harcourt family monuments spanning four centuries, the earliest of which are those of Sir Robert Harcourt and his grandson, also Sir Robert (pictured here), who died in 1509.

Bottom: The Grade I Listed church of St Michael is an integral part of one of the region's most perfect architectural groupings, completed by the buildings of the medieval manor house and 'Pope's Tower'.

Right: The moorings set alongside the river's bank upstream from Swinford Bridge and Eynsham Lock look deceptively easy to access, but in reality they require more finesse on the tiller than inexperienced holiday bargees realise

Opposite: Swinford Toll Bridge may be an elegant eighteenth-century structure but the archaic methods of collecting tolls by hand from a booth in the middle of the road causes traffic mayhem during the morning and evening peak times.

south transept and the fifteenth-century Harcourt Chapel are recumbent effigies of family members covering a time span of several centuries. Arguably the most notable is that of Sir Robert Harcourt, standard-bearer to Henry Tudor (the future Henry VII) at the Battle of Bosworth Field in 1485. A faded and tattered flag leans against the wall above the tombs of the knight and his wife Margaret, and although it is uncertain whether this actual standard was the one waved in triumph upon the defeat of Richard III and the House of York, it certainly looks the part.

From Stanton Harcourt, the way onwards towards Oxford is straightforward for walkers but becomes progressively more difficult for motorists. Oxford is not a vehicle-friendly city, and has armed itself with an almost impenetrable defensive cordon of ring roads and bypasses, and although one is urged to use the hugely efficient 'park and ride' system, that does not allow interesting places on the city's outskirts to be visited easily.

However, there are a few more miles to cover before such matters need be addressed, and so drivers can head towards Eynsham and the Swinford Toll Bridge via the B4449. Walkers will not need to retrace their steps back to Bablock Hythe, as a public footpath takes a direct route back onto the Thames Path. There follows one of the numerous unremarkable stretches along the Thames that are just what they are: stretches of rural England covered with trees and shrubs that just happen to be either side of a meandering river. In this particular instance, any dampened spirits are soon lifted by the distant view of Swinford Bridge which, as its name implies, was a recognized fording place where pigs were driven across the river.

It is sad that many year's growth of tree branches and other foliage have encroached so far across either end of Swinford Bridge, rather tending to truncate the bridge's Georgian elegance. However, the arches over the main river channels remain unaffected, allowing a reasonable degree of visual appreciation of one of the more aesthetically pleasing bridges across the river, but what cannot initially be seen from ground level is the small, glass-sided kiosk set in the middle of the road on

the bridge's northern end. Swinford is one of just two surviving toll bridges on the Upper Thames (Whitchurch being the other, see page 138), charging a minimum toll of 5p per vehicle.

The bridge replaced an existing ferry adjacent to the shallows of the ford and was opened in 1769, having been funded and built by wealthy local landowner, the Earl of Abingdon. He considered it to be a worthwhile investment rather than merely a public service, but his revenue from tolls proved less lucrative than anticipated. Paying for new bridges had become a major problem, especially after Henry VIII's Dissolution of the Monasteries in 1536, largely because structures such as bridges had been under Church and religious patronage since medieval times. Monastic orders were well endowed with funds from wealthy patrons keen to buy their way into heaven and, to those stonemasons and architects responsible for the largest cathedrals and abbey churches, a mere river bridge would have presented relatively few problems.

A well-meaning, but ultimately flawed segment of the Magna Carta stated that money could not be extracted from ordinary members of the public to pay for the building of bridges that had not previously existed. They could be charged tolls to pay for the upkeep of an existing one but if a new river crossing was deemed essential, it had to be funded either by the Crown or wealthy individuals. That latter part of the eighteenth century was the golden era of coach travel and road building once the concept of turnpikes (toll roads) had really caught on, and during that time around 400 turnpike acts were passed by Parliament within a space of twenty years. The highways from Gloucester and the west rather ground to a halt at Witney, as without a river crossing there was no direct link through to Oxford via Eynsham and the River Thames.

It required the full might of an Act of Parliament to sanction the building of the bridge and to also set out the terms and conditions. Deviating away from customary practice, the ownership of the bridge and receipts from any tolls charged were assigned to the Earl and his heirs 'in perpetuity'. No tax was payable either, and as it was all contained within an Act of Parliament, that status applies to this day. At the time of writing in 2009, the bridge is being offered up for sale with an asking price somewhere in excess of £1.5 million, but set against a rising tide of dissent over the presence of a 5p toll bridge in twenty-first-century England, it might not be such a cast-iron investment. There is a view that it should be acquired by the Local Authority, as the queue of traffic at peak hours extends way back over a mile into the heart of Eynsham village. Objectors suggest that pollution levels from idling engines pose a real threat to both health and the environment but one wonders whether it will constitutionally require another Act of Parliament to revoke the eighteenth-century original before any further measures can be taken?

The Trout Inn sits on the banks of the Thames facing the ruins of Godstow Priory, and both have associations with iconic figures; the former having been a favourite haunt of Inspector Morse and the latter haunted by the spirit of Rosamund Clifford, the 'Fair Rosamund' who was mistress to Henry II and died at Godstow.

The view downstream from the bridge comprises Eynsham Lock and weir in the foreground, set against the backdrop of Wytham Great Wood, whose densely tree-lined slopes plunge almost as far as the water's edge in places. Areas of shade combined with rain and spring water running down through the wood make for a very slippery Thames Path, and walkers do need to tread with care along the muddier sections. When the path breaks out into more open ground, the Thames is joined on the left by the River Evenlode, the last of its four main tributaries flowing down from the Cotwolds. After a further uneventful length of river, the path arrives at King's Lock, the most northerly point on the Thames. Although pedestrians will continue without let or hindrance towards Godstow (and without changing banks), an aerial view or satellite map image reveals that King's Lock marks the start of a quite complex network of streams, channels cuts and canals in the vicinity of Oxford. A man-made channel, Duke's Cut, leads away from the main river channel to provide the first of two links between the River Thames and the Oxford Canal. It was built by the Duke of Marlborough and opened in 1798, providing easier navigational access between the two waterways than the alternative at Isis Lock near the city centre.

Motorists can get from Swinford Bridge to Godstow by a choice of routes but perhaps the better option is to head away from the river and back towards Eynsham; follow the plentiful signs and take the main A40 to Oxford. At the Wolvercote roundabout, take the fifth exit signposted to Wytham and that road will lead straight to the car park of The Trout Inn, one of the river's most pleasant waterside pubs. It is set immediately next the older of the two Godstow bridges, a later version being constructed around 1792 to carry the road over a newly opened lock cut. Although The Trout Inn is known to many television viewers as a 'watering hole' favoured by the famous detective Inspector Morse, Godstow is most famous for its twelfth-century nunnery, the ruined walls of which are located between the bridges and Godstow Lock.

Godstow is irrevocably linked with Rosamund de Clifford, mistress to Henry II and universally referred to as 'Fair Rosamund' in the highly romanticized and largely fictional versions of the affair. The saga was 'spun' into a battle between the two contrasting women in Henry's life: the austere Queen Eleanor of Aquitaine and the soft English rose tracked down by the vengeful queen and murdered in a secret labyrinth housed beneath a royal palace at Woodstock (near the current Blenheim Palace).

The legend of Rosamund certainly captivated the imagination of writers, poets and especially some of the Pre-Raphaelite painters, for whom the Mills & Boon type story proved utterly irresistible. Dante Gabriel Rossetti, Edward Burne-Jones and John William Waterhouse painted either vivid portraits of Rosamund or the alleged final confrontation, in which Eleanor is proffering a vial of poison. Rossetti's portrait is by far the most striking, endowing Rosamund with luxuriant red hair and the ruddy cheeks of someone who has spent years on a farm. That definition might not be too far removed from reality because of the few elements of fact extractable from this story, the first is that Rosamund was the daughter of a Marcher knight, Walter de Clifford, and probably first met Henry at her father's castle in the Wye Valley. The second known fact is that having been exposed and humiliated by her liaison with the king, she retired in shame to the sanctuary of Godstow nunnery and died there in 1176.

It was reported that her tomb was placed near the high altar of the nunnery's church and became a popular shrine at which both nuns and members of the public prayed, adorning it with flowers and other tributes. That practice allegedly continued until a couple of years after Henry's death in 1189, when an outraged Hugh, Bishop of Lincoln, ordered her remains to be interred in the normal burial ground. If Rosamund did get a headstone erected over her new grave, it might well have joined others in being used for paving slabs when a footpath was laid to the nearby village of Wytham. After the Dissolution, the buildings were given to Henry VIII's physician, George Owen whose family converted them into a country mansion but, as a Civil War stronghold, it was virtually destroyed in 1645 and the ruins thereafter used as a source of free building material by the locals. The scant ruins of Godstow now comprise some curtain walls and the remains of a sixteenth-century chapel.

In many respects, the scenery around Godstow will have changed little since the late 1850s, when a writer named Charles Hodgson began visiting the area on rowing trips from Oxford. Hodgson's 'day job' was a lecturer in mathematics at Christ Church College in Oxford but, at the same time, was successfully writing under the pseudonym of Lewis Carroll. He became close friends with the college's new Dean, Henry Liddell, and would often row members of his young family out of town to places such as Godstow or Nuneham Courtenay. One of the Dean's daughters was called Alice Liddell and, as the saying goes, 'the rest is history'. From the germ of an idea, a story told to pass the time during a day on the river, the worldwide best-selling novel *Alice's Adventures in Wonderland* was created, the not unreasonable assumption being that the work's heroine was modelled upon his young friend.

From Godstow Lock, the Thames Path continues along the same side of the river towards the village of Binsey, with the vast expanse of the 440 acres of Port Meadow stretching out on the opposite bank. It is both extraordinary and refreshing to see such a large area of untouched land lying so close to a large and expanding city such as Oxford, but, as property developers throughout England have discovered to their chagrin, ancient grazing rights assigned to a piece of land cannot be easily overturned. William the Conqueror gave those rights to the Burgesses of Oxford and they are listed accordingly in the Domesday Book of 1086. Not only does the meadow serve as an outstanding area for recreation, it is also a priceless resource for flora and fauna, having never been farmed or ploughed throughout its entire history.

Before continuing the narrative for walkers along the Thames Path, I must briefly suggest that anyone in a car who has reasonable mobility should go back to the Wolvercote roundabout and use Oxford's excellent park and ride system. Yes, it can be inconvenient having to decide what to take and what to leave behind, but not quite so tiresome as being stuck in queues for a car park or trying to find the correct road back out of the inadequately signposted city afterwards.

The scant ruins of Godstow Priory sit directly on the Thames Path near Godstow Lock. The legend of Fair Rosamund has probably been embellished and romanticized over time but, as Lewis Carroll discovered centuries later, the setting could not be more perfect for story telling.

Right: Most visitors to Oxford will almost certainly never catch sight of the old Gasworks Bridge, even though it is only a short stroll from Folly Bridge and Christ Church.

Opposite: Folly Bridge, with its castellated nineteenth-century building adorned with statuary, is one of Oxford's major landmarks and the conveniently located starting point of many walking and river tours.

The walk into Oxford is most illuminating because it gives an insight into a city that is so much more than the collection of historic educational establishments, housed in the architectural splendour for which it is world famous. As the path gradually converges with the city's main railway line, the first buildings encountered are the old brick terraced cottages, facing a network of garden allotments directly across the river. It is at this point that the other access point to and from the Oxford Canal is reached and crossed by a footbridge. It is well worth a detour to follow the path running alongside that connecting cut, but only if one has the ability to walk bent absolutely double beneath a steel girder bridge bearing the railway.

From the footbridge over the canal, the main path continues along the Thames to Osney Bridge, an unremarkable structure carrying the main A420 road into the city centre. Motorists probably think nothing of it but, as the bridge with the lowest headroom on the Thames at just 7 feet 6 inches, it is the bane of leisure boaters' lives. I watched the person at the tiller of a traditional canal longboat duck as his vessel just scraped beneath the bridge but to those piloting most motor cruisers, Osney Bridge is an insurmountable barrier that determines the length and scope of any future expeditions, forcing boat owners to choose whether their vessels will be moored upstream or downstream from Oxford. Owners who deemed their boats to be not too far above the height restriction have been know to partially dismantle the superstructure in an attempt to pass under Osney, forgetting that the published height applies only to the centre of the arch. The river bed at this point is probably littered with countless lamps, rails and other accessories that did not make it through to the other side.

Old riverside mills, newer factories and industrial estates line the river on the far side of Osney Bridge but they simply act as a reminder that this is a living and working city, rather than a historical monument set in aspic. That presence is not obtrusive and the path soon meanders out of site towards Folly Bridge, The Head of the River and the termination of this particular leg of the journey, although one final remnant of an industrial legacy remains in the form of the Old Gasworks Bridge. It was constructed in 1882 by the brilliantly named Oxford Gaslight and Coke Company to transport coal to their works across the river but the site was dismantled in 1960 and eventually regenerated and transformed into the Grand Pont Nature Reserve.

The name Grand Pont actually refers to the Norman bridge and extended arched causeway, originally carrying the road over the river and safely onwards across those meadows most prone to flooding on the route to Abingdon. The current Folly Bridge is in two parts and dates back to 1828, although traces of Saxon stonework remain incorporated into the later version. The original bridge had a fortified gateway or tower which, during the thirteenth century, was the home, study and observatory of Franciscan Friar, Roger Bacon (not to be confused with Francis). He was apparently so far ahead of his time that the locals associated his work with witchcraft rather than science. Bacon died in 1292 and the tower was later repaired with the additional of an elaborate top storey, a structure eventually replaced by the quasi-Venetian style brick building in 1849, the exterior of which is adorned with statuettes, gargoyles and other strange statuary.

Folly Bridge is an excellent place from which to start a walking tour of historic Oxford and how much one takes in simply depends on available time and stamina. If it is possible to spend more than one day, I can heartily recommend getting up at dawn and exploring the deserted streets while nobody is around. There is a magical, timeless feel to places such as Oxford when viewed without the noise, clamour and intrusion of traffic.

Christ Church is but a short stroll up towards the city centre from the river and also happens to be Oxford's grandest college, owing its origins to the vanity of Cardinal Wolsey, Henry VIII's chief minister. Not content with building Hampton Court (see pages 192–3), he wanted to build something comparable in Oxford, to be named Cardinal College, and ruthlessly suppressed St Frideswide's Priory to accommodate his grandiose plans. The scale and grandeur of the buildings is quite breathtaking and little wonder that Charles I selected Christ Church as his personal headquarters during the Civil War. The largest quadrangle in Oxford, Tom Quad, is entered through a magnificent portal dominated by Tom Tower, the seventeenth-century bell tower designed by Christopher Wren.

Wolsey's fall from grace in 1529 meant that it was taken over by Henry VIII, who elected to designate the old priory church as Oxford's cathedral when making it

Above: Hertford Bridge in New College Lane is universally referred to as the 'Bridge of Sighs' due to its alleged similarity to the famous bridge in Venice.

Below: The Sheldonian Theatre was designed by Sir Christopher Wren and built during the mid-1660s as a secular venue for meetings and public ceremonies of the University. It was named after Gilbert Sheldon, Chancellor of the University at the time the building was funded.

Opposite above: Broad Street's many shops include the world famous Blackwell's bookshop, but Broad Street has a darker history because it was here that the Protestant 'Oxford Martyrs', Hugh Latimer, Nicholas Ridley and Thomas Cranmer were all burnt at the stake in the mid-sixteenth century.

Opposite below: Early summer mornings are the best time to savour the atmosphere and architecture of Oxford.

a diocese in 1546. Because St Frideswide's Church had been truncated by two bays of the nave to accommodate the quad, it became, and remains to this day, England's smallest and most discreet cathedral. Because there are so many excellent guidebooks and other sources of information on Oxford, I do not propose to suggest a complex and detailed itinerary after the obligatory visit to Christ Church. However, if time is pressing and one simply wants to savour the very essence of collegiate Oxford, I can suggest a compact walk that would do the job very nicely.

From Christ Church, turn left and then left again into Broad Walk, a wide gravel path running past the college and along through Christ Church Meadow. However, do not follow it right through, but turn left again in front of a large area of playing fields towards the chapel tower of Merton College, one of the oldest and most venerable colleges. The intimacy of its buildings clustered around the university's oldest quad provide a marked contrast to its near neighbour, Christ Church.

With your back to Merton College, proceed left along Merton Street for a short distance and turn right into Magpie Lane and onwards past Oriel College – the university's fifth oldest, founded by Edward II in 1326. At the end of Magpie Lane, cross over the High Street,

The Varsit Shop
THE BUTTERY HOTEL
THE BUTTERY HOTEL
Oxford Campus Stores
OMC
Except for loading 6 pm - 10 am
LET

SILENCE
PLEASE

Left and below: Narrow streets such as Brasenose Lane lead away from the great circular dome of Radcliffe Camera. The thoroughfares are punctuated by college entrance portals and, although it is fascinating to explore on foot, visitors should also be mindful that when they encounter signs saying 'Silence Please'; somewhere near by is a hall full of undergraduates sweating over potentially life-determining exams.

veering diagonally right and, having passed the back quadrangle of the fifteenth-century All Souls College, enter Radcliffe Square. The small enclosure is dominated by the glorious dome of the Radcliffe Camera, built by James Gibbs in 1737–49 to house a library endowed by physician John Radcliffe, and it is now used as one of the reading rooms for the Bodleian Library, located at the north end of the square.

Continue up the right hand side of Radcliffe Square (Catte Street) and turn right into New College Lane to admire the 'Bridge of Sighs', built in 1913 to connect the older part of Hertford College with a later addition. The bridge actually appears as a curious hybrid of Venice's two most famous bridges, the Rialto and the Ponte dei Sosperi but despite obvious similarities, it was allegedly not designed as a replica of either!

Return back towards Catte Street and continue ahead into a large gravel enclosure flanked by railings that houses the Sheldonian Theatre and Clarendon Building – the former built by Wren in 1669 and the latter, which is now part of the Bodleian Library, by his pupil Nicholas Hawksmoor in 1715. By cutting back into Radliffe Square, one can then either exit to the right via Brasenose Lane or, for anyone with a head for heights and a desire to see one of the best views in England, head straight ahead to St Mary's Church and pay to climb the tower.

If the Brasenose option is pursued, pass by Lincoln College and Exeter Colleges, turn left into Turl Street, cross over the High Street into Alfred Street, right onto Blue Boar Street and you are back at Christ Church. If you have visited the church instead, simply follow the High Street until meeting Alfred Street, and retrace one's route that way. There are so many different ways to see Oxford and so much more to explore than the brief encounter offered above that the best solution is a good map, a decent pair of walking shoes and a comfortable bed.

However, when Oxford has been explored and enjoyed, there is the small matter of a trip down the Thames to consider and so steps must be retraced back to Folly Bridge to commence the next stage of the journey to Reading.

CHAPTER 4

Controlling the Flow
Locks, Weirs and Cuts

Locks are a familiar feature on many English waterways and although canals could not function without them, rivers have always flown naturally from source to sea without let or hindrance from man. The Thames could quite happily still be wending its unfettered way across the landscape, but had it not been for human intervention, many of the towns, villages and rural industries that have grown up along its banks would not have become so well established. Most only flourished by the Thames as a direct result of being able to harness its power to drive machinery or import and export goods and raw materials via water-borne transport. It is also easy to forget that without the degree of control currently exercised over the Thames, the river would not have evolved into the safe, well-managed venue for all the sporting and leisure activities that we simply take for granted today.

Britain's earliest settlers had established themselves by the river and as boat building techniques advanced, the Thames became more important as a means of trade and communication, particularly during the latter stages of the Celtic Iron Age from around 100 BC through to the Roman occupation of the first century AD. The Roman influence gradually extended upstream from London and at strategic points along the river, used their technical expertise to erect pile-driven wharves capable of handling heavy goods such as timber and building materials. Although the Romans had made the Thames a

Iffley Lock on the outskirts of Oxford was one of the three early 'pound locks' to be built during the seventeenth century. It was rebuilt in 1924 and, with its decorous weeping willow and immaculately tended gardens, is the epitome of a modern Thames lock.

more viable shipping route, it was the later Saxon settlers who originated the process of diverting water to power riverside corn mills. The Domesday Book recorded over 5,000 mills throughout England in William I's post-Conquest 'stock taking' and the middle and upper Thames featured prominently on that list.

As windmills had not yet appeared on the English landscape, the vast majority relied on water to drive their grinding wheels, and so for every mill, their would almost certainly have been a weir to harness and direct a constant flow of water onto the waterwheel. It was the introduction and manipulation of weirs that would ultimately be the cause so much friction between the mill owners and other river users. Medieval landowners regarded any stretch of river flowing across their land as private property and although the initial investment in buildings and machinery was costly, the potential for long-term return profit was excellent. The feudal system also gave those landowners the right to compel their agricultural tenants to bring their grain to the manorial mill, regardless of whether the percentage of flour taken as a toll by miller for both himself and the owner was fair. The only way to make the business pay was to keep the mill constantly operating and to ensure there was always a good head of water, millers built great weirs across the river.

Weirs were the forerunners of locks, but as they were constructed for the benefit of millers, boat users were not only seriously inconvenienced but also found themselves being charged hefty tolls for the privilege of passing through the barrier. Those earliest weirs were basic manipulations of the river's flow, often created by using parallel logs, timber beams, woven slats and other debris to block off the flow. The only obvious gap in the weir would have been the sluice where a torrent of water continued to flow through its narrow aperture. It was inconceivable that barges and other boats could hurtle through that gap in the manner of a slalom canoe racer and as a result the 'flash lock' came into being. One part of the weir comprised a movable, hinged gate of stout

vertical timbers known as 'rymers', in between which were slotted wooden 'paddles'. When those components were in place the weir functioned as normal, with water flowing through the central sluice and the mill stream channelled off to one side to power the waterwheel.

When a boat wanted to pass through the 'paddle and rymer' or 'flash lock', paddles were withdrawn from their slots, allowing water to run straight through the gate, which could then be opened to create a sudden 'flash' of water. As soon the initial torrent subsided and the river had recovered some of its equilibrium, boats travelling downstream could ride the surge of water through the gap. Vessels making their way upstream against the current faced a far more difficult passage through the weir and had to be either physically manhandled through the gap or hauled through on a permanent winch fixed to the bank.

The millers who had built the weirs were naturally reluctant to let boats through because when the flash lock was in use, water pressure down the millstream dwindled to nothing and the waterwheel driving the quern stones fell silent. Some millers would levy exorbitant tolls to recoup losses incurred by an idle mill, but even then regarded that as poor compensation for time lost. It could take several hours for the upstream boats to be hauled though and it became common practice to stack vessels up in a queue before releasing the flash. In that way, the miller not only received a decent lump sum for one operation (albeit a protracted one), but might also have cleared the river of traffic for some time and he could get back to milling undisturbed. Shooting the flash locks must have been both exhilarating and dangerous in equal measures, especially if following others through the gap and there was also a collection of boats lying around on the other side waiting to be hauled upstream.

Below: Looking down onto the torrent of water passing over a Thames weir clearly highlights why medieval millers were anxious to harness such a source of power to drive their waterwheels.

Right: An example of how the difficulties and perils of navigation on a river whose levels were uncontrolled can be seen at the bywater near Duxford on the upper reaches of the Thames.

Hambleden Mill may now be converted for residential use but is nevertheless surrounded by weir pools and mill races to give an impression of what the working Thames was like many centuries ago.

However, flash lock operations were not only difficult for those in the barge. Official records from a late-fourteenth century inquest into the deaths of two river workers killed while hauling a boat up Hambleden Weir cited a tow rope snapping so violently that their skulls were fractured by the whiplash. One has only to stand above the mesmerizing torrent of Hambleden Weir to get some idea of the awesome force generating by a moving body of water channelled into a restricted space. As it approaches the Hambleden Mill and weir complex at the end of Henley Reach, the river looks it normal unflustered self, just gliding serenely along, but stick a weir in its path and Old Father Thames becomes decidedly agitated and grumpy.

One of the major headaches for river users remained the inconsistency of the river's navigable depth, one cause of which was the protracted opening of a flash lock and the depleted upstream reach not being refilled quickly enough. This problem was further exacerbated by the natural phenomenon of an uneven riverbed and man-made obstructions such as elaborate and surprisingly substantial fish and eel traps. Some parts of the river were notoriously bad and carriers would actually offload their cargoes onto cumbersome horse-drawn carts to bypass the affected stretch rather than face the hassle and expense of a grounded and potentially damaged vessel. River levels were only maintained at navigable levels if the locks worked in tandem, but because they were all privately owned and operated on the whim of a miller rather than catering for commercial traffic there were great inconsistencies.

The non-tidal Thames of today and the forty-five locks between Lechlade and Teddington are carefully managed by the Environment Agency. In essence, the locks divide the river into a series of forty-four intermediate water filled steps to facilitate a measured descent from the first lock, St John's Lock at Lechlade (73 metres above sea level) down to the final lock at Teddington (whose height is just 4.3 metres above sea level). A safe navigable depth within each segment is maintained by controlling how much water is allowed to flow over the weirs set alongside each lock. The natural configuration of the landscape means that some locks have a greater fall than others, the steepest 'step' being the 2.69-metre fall at Sandford to the south of Oxford, and the shallowest at Cleeve near Goring, at just 69 centimetres.

However, the transition from the days of badly sited and haphazardly operated flash locks to the current ordered network was a long, slow process. As England entered the Tudor era, the river's importance for trade increased, especially as coal was becoming more widely used for heating and the demand for building stone continued to rise. Both commodities were totally unsuited to being transported in any meaningful quantity by road carriers and it therefore became imperative to clear the Thames of debris and control the number of weirs, channels and cuts used by the mills that were increasing

Above: Eton Weir was the last of the old flash weirs on the Thames, dismantled in 1936. Some of the old cuts are still used for moorings but others have been filled in. Access to the 'island' is now via an arched footbridge.

Right: The commemorative bridge and boat rollers at Iffley.Lock. Boat rollers appear intermittently at locks on the Thames, usually where there is high percentage of sporting activity on the river.

in both number and size. Substantial progress had been made and the river was deemed navigable for large barges as far as Burcot (just to the west of Dorchester), but the route upstream to Oxford was still difficult. As Oxford was desperate for coal and London was equally anxious to secure good-quality stone from quarries located near the city, James I set up the Oxford–Burcot Commission in 1605 to try to resolve the problem.

The Act empowered the Commissioners to clear the river and its banks, and also granted rights of access onto private land for the men, horses or winching devices needed for hauling barges upstream, but it would appear that the work was spasmodic at best and had stopped altogether by 1611. A differently structured body of Commissioners with powers of local taxation to fund the project was set up under the terms of a revised Act in 1623 and their most important achievement was the introduction of the first pound locks on the Thames at Sandford, Iffley and Culham in the early 1630s.

Pound locks are simply man-made chambers lined in brick or stone with heavy wooden gates at either end, each of which is fitted with its own sluice gate to allow water to be either let into the lock if boats are travelling upstream and need raising, or drained from it to match the level of the river on the downstream side. The first pound locks built in Europe are thought to have been in the Netherlands during the fourteenth century and although the early models were technically fairly basic, the later introduction of the mitred gate was a huge advance. It will come as no surprise to discover that Leonardo de Vinci's papers contained plans and drawings for such a system. The pointed end of the mitre faces the river's current and is therefore kept tightly shut by sheer water pressure. When the water levels on either side of the lock gate have been equalized, they are then easily swung open.

Despite the undoubted advantages of pound locks over their more basic predecessors, the seventeenth-century trio near Oxford stood as an isolated experiment for another 140 years until the advent of the Thames Navigation Commission, a new river management body created in the mid-eighteenth century under the auspices of George II. It became imperative to take the Thames forward into a rapidly advancing age of industrialization that would require the smooth, unfettered passage of goods and raw materials, rather than having laden barges lying idle for days while being held to ransom by mill owners. Under the Thames Act passed in 1770, the new Commission had substantial powers that included the crucial right to purchase land compulsorily for locks and weirs.

A later version of that same Act in 1795 also gave Commissioners the right to purchase riverside land for the creation of a towpath, but it inexplicably included a clause preventing such acquisition should there be a house, garden or orchard close to the river. That short-

Eynsham Lock photographed from the Swinford Toll Bridge. It was built in 1928 and one of the last locks to be added to the non tidal Thames, ensuring a continuity of smooth navigable water upstream to Lechlade.

Above: Buscot Lock is one of the smallest on the Thames. The manual, beam-operated pound lock was built in 1790 and, along with most of the Buscot Estate, appears to have changed little during the last two centuries.

Below: Sonning Lock is the first to be encountered downstream from Reading and lies amid a glorious setting comprising woodland, weir pools and the historic Sonning Mill and village.

sighted omission is one of the reasons why the towpath constantly changes from one bank to another, causing bargees immense logistical problems by having to keep swapping their horses but, looking on the bright side, also providing extra work for rural ferry operators and their large, flat-bottomed vessels. The first of the new pound locks opened in 1772 was Boulter's Lock near Maidenhead, and before the eighteenth century drew to a close, well over twenty more had been added, either as direct replacements for flash locks or re-sited to more operationally efficient locations. Some flash weirs did remain in operation long after most of their peers had been made redundant and the most notable example was at Eynsham, dismantled only in 1931 after a pound lock was built nearby.

Many of the late-eighteenth-century stone pound locks were subsequently rebuilt and although one of those was the isolated Rushey Lock, set midway between Radcot and Tadpole Bridges, it is one of only three on the river whose weir has retained its paddle and rymer system and although the framework of the weir itself has been updated, the principle of how the river's flow was manipulated remains the same. Watching the

A detail of the paddle and rymer system still in operation on the weir at Rushey Lock.

foaming white water forcing its way past the paddles really emphasizes the raw power of a flowing river and actually how skilfully constructed those medieval flash locks and weir must have been to not simply have been swept away on the current. Although aesthetically not as pleasing as the old rymer and paddle systems, concrete and hydraulically operated metal gates are now more commonly used for Thames weirs, but regardless of how the weir is constructed, they all do the same job.

Some weirs do have public access via securely railed walkways, especially where ancient rights of way across the Thames needed to be maintained. However, despite the presence of handrails and secure steel mesh sides, walking across weirs still somehow manage to generate a vertiginous sense of panic. It is probably just a combination of the unremitting roar and the foaming mass of white water in one's peripheral vision that causes such anxiety. However, for twenty-first-century century pedestrians, any worries about personal safety are purely illusionary but the same probably could not have been said in the old days of Thames weirs. Victorian photographers such as Henry Taunt captured images of some surviving flash weirs and the couple of rough wooden planks laid across the structure as a walkway hardly inspire confidence in the likelihood of a successful transition from one bank to another.

The actual configuration of lock sites will obviously vary due to topographical differences in the river and its surrounding landscape, but most will have a constant – the lock keeper and their cottage. No two lock-side dwellings are the same because they were all built at different times and, unlike the keeper's dwellings on some canal networks, there is no 'house style' on the Thames. However, what does unite them all is the immaculate condition of the lock surroundings and gardens. Although the lock keeper and his or her family might be perceived as having all the time in the world for pottering around in the garden, there is significantly more to the job than simply overseeing the transit of boats through the lock itself. Safety is always a very real issue and, although many river users are experienced boat handlers, an increasing majority are simply on holiday in a hired motor cruiser or narrowboat and apart from an introductory briefing at the time of rental, might never have previously set foot on a boat.

Transiting the majority of locks is not the arduous manual task it was prior to the introduction of hydraulic machinery and electrical controls to operate lock gates. Many of the old oak beams that were such a feature of a lock's architecture have now been rendered redundant and removed. However, even though the passage through a Thames lock has been made technically easier, the procedures, protocols and etiquette of lock use can only be acquired with experience and a busy lock on a summer Sunday afternoon is not the ideal place to begin the learning process.

Opposite: Goring Weir at sunrise. No two weirs on the Thames are the same and their size and construction has to be tailored to the topography and prevailing conditions of the river in the vicinity of the locks they serve. Some are more aesthetically pleasing than others and although Goring may look more industrial rather than rural Thames, it was built to do a job, not to look pretty.

Lock keepers are also the front-line guardians of the river, ensuring that no debris is blocking the navigation channels or lock gates, keeping the weir gates free from obstruction and perhaps most importantly, constantly monitoring river levels in times of increased flood risk. Local villagers will probably ring the lock keeper before contacting any centralized agency, as they are the ones who instinctively know how the river is likely to behave under a given set of circumstances. Apart from actually operating the lock gates, the keeper's other main duty was the collection of tolls from vessels using the lock and, in the earliest days of the pound locks, they were known as 'turnpikes', the term applied to tolls roads in the coaching era. However, times have moved on and lock fees are now included in the mandatory annual licence boat owners have to buy and display in the same manner as motor vehicle tax discs. Users of unlicensed craft face prosecution in just the same way that a car driver would, and lock keepers are also trained in the Police and Criminal Evidence Act 1984 and empowered to administer the appropriate PACE caution to offenders.

The gradual introduction of the pound lock system to improve navigation on the Thames necessitated the cutting of new channels in places such as Culham and Shifford, where the river's natural course was far too convoluted and shallow to accommodate a lock and weir. Although the cuts themselves appear as significant engineering works, when one considers that most were dug during the heyday of an English canal network that forged its way across hundreds of miles of virgin countryside, 100 metres or so would have been a mere bagatelle. The management of such lock sites on the Thames and other river navigations such as the Wey is quite a complex business involving careful monitoring to ensure the correct distribution of water between the river's original stream and artificially dug lock channels.

Anyone exploring the Thames and its tributaries by boat will quickly discover that no two locks are identical in terms of size and character but most fall within a given set of parameters designed to cater for river traffic of varying length and width. Those general rules seem to have been dispensed with at Teddington, the lock complex marking the division between the tidal and non-tidal Thames. As one might expect, Teddington is all about sizes and volumes and comprises a vast barge lock almost 200 metres long and a weir that during peak flow, sees around 54 billion litres of water cascade over its gates, although the more modest summer flow is a mere 600 million litres a day.

But not everything about Teddington is oversized – the weir also has tiny fish passes built into it measuring just 75 centimetres square, but the scariest feature is the skiff lock, known ominously as 'the coffin'. It has been given that nickname because of its depth and narrowness (less than 2 metres wide) and when drained it is allegedly like looking out of a coffin. Assuming that reference is to one that has already been lowered into a grave, who actually went down to establish that particular visual analogy but still managed to get out again? Skiffs and other rowing boats are an integral part of the Thames scenery and even though many rowing clubs or individuals are able to derive sufficient pleasure, exercise or competition from their own particular reach on the river, boats do need to be taken through locks. The arrangements to cater for them vary and although some locks still have sets of boat rollers used to manhandle small craft, others simply accept muscle-propelled boats as part of the everyday traffic. A rule relating to conduct within Thames locks that will be appreciated by skiff users is the one requiring powered vessels to turn off their engines while inside the pound chamber. Not too many rowers would feel fit enough to continue with any vigour after having spent ten minutes in an enclosed space filled with diesel fumes.

As with any mechanical system introduced during the formative years of engineering technology, locks have constantly needed repair or upgrades of machinery. Fortunately, the Environment Agency is committed to ensuring that the smooth and safe passage of boats along the Thames continues. But even though there might be an increasing reliance upon technology to operate the system, the authorities will dispense with full-time lock keepers at their peril. Imagine what state the Thames would end up in if locks became like London's suburban rail stations, if they were totally devoid of staff and if the only help available was via a call centre with advice delivered verbally via a crackling speaker set on the lock side . . .

CHAPTER FIVE

Meandering through History
From Oxford to Reading

The distance between Oxford and Reading via the Thames Path is just a little over 40 miles, and maybe a dozen less if one takes the most direct route by road. However, that total does not take into account any diversions, detours or doubling back to access places of interest. This is a different Thames from the narrow, meandering stream encountered to the west, due partly to an increase in stature once joined by the waters of Oxford's other river, the Cherwell, and also significant changes in the terrain, not least where it has forged a path between the Berkshire Downs and Chiltern Hills at Goring Gap. The hand of man has also made a greater imprint upon the landscape, with more villages, historic market towns such as Abingdon and Wallingford, numerous medieval churches and a significant number of grand country houses.

A footbridge leads down from Folly Bridge past the famous Salters' Steamers offices and moorings. The name is synonymous with travel on the Upper Thames, as the family have been associated with river transport since taking over the boatyard in 1858. Although watching the river and surrounding countryside drift by from the top deck of a motor launch is hugely enjoyable, it can be equally frustrating to pass a point of particular interest without being able to investigate further. As this is primarily a journey for those on foot or behind the wheel of a car, that problem should not arise.

Wallingford Bridge and the needle-thin spire of St Peter's Church.

Sunrise over Christ Church Meadow. The moored boat is one of the dwindling number of old college barges that were once an integral part of Oxford's sporting and social scene. Some are being restored but many of the timber vessels have succumbed to old age and decay.

The Thames Path's exit from Oxford along the south bank could not be more different from its arrival. Industrial sites, workers' cottages and railways lines are replaced by the serenity of Christ Church Meadow, with glimpses of college towers and spires through avenues of mature trees. Christ Church Meadow is bordered by one of the divided streams of the River Cherwell and crossed by an arched footbridge leading to the university boathouses clustered on the triangular island created by the bifurcated tributary. Walking the towpath along this stretch of the river needs maximum concentration to avoid being run down by cycling or running undergraduates out on training runs. Even more potentially lethal is the cycling rowing coach, bellowing through a megaphone at their charges in midstream, and the expectation is that pedestrians will be the ones taking evasive action rather than the other way round.

Depending on the time of year, one or more of the old college barges can be seen moored near the boathouses, once used as both grandstands along the rowing reach and lavish hospitality venues. Many of those elegant and elaborate vessels were reminiscent of a bygone era, some acquired from London City Livery Companies and dating back to the days when the Lord Mayor's Procession was a water-borne pageant. They had windowed prows like Nelson's *Victory* but, being made entirely of wood, they could not last forever, although several colleges are attempting the restoration of their own particular barges.

Most of the Oxford college boathouses are located in a cluster near the Cherwell's confluence with the Thames beyond Christ Church Meadow. Inter-collegiate rivalry is intense and during race weeks the viewing terraces are crammed with cheering spectators.

As the river passes beyond the boathouses, it bends and narrows; this is the 'Gut', where much of the 'bumping' takes place during the university's major rowing event, Summer Eights Week (page 151–2). Donnington Bridge is a dreary concrete affair, but it does get traffic from one side of the Thames to the other and is soon left behind *en route* to Iffley Lock, one of the first pound locks to be built by the Oxford–Burcot Commissioners in the seventeenth century. It has been rebuilt several times, the latest as recently as 1924, when opened by Lord Desborough, Chairman of the Thames Conservancy Board, an event marked by an elegant stone bridge and a large bronze bull's head, presented as a starting for the various university rowing races that start at the lock. The towpath bridge is a reduced scale replica of the 'Mathematical Bridge' at Queens' College in Cambridge.

However, the unmissable highlight for pedestrians and touring motorists alike is Iffley's parish church of St Mary the Virgin, set high above the river in the heart of the village. It is a stunning example of late-Norman architecture dating back to 1170, whose west and south doors are adorned with some of the most elaborate and ornate carved detail to be found on any Romanesque church in England. The familiar zigzag and sawtooth patterns are augmented by other beakhead designs, quatrefoils and grotesque animals that are more the stuff of nightmares than guardians of a Christian place of worship

Upon leaving the lock, the path passes under the Iffley road bridge and shortly thereafter crosses the Hinksey stream flowing into the Thames from the right via a substantial wooden footbridge. The river below Iffley becomes rather featureless and motorists will have missed nothing of import if heading straight from Iffley to the riverside village of Sandford-upon-Thames. Walkers will know they are getting closer to Sandford by the increasingly loud noise created by a large volume of water going somewhere in a hurry. The weir is justifiably known as Sandford Lasher and its weir pool was notorious for drownings, a sad fact confirmed by the presence of a stone obelisk memorial set above one of the weir's concrete gates.

The author Jerome K. Jerome, author of the Thames based classic *Three Men in a Boat* observed that 'the pool under Sandford Lasher, just behind the lock is a very good place to drown yourself in'. On a hot summer's afternoon and after a few beers, one could understand the temptation of a quick dip in the pool, but the invisible undercurrents created by the weir have certainly claimed the five undergraduate victims remembered on the memorial, and possibly many more have had narrow escapes. The most recent of those student fatalities was Michael Llewellyn-Davies, whose guardian was Sir James Barrie, the writer of *Peter Pan*.

The scene around Sandford Lock has changed immeasurably over the centuries since a corn mill was

Above: The reopening of Iffley Lock in 1924 was celebrated by the inclusion of this elegant stone bridge over the lock cut.

Left and below: Both inside and out, St Mary the Virgin, Iffley, is one of England's great showpieces of late-Norman church building, dating from around 1170. Its west front is rich in beakhead and zigzag carving and the dark, aisled interior has two equally richly decorated arches from the same period.

The lock at Sandford has the greatest fall of water on the Thames, and its turbulent weir has long been referred to as the 'Sandford Lasher'. Even under benign summer conditions, the volume of water shooting the weir is impressive and quite hypnotic. It is perhaps as well that the tall metal gates at either end remain securely padlocked.

established there by the monks of the Benedictine abbey of Abingdon, the site then passing to the Knights Templar towards the end of the thirteenth century. The practice of harnessing the Thames to drive milling machinery continued through into the industrial era of the early nineteenth century, when a paper mill was built at Sandford, but that too is gone. Modern flats now occupy the site, although to be fair to the developers, they have kept the design and execution of the plans in keeping with an old riverbank mill complex. The King's Arms pub stands right next to the lock and has been a popular place from which to watch the world float by for walkers, boaters and day trippers from Oxford for well over a century.

As the river at Sandford flows almost directly due south, it is the west bank along which the Thames Path continues in the direction of Abingdon, passing Radley College boathouse and precious little else in the way of buildings or other diversions *en route*. However, from the vicinity of the boathouse there is one spectacular view across the river to the to the glorious 'Capability' Brown-designed parkland of Nuneham House, the eighteenth-century mansion built for the first Lord Harcourt when the family moved from Stanton Harcourt. Although the absence of any river crossings in the vicinity means that walkers are restricted to admiring the carefully sculpted composition from afar, drivers will automatically pass through the village of Nuneham Courtenay if following the A4074 road from Sandford towards Reading.

In common with several other medieval villages around the country that had the misfortune to be perceived as a blot on the landscape by wealthy landowners building their grand country houses. The former village stood between the old house and its church; cottages, larger houses and an inn clustered around a triangular green, but when the 2nd Lord Harcourt inherited, Nuneham was razed to the ground and rebuilt as a model village on what is now the main road. It seems somewhat ironic that the village's name actually means 'new village' – but it was already new before being relocated. Of course one has no real idea whether the original was a thriving utopian community living in more than adequate accommodation, but it might be a reasonable assumption to suggest that agricultural workers would not have been living in any degree of luxury! The current occupants of the military-straight line of cottages must rue the fact that they live on such a busy highway with lorries and cars thundering past throughout the day, but visitors can turn off that main road and drive along narrow estate roads to Nuneham House.

Although starting out as a classical Palladian villa, Nuneham was extended and remodelled over time by successive generations right through into the twentieth century, finally being sold to the University of Oxford in 1948. By 1980 it had been completely restored and renovated and is now leased to the Brahma Kumaris World Spiritual University and serves as the Global Retreat Centre. Obviously the house is not open to the public, but visitors may access the remarkable church that appears more like a temple than an English parish church.

With its prominent Palladian dome and pedimented Ionic portico, All Saints' might be a successful exercise in architectural classicism, but even its well-preserved state courtesy of the Churches Conservation Trust does not make its interior any less cold or unlovable.

Because I am essentially following the river footpath, the next major halt on the route is Abingdon, but drivers will have to engage in a bit of a diversion, cutting across from the A4074 via Clifton Hampden (a village that appears downstream from Abingdon in the narrative). The Thames Path continues past Nuneham in a tight sweeping curve to the right, passing a weir on the opposite bank that marks the entrance to Swift Ditch, believed to be the river's original course. The current channel was thought to have been partially engineered by the Benedictine monks of Abingdon Abbey, the foundation of which dates back to the late seventh century. Abingdon Lock is just upstream from the town centre, and it here that the footpath changes banks (again). The tall, elegant spire of St Helen's Church is now a prominent feature, combining with the town's outline and river to create one of the Thames's most iconic images.

Abingdon Bridge is an early-twentieth-century version of the original fourteen-arch stone bridge built by the Fraternity of the Holy Cross in 1416, replacing earlier wooden structures. That large number of arches once

Above: The model village of Nuneham Courtenay now lies on the main Oxford to Reading road, having been relocated and rebuilt when the original was obliterated from the landscape of Nuneham Park by the 2nd Earl Harcourt during the latter decades of the eighteenth century.

Below: All Saints' Church lies in the grounds of Nuneham Park, and was built in the style of a Palladian temple. Its dark, soulless interior is full of Harcourt memorials, including the poignant alabaster figure on the tomb of Julian Harcourt, who died in infancy in 1862.

The Thames at Abingdon on a frosty autumnal morning. The distinctive spire of St Helen's is one the river's more recognisable landmarks and photographers treasure mornings such as these.

Below: Abingdon Bridge is really three separate bridges linked together, and Abingdon Bridge proper goes over the backwater nearest to the town centre. This is Burford Bridge, crossing the main stream of the Thames, and Maud Hales Bridge, taking the road over marshy ground to the south.

Opposite left: Following the Dissolution, the gatehouse to Abingdon Abbey was purchased by the town's council, who used the upper rooms as the borough prison for over 250 years. The wall on the left of the picture belongs to the twelfth century church of St Nicholas, built for the lay servants of the abbey.

Opposite right: As one of the wealthiest abbeys of medieval England, Abingdon Abbey occupied a significant site but all tangible remains have disappeared. The layout of the walls is now marked by stone blocks, backed up by interpretation boards. The ruins in the abbey gardens are sadly little more than an atmospheric early-twentieth-century folly.

again emphasizes how vulnerable such crossings and their approaches were to flooding. There was little point in going to the vast expense of simply constructing a stone bridge over the river itself if winter floods rendered the roads and tracks on either side virtually impassable to heavy-wheeled carts.

The modern town spreads out to the north and west away from the Thames, and although there are the inevitable industrial estates and retail parks on the fringes, at least Abingdon has retained a substantial part of its historic past, readily accessible and within just a short stroll from the bridge. Perhaps the most impressive remnants are the fifteenth-century abbey gateway attached to the medieval church of St Nicholas, built by Abbot Nicholas of Culham in 1289–1307. Although the gateway has obviously been substantially restored, its presence serves to emphasize the wealth and power associated with many medieval monasteries. Unfortunately, none of the

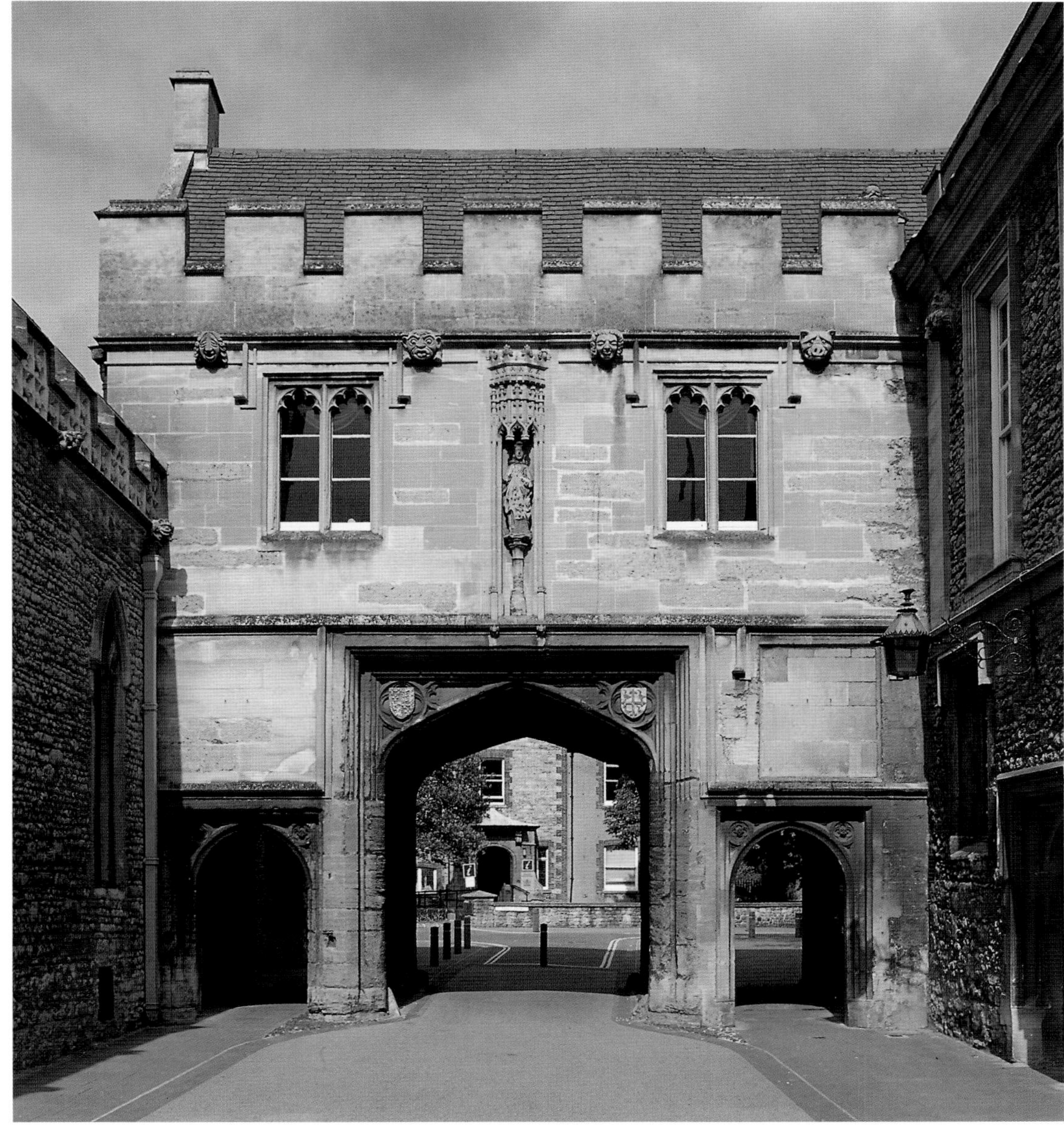

monastic buildings or the abbey church has survived although some domestic buildings have been restored and are in use. The Long Gallery has a spectacular timber-framed interior that is worth taking time and trouble to visit and another extant monastic building has been restored and converted into a theatre.

Other buildings worthy of note include the seventeenth-century Baroque-style County Hall set opposite the abbey gate and, of course, St Helen's Church, whose configuration of five parallel aisles make it a rare example of a church that is broader than it is long. The church is predominately fourteenth- to sixteenth-century Perpendicular gothic, with an impressive painted roof, but despite those arresting features and its interesting location among a cluster of almshouses, the beauty of St Helen's remains its aesthetic contribution to Abingdon's riverside setting.

The route for both walkers and motorists is back over Abingdon Bridge, the footpath then heading along the riverbank past St Helen's, over a footbridge carrying the southern exit of Swift Ditch into the Thames, and onwards in the direction of Culham Lock. The 'old' Culham Bridge, built at the same time as Abingdon's, can be seen away to the left at this point. Both path and river take an acute turn to the left at a point where the original channel continues on a more sedate course, leaving the Thames Path to follow Culham Cut, dug in 1809 to accommodate the lock. Midway along that channel, a footbridge leads across to the delightfully secluded Sutton Pools, created around the weir, and onwards into the village of Sutton Courtenay.

Drivers can head for that same destination by taking the A415, turning right at a signpost marked Culham and Sutton Courtenay, thereafter crossing a pair of bridges downstream from the lock, carrying the road over the canalized channel and then the narrower stream of what was once the Thames, but is now relegated to being the weir stream. A right turn at the subsequent T-junction brings one into the eastern end of Sutton Courtenay, where clearly marked footpaths lead across the old mill

Above: The view downstream from Abingdon in early summer, with the chestnut trees in full bloom.

Right: Sutton Pools, a haven of peace and tranquillity for both humans and wildlife.

Opposite: The parish church of All Saints', Sutton Courtenay, is typical of many village churches, a building that was begun in the twelfth century and grew gradually over the centuries.

stream and onwards into the willow-fringed haven of Sutton Pools.

Sutton Pools is one of the most beautiful backwaters on the Thames, fortuitously created when the lock channel was cut to avoid the stretch of barely navigable river caused by the nearby weir and the exorbitantly high tolls charged by the mill owner to pass through it. The 'Sutton' in the village's name can be translated as 'south farm' (or settlement) and the 'Courtenay' suffix refers to Reginald de Courtenay, ancestor of the Earls of Devon, who was granted the manor by Henry II in 1161. It was one of Reginald's descendents, Hugh de Courtenay, 9th Earl of Devon, who gave his name to Nuneham Courtenay (the village we passed through a few miles before Abingdon). Sutton has a long village street containing some houses dating back to Norman times and which, although modified and enlarged, unusually retain many of their original features.

All Saints' parish church dates from around the same time and, although it is not endowed with any one particularly outstanding architectural feature, its gradual growth through the centuries has resulted in an interior conveying a harmonious ambiance of gentle textures and colours. Sutton Courtenay is arguably better known for its churchyard, being the final resting place of Herbert Henry Asquith, 1st Earl of Oxford and Asquith (1852–1928), the last Prime Minister of a Liberal Government (1908–16), who allowed Lloyd George to lay the foundations of Britain's Welfare State. The other most notable long-term resident is buried beneath a simple headstone inscribed with the name Eric Arthur Blair, better known as the writer George Orwell (1903–50).

It is in this vicinity that it becomes increasingly difficult to avoid mentioning the 'elephant in the room', because Didcot Power Station now looms extremely large on the horizon. There have been occasional glimpses of its giant cooling towers as the Thames progressed in its south-facing leg from Oxford, but its presence is now very much part of the landscape. Because Didcot is such a large industrial site set in isolation it does have a huge visual impact upon the landscape, but (and this is only my opinion as a photographer) it is more like a piece of a sculpture than an eyesore. Unfortunately, power generation and distribution also means electricity pylons, and while I can cope with the presence of one power station, the armies of nasty, ugly steel pylons marching across even the most sensitive parts of our countryside, do drive me to distraction.

The main route can be picked up easily by rejoining the Thames Path via the Sutton Bridges and thereafter both road and footpath converge upon the famous village of Clifton Hampden, legendary for its close association with Jerome K. Jerome and *Three Men in a Boat*.

Although it will patently take walkers considerably longer than motorists to reach that destination, that additional time and effort will be rewarded by one of the most pleasing ensembles on the Upper Thames: Sir George Gilbert Scott's mellow red-brick bridge set against a small cliff upon which sits the church of St Michael and All Angels. Scott's bridge was commissioned by Lord of the Manor, Henry Hucks Gibbs, to replace the existing ford and ferry and was completed in 1864. There is definitely more than a trace of Norman-style architecture about the bridge, which, although modelled upon the past, is nevertheless surprisingly narrow for a late-nineteenth-century structure and is barely wide enough to carry modern vehicles. On the far side of the bridge and past the house that once served as the toll booth is The Barley Mow Inn.

Many visitors to The Barley Mow mistakenly attribute it as having been one of the places where Jerome K. Jerome settled down in the snug bar to write passages of *Three Men in a Boat*, but such notions are sadly incorrect. He mentions his visit in the book, albeit when obviously in one his mawkish moods, citing the place as being 'the quaintest, most old-world inn up the river. Its low pitched gables and latticed windows give it quite a storybook appearance, while inside it is even more once-upon-a-timeyfied'. The Barley Mow originated as a fourteenth-century, half-timbered, cruck-framed building, but although some of the interior panelling is several centuries old, the original building suffered a catastrophic fire in 1975, was then restored but later rebuilt and re-thatched some two decades later. Despite the building being a revised version, it retains the anticipated atmosphere and for tall people, the doors still require careful navigation. As the warning sign by the door indicates – 'Duck or Grouse'! Cruck frames were a common form of construction in this region during the Middle Ages and there are numerous examples extant in riverside villages such as Clifton Hampden and a little further downstream at Long Wittenham.

George Gilbert Scott was also responsible for twice restoring the church, the first occasion being in 1844 and again around the same time as work was progressing on the bridge below. Relatively little remains of the church's medieval origins but Victorian architects inflicted far worse restorations many of England's rural

After several bridges of mellow limestone, George Gilbert Scott's nineteenth-century red-brick crossing of the Thames at Clifton Hampden is something of a surprise, which, although appearing rather too vibrant on sunlit days, still forms an agreeable ensemble with the village church.

parish churches and the proportions of the small spire and bell tower act perfectly well as a visual foil for the bridge. The long climb up several flights of steps to reach the church from the Thames is well worth the effort, even if only to savour a beautiful retrospective view of the bridge and river from the vantage point of the churchyard.

If time, transport or stamina permits, the village of Long Wittenham is a highly recommended detour, readily accessed by continuing on past The Barley Mow Inn. There are two Wittenhams in close proximity and both perfectly reflect their prefixes of 'Long' and 'Little'. Long Wittenham certainly is a linear community, whose single main street extends for about half a mile and is lined with houses from several periods. Unfortunately, a devastating fire in 1868 destroyed many of the old dwellings, but the parish church and its remarkable Norman lead font survived intact and the medieval village cross stands midway along the High Street.

Many similar crosses were known as preaching crosses and very much associated purely with religion, but Wittenham's is thought to have served almost exclusively as a market cross, known as a chipping or bargaining cross. Notwithstanding such a cross's isolated, rural location, any vendors or buyers who carried out transactions in its vicinity knew that they were subject to the same trading laws that applied to more formal covered markets in the larger villages and towns.

Above: Sunset on a winter's afternoon from the Thames Path near Clifton Hampden

Opposite: Love them or loathe them, the cooling towers of Didcot power station leave an indelible mark on the Thames landscape, especially when viewed from the vantage point of the Iron Age hill fort on the Sinodun Hills.

A quick glance at the horizon in the vicinity of Long Wittenham will show its southern aspect to be still occupied by cooling towers but further east by a pair of almost geometrically sculpted hills. These are universally known as the Wittenham Clumps, from the eighteenth-century beech trees planted on their summits, but they are actually the Sinodun Hills and they make a welcome and rather dramatic appearance in a landscape that at times would have lost out to a pancake in a flatness competition. As with all landscape features, shapes and outlines can alter as the viewer changes their own position, an observation that very much applies to the Clumps. When seen from certain angles they lose that almost conical shape, simply reverting to an elevated area of land; from another direction, one can readily appreciate how they also came to be known locally as the Berkshire Bubs (even though county boundary changes have now placed them in Oxfordshire) or the even more ribald title of Mother Dunch's Buttocks!

The woman in question was the wife of an unpopular local landowner, whose family had been associated with nearby Little Wittenham since before the Civil War. The Dunches were related by marriage to Oliver Cromwell so one might safely deduce from the insult that the area was not for the Parliamentarians during that conflict. However, regardless of their shape or nickname, the hills really should be climbed for a spectacular view of the Upper Thames valley and to appreciate why they were chosen as viable defensive positions from the Bronze Age onwards. One of the two hills is named Castle Hill and archaeologists from Oxford University have been conducting research on an Iron Age Hill fort that occupied the site.

Despite their commanding position, Wittenham Clumps are actually easier to access, both on foot or by car than might be initially supposed. Drivers simply need to head for Little Wittenham and follow signposts to the car park provided by the Northmoor Trust, who own and manage the Wittenham Clumps. As the lane leading up to the car park is quite long and steep, it will be the car doing most of the work and its occupants will face little more than a gentle uphill stroll to reach the summits. Having visited the Clumps, I would advise drivers to retrace their route back to Clifton Hampden and pick up the A415 again, heading in the direction of Wallingford and Reading but, having passed through the village of Burcot, divert off the main road to the right and follow the signs to Dorchester.

Walkers on the Thames Path actually have a couple of viable route options from Clifton Hampden, one of which will entail forsaking the river bank during its long meander round to Day's Lock. It is easy enough to walk alongside the road to Long Wittenham before then cutting across to Little Wittenham and the Clumps. Cutting off the river's meander is a shortcut in terms of distance travelled but it would mean missing out on a sighting of Burcot on the opposite bank at the furthest point of the loop. The village itself is unremarkable but, as detailed in the previous chapter, it occupies a significant place in Thames history through the seventeenth-century Oxford–Burcot Commission.

Day's Lock is situated by Little Wittenham village and was named after a well-known local seventeenth-century family of Catholic yeomen, although there are early documentary references to it as Dorchester Lock. A two-part footbridge via an island just downstream of the lock carries the Thames Path over to the north bank and, while this is normally a tranquil place, pandemonium breaks out here every March (and has done since the inaugural event in 1983) when the annual World Poohsticks Championships are held around Day's Lock. Ever since A.A. Milne's teddy bear Winnie-the-Pooh tripped, lost grip of his fir cone on the bridge at the edge of the Forest and thereby accidentally invented a game, poohsticks has been beloved by both young and old. The 'World Championships' were the brainchild of lock keeper Lynn David who noticed that visitors were breaking twigs of nearby trees and bushes and playing poohsticks from the footbridge.

As a staunch supporter of the RNLI (Royal National Lifeboat Institution) and always on the lookout for fundraising ideas, he collected a large pile of twigs and left a voluntary donations box alongside and having established that people would actually pay money to throw sticks into a river, the idea was born. It is just one of those silly, quintessentially English activities and pastimes that has television crews from around the world converging on Day's Lock to provide a few second's footage for the 'and finally' items that now seem to have become an obligatory lighthearted ending to news programmes normally containing excessive gloom.

Dorchester-on-Thames lies but a few fields away from the river, a short walk that is arguably one of the most rewarding detours along the entire length of the Thames Path. A public footpath heads diagonally away from the lock, crossing and then running parallel with a double line of Iron Age earthworks known as the Dyke Hills. The path soon arrives near the heart of Dorchester and its ancient abbey but one wonders whether it is correctly named, being located immediately next to the River Thame (see pages 49–51), whose confluence with the Thames is just to the south. Many people driving over the quite substantial Dorchester Bridge wrongly assume that they are crossing the Thames but walkers peering over the parapet will see only a narrow stream.

Day's Lock photographed from the Sinodun Hills (more commonly referred to as the Wittenham Clumps). Frozen flooded gravel pits lie behind the course of the Thames, and Dorchester Abbey is just a few hundred metres away to the right. River conditions permitting, the lock is usually swamped with visitors each March for the annual renewal of the World Pooh Sticks Championships.

Right: The main street of Dorchester-on-Thames, with the abbey tower in the background.

Opposite and below: The abbey church of Dorchester is dedicated to St Peter and St Paul and is magnificent in both proportions and detail. The majority of the building is from the Decorated period and the sense of light and space generates a special atmosphere. Some of the glass is outstanding, not least the famous Tree of Jesse Window, in which stone and glass mingle to form a biblical 'family tree'. The thirteenth-century effigy of a knight drawing his sword is one of the best, most expressive pieces of early funerary sculpture in England.

The site's strategic position by a river crossing led to its development as a Roman military town on one of their main roads north from Silchester; fragments of mosaic pavements, coins and other relics discovered near by are in the care of the Ashmolean Museum in Oxford. Regardless of what importance the town had during the Roman occupation, it was during the Saxon era and the spread of Christianity through England that Dorchester flourished. It technically became a city when the Roman missionary, St Birinus, was granted a vast 'see' in AD 635 by his most powerful convert, King Cynegils of Wessex, and allowed to build a cathedral near the two rivers. Although there were necessary changes in how, and from where the see was administered due to threats of war between Wessex and Mercia and the ninth-century Danish invasion, Dorchester maintained its position as the largest in England well into the Norman Conquest.

Its first post-Conquest Norman bishop was Remigius, but his tenure in Dorchester was short-lived when it was decreed that all bishoprics should be in major cities rather than rural villages, regardless of their past status. Remigius therefore relocated to Lincoln and Dorchester probably reverted to being a parish church until founded as an Abbey of Augustinian canons during the mid-twelfth century. Much of it was destroyed at the Dissolution, but an altruistic intervention by a rich local merchant named Richard Beauforest saved the abbey church for the town and it stands today as one of the great ecclesiastical buildings in the southern half of England. The Norman church is represented by the nave's north wall but the additions from later periods are those that contribute so much to Dorchester's character.

Dating from the fourteenth-century Decorated period, the Jesse Window is a work of extraordinary complexity – intricately carved stone and stained glass combining to form a 'family tree' depicting Christ's descent from Jesse, father of King David. One of Dorchester's other great treasures is the thirteenth-century tomb effigy of a Crusader knight, which although unidentified on the tomb itself, is thought to be Sir John Holcombe who died in 1270. The torsion created in the figure is quite extraordinary for a piece of sculpture from that period, with one hand holding the scabbard and the other grasping the handle of his sword. There is a degree of ambiguity and uncertainty, as he could either be sheathing his sword at the end of life's battle, or maybe drawing it to ward off an advancing foe – maybe even Death itself. One other monument of particular note can be found in the south aisle, where a black stone tablet dedicated to Mrs Sarah Fletcher, who died in 1799, informs us that she was 'a martyr to excessive sensibility'. As Jane Austen's novel *Sense and Sensibility* was published in 1811, one could deduce that there was most definitely an excess of sensibility around the turn of the nineteenth century.

Dorchester has now been bypassed by the main Oxford to Henley road, and although some local businesses will possibly be suffering from the absence of through traffic, some semblance of tranquillity has been returned. It is difficult to wander at leisure past historic coaching inns from the sixteenth and seventeenth centuries and take in the atmosphere of hidden cul-de-sacs of half-timbered brick cottages with the roar of traffic as an accompaniment. The detour off the bypass is so straightforward and such a minimal detour that I think anyone who needs lunch or a sandwich knows perfectly well that Dorchester is still there!

Walkers leave Dorchester via a footpath running parallel with the Thame (no 's'), rejoining the Thames (with an 's') by the confluence of the two rivers. Drivers simply follow the old Henley Road until it rejoins the bypass and thereafter head for the next two ancient fording places over the river, Shillingford

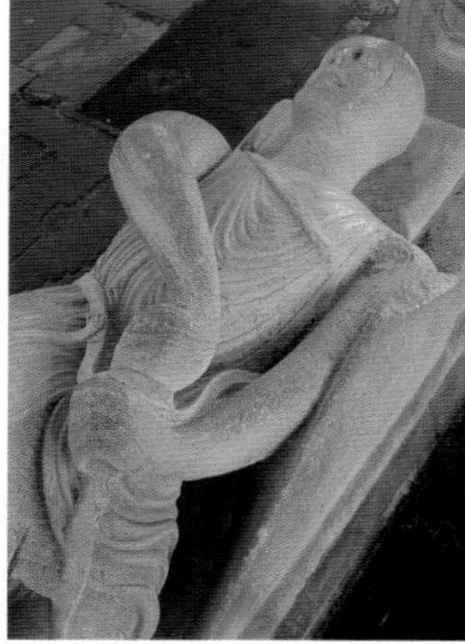

Below: The red-brick and flint Tudor village school at Ewelme has remained virtually unchanged since it was built in the fifteenth century, and still serves as the local primary school.

Right: Ewelme's almshouses also date from around the same mid-fifteenth-century period and were originally built under licence from Henry VI to provide homes for thirteen 'distressed men' (no mention of distressed women).

and Wallingford. Despite occasional glimpses of the Wittenham Clumps, this is a dreary, featureless stretch of river. At a point where a ferry known as the Keen Edge once operated, the Thames Path is diverted onto a designated path running alongside the main road until reaching Shillingford village. As the name Keen Edge has no logical relevance to a river ferry, one wonders whether it might have been a local dialect corruption of Cane Edge, in reference to the copious osier beds growing along the banks of this stretch of the Thames.

The pedestrian route then turns right down Wharf Road in Shillingford, and although well worth a visit by motorists to admire the thatched boathouse and stylish old building of Shillingford Court, they will have to do an about-turn because, as its name suggests, Wharf Road terminates at the water's edge. Shillingford Bridge is early nineteenth century, just one of several similar Thames road bridges built around that period that fall into the functionally elegant category. What Shillingford does have is a beautiful setting with a large riverside hotel, which, despite lacking the atmosphere of the old coaching inns in Dorchester, is not a bad place from

which to watch the river drift by on a lazy summer's day.

The official path does not cross the bridge, and drivers too should retrace their route back to the main Shillingford roundabout and follow the signs to Benson, Wallingford and Reading. Benson is not really a place to linger, and although the quickest route onwards to Wallingford by road would have been to continue over Shillingford Bridge, that would deny people the opportunity of making a detour eastwards from Benson to the remarkable village of Ewelme. I am mindful that the 4 miles round-trip from Benson could be a step too far for walkers, but even if that is the case, this insight will hopefully lead to a return visit at a more opportune moment.

When the B4009 leaves Benson in the direction of the Chilterns, it is running almost parallel with one of England's ancient tracks, the Ridgeway, and although no way near as old as that prehistoric route, the flint and brick village of Ewelme is renowned for three outstanding fifteenth-century buildings: a castellated church, village school and diminutive cloistered almshouses.

The church is a far more distinguished building than one would normally expect to find in a small, rural village but perhaps less surprising when one encounters the exquisitely carved alabaster effigy of Alice, Duchess of Suffolk (1404–75), set above a rare example of a cadavar tomb. The effigy portrays her in nun's garb but also wearing the ducal crown, yet beneath the elaborately decorated tomb there lies a second alabaster figure depicting the duchess in death as a partly shrouded, skeletal cadavar. Although somewhat macabre, it was device used to emphasize the fact that regardless of wealth or stature, all were equally humble in death.

Alice was the daughter of Thomas Chaucer (whose tomb lies in the same chapel) and granddaughter to one of England's most celebrated poets, Geoffrey Chaucer. She acquired her title when marrying William de la Pole, 1st Duke of Suffolk, and they jointly founded the school and almshouses, licensed by deed from King Henry VI in 1437. The formal title of the almshouses (and the charity that still administers them) rejoices in the glorious name of The Two Chaplains and Thirteen Poor Men of Ewelme. One of the chaplains officiated at the church and the other taught at the adjacent school, an institution that has survived to the present day and flourishes as a state-run primary school.

The almshouses are arranged around a cobbled courtyard with a well in its centre but, unlike their predecessors, the current recipients of the Ewelme Trust's hospitality do not have to attend church five times a day to pray for the soul of their benefactors. There are

A misty autumn sunrise on the Thames near Wallingford. I love the atmosphere of the picture but also know from bitter experience that days beginning perfectly tend to stay too hazy for good landscape photography.

now only eight occupants, due the fact that the dwellings were slightly enlarged in 1970 to allow each resident to have their own bathroom, but the designated number of thirteen has been maintained by the construction of five new almshouses elsewhere in the village. Although the church contains several magnificent funerary monuments, a more simple memorial located outside in the churchyard will be of particular interest to those on a journey down the Thames, for this is final resting place of Jerome Klapka Jerome (1859–1927), author of *Three Men in a Boat,* who lived in a farmhouse near the village during his later years.

For those rejoining the Thames at Benson (or indeed, those who never left it) the National Trail once again transfers onto what is now the west bank. The main road from Benson should be followed until directed to Wallingford via Crowmarsh Gifford. Both approaches to the fortified Saxon town will converge on the wonderful seventeen-arch bridge, of which six cross the river and the others eleven carry the road over the adjacent floodplain. Those travelling by road will pass a terrace of old whitewashed cottages on the right as the bridge approaches, one of which bears a blue plaque denoting a famous past resident. The occupant of this particular dwelling was Jethro Tull (1674–1741), who lived in Crowmarsh Gifford for ten years from 1700. When that name is mentioned to people of a particular age, the association might be with the flute-playing leader

of a 1960s rock band, rather than the inventor of a mechanical seed drill that effectively launched the eighteenth-century Agrarian Revolution.

The bridge itself was substantially rebuilt and widened in 1809 after severe flood damage, although substantial traces of the stonework of earlier versions survive in the some of the lesser arches over the floodplain. Despite that remodelling, the bridge is still only wide enough to carry a single line of vehicles, a bottleneck that created daily mayhem before a modern bridge was added to the south of the town. The first stone bridge to be erected over the Thames at Wallingford was surprisingly early; records showing that it was completed in 1250, during the reign of Henry III. As with the majority of the river's earliest bridges, repair and upkeep were frequently neglected until they were on the verge of collapse and at which point the issue of funding would then have to be addressed. Pontage, or tolls, were customarily exacted from travellers and traders, and at one stage in its history, the bridge had a toll house set over the central span.

As the one of lowest safe fords across the river, Wallingford has featured prominently in most of the wars, incursions and invasions that beset England from the Roman Occupation to the Civil War. Aulus Plautius would probably have marched his troops across *en route* to suppressing the Dobunni tribe in Gloucestershire; King Alfred made it one of his Saxon burhs; William the Conqueror used the ford in his circuitous route to

take London and the Royalist commander, Colonel Blagge, blew up four arches of the bridge and laid a wooden drawbridge over the void to improve the town's defences. Wallingford Castle was the last Royalist stronghold to surrender and was eventually destroyed by Commonwealth soldiers in 1652. Fragmentary remains of the castle walls can be see on rising ground to the right as one enters Wallingford along the Thames Path route.

Wallingford originally rivalled Alfred's capital, Winchester, in size and importance, with much of the town's surviving grid layout attributable to that period but, in spite of the legacy of defensive walls and ditches left by the Saxons, it was the Norman oppressors who began the castle that dominated the town's history for another six centuries. As with the majority of castles initially thrown up by the Norman conquerors as they sought to impose their will on the Saxon population, that first version would have been a motte and bailey. The motte, or mound, was topped with a defensive palisade and the earth dug out for the mound left a huge ditch around the base. Stone castles replaced those basic but effective structures over time and Wallingford's soon evolved into one of the largest and strongest castles in the country. It acted as Queen Matilda's main stronghold in the region during her war with King Stephen and the town was handsomely rewarded by Henry II in 1155 with a lavish Charter of Liberties in return for its support of his mother.

The town prospered as a result of its enhanced status and, by the thirteenth century, comprised eleven parishes, each of which had its own church. However, no amount of status or prosperity could defend it against the Black Death of the fourteenth century, when over a third of the population was wiped out. Eleven churches quickly became four and Wallingford has done well to lose only another one of those over the intervening centuries, although perhaps that should be one and a half – the eighteenth-century church of St Peter is now classed as redundant. Despite being no longer used for worship, St Peter's is Wallingford's most instantly recognizable landmark, its needle-sharp spire being an automatic part of most photographs taken of the bridge. One of the churches still in use is St Mary-le-More, which, although occupying a prominent position in the town's vast market place, is architecturally subservient to the seventeenth-century town hall, its open, ground-floor market area supported on extremely solid Doric pillars.

Having been briefly diverted through some of the town's narrow streets, the Thames Path stays on the west bank as the river flows almost due south towards Goring Gap. Drivers can opt for a direct route to the Gap on both

Opposite: The ruins of Wallingford Castle extend almost down to the Thames, serving as a reminder that this was one of the most important and strategic crossing points on the river to the west of London. Monarchs throughout the centuries added their own embellishments and fortifications but the castle finally succumbed during the Civil War.

Below and bottom: Wallingford's strategic importance was reflected in the size and scale of its fortifications and its stature as a major trading centre represented by the vast market square lined with buildings from the sixteenth to the eighteenth centuries. The open space is presided over by colonnaded town hall and the Perpendicular church tower of St Mary-le-More.

sides of the Thames via the main A329 to Reading, or a minor road on the opposite bank that passes through the villages of North and South Stoke. However, unless one is actually walking this particular sector, direct contact with the Thames is minimal, and it is the surrounding landscape that probably determines one's onward route.

Regardless of one's mode of transport, I do recommend a short walk downstream along the riverside meadow opposite St Peter's and Wallingford. This is a popular spot for visitors, and ample car parking is provided right down by the river. The juxtaposition of bridge and church spire from this vantage point is perfect and one can also admire (and possibly covet) some of the adjacent elegant Georgian houses, whose gardens slope gently down to the riverbank and perhaps a small motor launch moored alongside a jetty. As with most things in life there is also a downside to such apparent Thames-side bliss; there is a continuous drone of traffic from the town's bypass and those houses near the bridge are but a few metres from a new Oxford University boathouse, so there could also be the distracting sight of outrageously fit rowers skimming past at high speed. However, all things considered, there are probably worse things in life to endure.

Upon departure from Wallingford, the designated path and the road south run past the small suburb of Winterbook, associated with the writer Agatha Christie, who lived at Winterbook House for over three decades, dying there in 1976. The path goes under the new bypass bridge and thereafter reverts back into a mile or so of rural tranquillity. As the village of North Stoke recedes on the opposite bank, the footpath arrives at the site of what was the Littlestoke Ferry. The original slipway is now occasionally used by those wanting to launch small craft for a potter about on the river, but it is disappointing (although not surprising) to note that the access track is now named Ferry Lane rather than its original title of Papist Way. That original name refers to that time during the seventeenth century when Catholics were persecuted and had to meet clandestinely to celebrate Mass. The Hildesley family of Littlestoke Manor were one of the leading Catholic families in the area and the Thames became their secret lifeline.

Just up Ferry Lane (and also on the main road) lies the sprawling shell of the Victorian red-brick complex of Fairmile Hospital, which opened in 1870: a chilling reminder of the days when asylums were the norm and mental illness was so feared and misunderstood. The site is actually due for redevelopment but, knowing how long the planning and appeals process takes, the deserted buildings may not be demolished for some time. Regardless of Fairmile's longevity, a far better use of brick appears ahead in the form of Isambard Kingdom Brunel's 1838 Moulsford viaduct for the Great Western Railway. A replica was built parallel to the original when the tracks were extended towards the end of the nineteenth century.

Right: The view down into the Thames Valley at Goring Gap. Three adjacent areas of National Trust land overlook the villages of Streatley and Goring: Lough Down, Lardon Chase and the Hollies all give far-reaching vistas across the Thames and beyond to the Chiltern Hills.

Opposite: The Thames as it passes between the neighbouring villages of Goring and Streatley, connected by the bridge just visible behind the trees in the foreground.

It must be a sign of the times but the two most famous riverside pubs located between Wallingford and Goring are no more – well, perhaps not exactly deceased but reincarnated as rather chic waterside restaurants. The Beetle & Wedge at Moulsford has relocated from its original building into a beamed boathouse 'restaurant with rooms' on the site of the old Moulsford ferry. The 'beetle' in the name refers to neither car nor insect but is derived from the Old English word for a heavy mallet or hammer. The Leatherne Bottel lies on the opposite bank to the B&W, located a little further downstream towards Goring, and it too has been transformed from a centuries-old pub into a very smart restaurant.

The immediate environs of the Thames have been rather bland for the last few stretches but all that is about to change as it arrives at Goring Gap. This is not a gorge through which the river is transformed into a raging torrent when squeezed between impermeable rock strata, but a rather more sedate affair where the Thames has carved a valley out of a line of chalk hills that become divided into the Chilterns to the north-east and the Berkshire Downs to south-west. The transformation becomes even more apparent as one draws near to Cleeve Lock, where walkers might realize that it is some considerable time since they passed by a lock. The 6½-mile reach above Cleeve is the longest on the entire non-tidal Thames and the reason why it has such appeal to rowing clubs seeking long, unbroken stretches of water for serious competition training. They would fare less well on the reach downstream from Cleeve to Goring Lock, as that happens to be the shortest reach on the river.

Of the two ranges of hills, the Berkshire Downs are the more dramatic in the immediate vicinity of Goring Lock, where the whitewashed lock keeper's cottage is set against a backdrop of a steep, thickly wooded hillside. The Chilterns become more apparent as one progresses downstream. The large village of Goring is on the port side (left) if one were sailing down the river and directly opposite on the starboard beam is the smaller community of Streatley. This has always been an important crossing point of the Thames, a place where prehistoric tracks and trade routes came down to the wide but shallow fording place. The Romans built a causeway to facilitate the swift transfer of troops, but a ferry was later installed to cope with the demands of medieval commerce and social traffic between Goring and Streatley. Boats and alcohol have never formed a

Above: The ex-Magadalene College barge has taken up permanent residence outside the Swan Hotel at Streatley.

Below: The lock keeper's cottage at Goring Lock with the tree-lined escarpment of the Hollies and Lardon Chase behind.

Opposite: The Thames Path and old towing path share the same river bank leaving Goring *en route* to Lower Basildon. The woods opposite may give the impression of being an impenetrable mass, but behind the first few ranks of trees, the main A329 road to Reading runs parallel to the Thames.

safe working partnership, a fact sadly borne out after the annual Goring festival in 1674, when sixty people tried to cram onto the ferry for the short crossing but all perished as the vessel went out of control and plunged over the weir.

The two communities are now connected by a long, trestle-type bridge in two parts that seems entirely appropriate for crossing the complex network of weir pools, mill streams and the main river channel that make up the Thames at this point. The narrow slip road still leads down to the towpath past Goring Mill and one really does get a sense of what the old working river must have been like centuries ago. Goring may have been judged the winner of best village competitions (albeit on environmental issues as well as appearance) but it has to be said that the most appealing views in the vicinity are those seen when walking across the bridge towards its near neighbour, Streatley!

The lock and cascading weirs take the eye on that first section of the bridge, to be replaced in one's line of vision by the Swan Hotel, alongside which is moored one of Oxford's 'floating pavilions' – the Magdalene College Barge. The road then climbs away from the river, crossing the main Reading Road (the A329 from Wallingford) before tackling the steep hillside leading up to the vantage point of the National Trust-owned Lough Down or adjacent Common Wood on Streatley Hill. It is both fascinating and frustrating to view the work of late-nineteenth- and early-twentieth-century photographers such as the legendary Henry Taunt (1842–1922), noting just how many fewer trees there were to obscure views of the river a century ago. Whether working alongside the riverbank or from adjacent hillsides, it can be difficult to find places from which to gain a clear, uncluttered view. The riverbank has obviously changed immeasurably in so many ways since Taunt's time and even during the three decades or so that I have been photographing the English countryside, certain favourite views are now no-go areas due to excessive trees growth and other foliage.

If a detour up the hill has been made then cars should turn right towards Reading upon reaching the main road, while walkers cross back towards Goring and carry on along the downstream towpath. The pendulum

of fortune definitely swings in favour of motorists on the next leg towards Pangbourne and Whitchurch, as they will easily be able to visit the Palladian Mansion of Basildon Park, a detour perhaps too far 'off piste' for Thames Path walkers. The house was built in 1776–83 by John Carr of York for Sir Francis Sykes. After various owners, the estate was purchased in 1928 by the 1st Lord Iliffe, who promptly sold the house on to an eccentric American whose plan was to dismantle it stone by stone and have it shipped to the United States for re-erection. Happily he was either overcome by a bout of common sense or perhaps had simply received a quotation for the transportation costs.

Basildon Park then went into rapid decline. It was used by the army during the Second World War but, incredibly, was repurchased by Lord Iliffe's son and his wife, who set about the long process of saving the house. It was handed over to the National Trust in 1978 and has recently featured in several high-profile movies, most notably the 2005 version of *Pride and Prejudice*, for which it was transformed into Netherfield Hall. Many of England's old country houses are like our medieval churches and cathedrals, in that they all look wonderful to the casual glance but, beneath those awesome façades, the fabric is simply crumbling away, and we do rather tend to take our architectural heritage for granted. Having now stepped away from the limelight, the house is currently undergoing a major conservation project to prevent further decline, but without the efforts of the National Trust, English Heritage and other major conservation bodies, many historic buildings would have disintegrated long ago.

Lower Basildon lies on the Thames side of the main road, and it is worth heading down the lane leading to visit the late-thirteenth-century flint-and-brick-built church dedicated to St Bartholomew. Despite spending most of his life away from the parish, Jethro Tull was born in the parish, baptized here in 1674 and, at his behest, was returned after death to be buried in the churchyard. Although his memorial is a somewhat disappointingly modern headstone, an engraved memorial is certainly better than an unmarked grave. The church is yet another in the growing portfolio of redundant churches cared for by the Churches Conservation Trust, and although not usually open, the keyholder lives nearby and their details are posted on the church door.

Below: The shingled spire of St Mary's Church and surrounding cluster of half-timbered houses reflected in the mill pool at Whitchurch.

Bottom: The author Kenneth Grahame lived in the village of Pangbourne, and the landscapes of the riverbanks and surrounding woodland are often associated with his classic book *The Wind in the Willows*.

If anybody visiting the church wishes to continue on down to the river, a footpath leads from the church car park down to the Thames at a point almost directly facing Gatehampton Manor and the old ferryman's cottage. That particular ferry signified yet another place at which the river's old towing path transferred banks, and although there is a public right of way along the river from Lower Basildon, the National Trail continues on the opposite bank in the direction of the riverside community of Whitchurch-on-Thames.

Motorists *en route* from Streatley and Basildon Park will eventually arrive in the substantially larger village of Pangbourne, having enjoyed a glorious last mile driving almost parallel to the river. That broad reach above Pangbourne Weir is set with ancient trees, graceful Victorian villas and lined with boats of all shapes and sizes. The Swan Inn is located immediately next to the weir, and it was here that Jerome K. Jerome and his cronies abandoned their boat in a downpour and beat a hasty retreat via a considerably drier train back to London from the nearby station.

Pangbourne is set directly across the Thames from Whitchurch, linked to its neighbour by one of the two remaining toll bridges still in operation on the non-tidal river. The white, lattice girder bridge currently in place dates from 1902, but its predecessors had spanned the river since a private Act of Parliament was passed in 1792, granting the newly formed Whitchurch Bridge Company the right to replace the existing ferry with a bridge and to levy predetermined charges on pedestrians, livestock and carriages using that facility. Privately owned and run toll bridges have to be largely self-funding and the onus of repair and maintenance obviously lies with those who receive the monies accrued from tolls.

After decades of wear and tear inflicted by vehicles it was patently not designed to accommodate, Whitchurch Bridge has now become in need of significantly more than a fresh coat of paint, and is scheduled for reconstruction in 2013. As the cost is estimated to be in excess of £3 million, the company was granted government permission to raise tolls by 100 per cent, and from October 2009, the maximum payable became 40p. There are multi-trip vouchers and discounts for local residents, but the increase has been vigorously opposed in some quarters. However, given that the only other available bridges are either back at Streatley or significantly further downstream at Caversham near Reading, 40p still seems very good value, when considering that petrol and diesel seem destined to hover around £5 per gallon for the foreseeable future (and no, I am not a shareholder in the Bridge Company).

Although often perceived as a sleepy hamlet through the much-painted and photographed grouping of church, mill and thatched cottages reflected in the tranquil waters of its weir pool, Whitchurch is a significant community in its own right and was actually afforded greater status than its neighbour in the Domesday Book. However, easier road and later rail links gradually elevated Pangbourne into a bustling commuter town. But despite the roundabouts, traffic lights and clatter of trains, the tranquil 'Wind in the Willows' riverbank of 'Ratty, Mole and Toad' is never more than a short stroll away. Pangbourne was the home of that much-loved book's author, Kenneth Grahame, who had lived in Church Cottage from 1924 until his death in 1932. The legacy of *The Wind in the Willows* is tinged with sadness because it evolved from the imaginative bedtime stories created for Grahame's four-year-old son Alastair, who was tragically killed by a train in Oxford in 1920.

The riverbank path leading downstream from the Whitchurch–Pangbourne bridge is just one of many stretches along these upper reaches of the Thames that could have been the inspiration for some of the book's atmospheric locations. The work of artists, cinematographers and writers is constantly analyzed and dissected by aficionados, many of whom seem desperate to stand in the shadow of the easel, in the same spot as the movie camera or play detective by tracking down the real-life locations that allegedly provided the inspiration for fictional places in a book. One potential candidate for Mr Toad's rambling country residence, Toad Hall, lies downstream from Pangbourne, but the gabled Tudor mansion of Hardwick House is a private residence and barely discernable on the opposite bank from the Thames Path through its protective screen of mature trees. What people do sometimes overlook is the fact that, although Kenneth Grahame lived the last eight years of his life here in Pangbourne, he spent a far greater portion of his life in and around Cookham (see page 174) and so his influences were spread over a significantly greater stretch of the Thames than perceived by some of his readers.

Below: Moored motor launches upstream from Pangbourne Lock in the aftermath of a thunderstorm.

Right and left: The rewards offered to those who make the effort to access Mapledurham are immense as this is an historic place seemingly untouched by the passage of time. The Elizabethan mansion, church and fully operational water mill are set close by the Thames, at the end of a narrow street lined with early seventeenth-century almshouses.

Below: The bridge at Caversham marks the end of a memorable stage of the Thames Path. The early twentieth-century concrete structure links Caversham with Reading, and replaces a succession of earlier crossings extending back to twelfth century, one of which housed a chapel dedicated to St Anne.

The main road from Pangbourne declines to follow the great northern loop executed by the Thames between Pangbourne and Mapledurham, opting instead to pursue a dreary route through the rapidly expanding Reading commuter belt that comprises the communities of Purley and Tilehurst. A much more rewarding option is to invest 40p in a river crossing over Whitchurch Bridge, follow the road up Whitchurch Hill towards Goring Heath and Reading, and thereafter follow the clearly marked road signs to Mapledurham House and Mill. If Thames Path walkers rigorously adhere to the marked trail from Pangbourne, they will have the pleasure of strolling through the National Trust-owned riverside meadows opposite Hardwick Park but, when the path reaches Mapledurham Weir, they will be temporarily directed 'inland' to Purley, picking up the Thames again near Tilehurst rail station. Because there is no pedestrian access to Mapledurham across the weir and lock, walkers will get only the briefest glimpse of the outstanding Elizabethan house.

There is a viable pedestrian option which, although involving some road walking, is predominately upon bridle tracks through the outstandingly beautiful wooded countryside of the Hardwick and Mapledurham estates. The route initially follows that adopted by motorists over the Whitchurch Bridge but soon picks up the private road to Hardwick House, which is also a public bridleway and footpath. This eventually emerges at Mapledurham, and on a quiet weekday out of season, it really does feel as though the clock has been wound back a few centuries. However, people should be aware that although the house and mill are open to the public, those days are generally restricted to summer weekends

and Bank Holidays. Even if the house itself is closed, the atmosphere of the place is something to savour anyway.

Mapledurham House is perceived as another potential candidate for Toad Hall, but regardless of its status in that literary role, its water mill certainly featured prominently in the Michael Caine film *The Eagle has Landed*. The mill has been restored to full working order and gives an invaluable insight into one of the river's most important industries – the production of flour. Windmills are obviously rendered impotent by calm weather but riverside mills have a constant source of energy at their disposal and have therefore made a significant contribution to rural economies. The mill shaft is made of oak, its waterwheel from elm and its undershot wheel drives a pair of millstones capable of grinding a tonne of flour in six hours.

The Blount family and their descendents have occupied Mapledurham House since it was built in 1588, and their ownership of the manor predates that by another two centuries. The mellow brick-built house has wings flanking a shallow courtyard and porch leading into an entrance hall dominated by a portrait of Sir Charles Blount, a prominent Royalist who managed to defend Mapledurham to good effect during the Civil War as it suffered comparatively little damage during that conflict. However, given the site's remoteness, it would have been a most determined foe who troubled himself with such an arduous expedition for the sake of one renegade outpost. The same principle might have applied to those charged with the persecution of recusant families such as the Blounts; the presence of 'priest holes' and secret passages confirm the fear felt by England's Catholic families during that time of religious intolerance. Mapledurham House has its own chapel but the parish church of St Margaret set close by the house also contains a curious legacy of the family's religion: a separate Catholic chapel formed from the church's south aisle. It has been unused for centuries and is divided from the nave by a combination of impressive Blount memorial tombs and some rather dour black railings.

For those walkers who opted out of the Mapledurham detour, the route continues along the river's south bank towards Caversham and Reading. The views across the river away from the footpath are significantly more pleasing than the rather built-up environs of the Thames Path itself, an observation that applies in reverse to anyone walking the bridle paths onwards from Mapledurham. At least the final stage of the path is alongside open spaces and a civic park prior to arrival at Caversham Bridge – the same landmark and river crossing that awaits those traveling by road from Mapledurham. Reading and Oxford share similar traits in that the Thames actually flows around their peripheries rather than being an integral part of the city centres, but there the similarity ends. The view from Caversham Bridge encompasses no medieval spires or towers adorning ancient academic foundations but there is just a glimpse of the grim, red brick of Reading Gaol, hidden amid the concrete and glass with which Reading has been reconstituted from a post-industrial mess into a thriving modern commercial centre. Strictly speaking, Reading is on the River Kennet rather than the Thames, and as I have already included a more detailed description of the town's history and architecture on page 53 the graceful shallow arches of Caversham Bridge seem an eminently suitable place to end this section of the journey.

The grim, castellated tower and walls of the mid-nineteenth-century Reading Gaol once famously housed Oscar Wilde. There is a strange correlation between the Victorian gaol and the extant walls of the medieval Reading Abbey, as the inhabitants of both institutions were seeking redemption, although one kind was arguably more tangible than the other.

CHAPTER SIX

Messing About in Boats
Sport and Leisure on the Thames

When man first realized that a floating hollow log could transport him safely and dryly across water, would go faster when propelled by a flat stick rather than hands and then told others of his discovery . . . competitive water-based sport was born! Of course back in the days of prehistoric man, any notion of competition existed solely in pursuit of survival. The man who could paddle fastest and be first to the prey would have more food for his own family when the 'law of jungle' prevailed among the earliest civilizations. When sea-borne trading became the norm, the skipper who could read the tides, wind and weather and trim his sails better than rival boats would be the first back to port with a cargo and most likely the one to pick up the next charter as a result. The same logic applied on the river: the professional waterman engaged in light transport or ferry services who was fastest across the river got first pick of the next job.

On the occasions when the everyday economic pressures of work could be set aside, the notion of friendly amateur rivalry did eventually become part of life on the Thames. Many of the earliest recorded rowing contests were actually heavily wagered upon prize matches rather than the type of gentlemanly competition that evolved with rowing clubs such as the Leander Club at Henley-on-Thames. Founded in 1818, it is acknowledged as the oldest public rowing club in the world, but it took until the end of the nineteenth century before women took to the river in a formally organized manner, when a seventy-one-year-old doctor, Frederick Furnivall, founded the Hammersmith Sculling Club for Girls in 1896.

Although there were isolated occasions when women competed for money in sculling races during the 1830s, nineteenth-century society's attitude certainly precluded them from daring to venture into the hitherto exclusively male domain of river sport. Not only was Furnivall fervently against such gender discrimination, but he had also been concerned about the poor physical condition of the girls who worked in his favourite local teashop and wanted to encourage them and other women to become fitter. The club opened its doors to male rowers just five years later and still flourishes successfully today as the Furnivall Sculling Club.

The Thames hosts competitive rowing events, amateur regattas and sailing matches along much of its length between Oxford and the estuary, progressing

from events based upon the legacy of the working river through to the organized chaos of University Eights Week. Almost no formal competitive sport takes place upstream from Oxford, and this is the favoured territory of the motor cruiser and narrowboat fraternity, whose greatest exertion on any given day might run to little more than untying the mooring rope to drift though another idyllic day of storybook Thames. That is the joy of the river; there is room for everyone to do more or less as they please without let or hindrance.

One place where there is most certainly plenty of room is out beyond Gravesend, where the Thames expands from river into estuary and it is there that a sailing match takes place to celebrate the survival of one of the river's oldest traditional vessels. The **Thames Sailing Barge Match** is an annual event that is just one leg in a series of races held on the Thames, Medway and other Essex coastal estuaries between May and September. It was first run in 1863 and the brainchild of Henry Dodd (1801–81), known locally as the 'Golden Dustman', who started his working life as a ploughboy before taking to the river and making his fortune by carting rubbish away from London. The races are run exclusively for the traditional Thames cargo barges, whose distinctive red sails were once a common sight on the river as they plied their trade around the notoriously difficult waters of the outer estuary and the Kent and Essex coastlines. The boats were uniquely designed to cope with the region's shallow tidal estuaries and creeks, could float in little more than a metre of water, and if grounded at low tide, would not keel over like other vessels. Thames barges also had the advantage of being sufficiently well balanced to enable them to safely sail without ballast and were also designed to be sailed by just two men if absolutely necessary.

There were some 2,000 in operation around the turn of the twentieth century, carrying bricks, coal, grain, agricultural products and other general commodities, although they inevitably declined in number as rail and road transport began taking trade away from rivers and canals. The Thames Sailing Barge Match is the second oldest in the world, predated only by the Americas Cup that originated in 1851. However, there are those within the sailing barge community who suggest that the Americas Cup has changed out of all recognition since its inception, whereas theirs has not and so consider the Thames event worthy of that historic accolade.

The starting point in on Lower Hope Reach, some 4 miles downstream from Gravesend and set alongside the bleak marshes of the Hoo Peninsula. The course runs out past Southend-on-Sea to the North Oaze Buoy, located way out in an area of the estuary that is somewhat bizarrely known for its architectural features. The gaunt outlines of old Second World War anti-aircraft towers,

Competitors in the annual Thames Sailing Barge Match (usually from Lower Hope Reach on the seaward side of Gravesend), sailing a course that will take the vessels far out into the Thames estuary.

later occupied by 1960s pirate radio stations, share the horizon with an offshore wind farm. The distance for the race is 43 nautical miles and it takes around eight hours to complete, although the race stewards can adjust the course if wind conditions are so unfavourable that competitors would be unlikely to make it back to the finishing line in Gravesend before dark. Some of the sailing barges that have recently competed in the race are over a hundred years old and the survivors of the original fleet are restored by dedicated enthusiasts, just about able to make the necessary ongoing maintenance viable by running day charters for visitors and fellow sail boat admirers.

The **Doggett's Coat and Badge Race** is considered to be the oldest continuing sporting contest in the world, having been founded in 1715 by Thomas Doggett (1654–1721), an Irish actor who followed his considerable success on the stage by going on to manage the Drury Lane Theatre in the heart of London. The race was established for six newly qualified Thames Watermen and Lightermen in their first year of freedom after apprenticeship and the prize put up by Mr Doggett was a splendid red waterman's coat with a lavishly engraved

Above: A handful of tourists on the London Millennium Footbridge near St Paul's become unwitting spectators of the historic Doggett's Coat and Badge Race as the rowers pass beneath them *en route* to the finish in Chelsea, almost 5 miles away from the City.

Below: The Thames Barge Driving Race was instigated in the 1970s to showcase the skills of Thames Lightermen and Watermen. Propelling heavy barges from Greenwich to Westminster using oars alone is not for the fainthearted and the rowers have to constantly rotate to avoid total collapse from exhaustion.

silver badge. The Watermen who competed in the race were the eighteenth-century equivalent of today's taxi drivers and, as he lived several miles upstream at Chelsea, it is thought that Doggett came to know and like many of those who ferried back and forth along the Thames.

The first race was held on 1 August to celebrate the anniversary of the accession of George I in 1714 and rowed from London Bridge to Chelsea, a distance of nearly 5 miles. It was stipulated that all competitors should row the traditional Thames wherries or whatever type of boat should later succeed them. The wherries were heavy boats and, until the rules were changed in 1873, the race was rowed against the tide, a task that in adverse weather conditions must have made it an almost impossible test of strength and endurance.

Thomas Doggett sponsored the race until his death in 1721 and made provision in his will for its continuation, stipulating that the race be maintained in perpetuity and that the cost of each year's coat and badge should be met from his estate. His executors were rather less enthusiastic and came to an arrangement with one of London's ancient Livery Companies, the Worshipful Company of Fishmongers, who agreed to ensure the race's longevity – a pledge the Company honours to this day. One suspects that the £300 originally paid from Doggett's estate has long been swallowed up, and the Company should be applauded for its willingness to place a higher value on tradition rather than count its pure monetary cost.

Although the race was understandably suspended between the war years of 1939–46, nine races were held in 1947 to allow those Watermen who had qualified during the missed years to actually race for the honour of the coat and badge, thereby ensuring an unbroken list of winners from 1715. The Doggett's Coat and Badge Race is now held in July, rowed with the incoming tide, rather than against it and most competitors now take just about 30 minutes to complete the course in sleek, single racing sculls rather than more traditional boats. It may be steeped in history, but the event doesn't really make much of a spectator sport and tourists crossing the Millennium Footbridge from St Paul's to Bankside have little idea that they are watching such a historic event unfolding beneath them. The flotilla can be already quite well strung out by then and the only clue that a race is taking place is offered by the official umpire's launch following in the competitor's wake. The rules for the Doggett's race may have been tempered over time to make things slightly easier for the competitors, but another more recently introduced competition for Thames watermen and lightermen makes no such concessions and represents the sternest imaginable test.

The **Thames Barge Driving Race** was first held in 1975 and is organized by Transport on Water, an association of lightermen and watermen formed in 1974 whose main stated aim was to 'reverse the decline in commercial water-borne traffic on the nation's rivers and canals'. Transport on Water decided to devise an event that showcased not only the physical and navigational skills of watermen and lightermen, but also that intuitive ability to 'feel' the river. Powered vessels go in the direction determined by the helmsman but the 30-ton barges used in the race are propelled only by three 20-foot oars and consequently at the mercy of every tidal shift or gust of wind that blows across the Thames.

The 7-mile long course runs between the palaces of Greenwich and Westminster, passing through several bridges with large concrete or cast-iron piers and, while the barges themselves may not suffer unduly in any collision, the culprit would be heavily penalized for such a navigational error. Only three crew members may row at any one time, two using the oars, known as 'sweeps' to propel the barge forward with a third used as rudder to steer.

Although the crews can select their own course along most of the route, they are required to collect at least one pennant from barges moored along the course, most of which require a significant shift in direction to access them. For the more experienced crews, there are additional trophies on offer for collecting either two or three pennants, although having witnessed the pain etched on the faces of some oarsmen, one suspects that simply finishing the course with the mandatory single pennant is achievement enough.

The race really does hark back to the days when the port of London relied exclusively on manpower. Before the construction of London's enclosed docks from the early nineteenth century onwards, most vessels moored in the centre of the Thames and their cargo was unloaded into flat bottomed barges called lighters, hence 'lightermen'. The watermen were responsible for passenger traffic and when one considers that until the building of Westminster Bridge in 1750 London Bridge was the sole crossing point over the Thames, 'water taxis' would have been very much in demand. However, the issues of safety and pricing became an increasingly major concern and the passing of an Act of Parliament in 1555 led to the founding of the Company of Watermen. The establishing of that professional body ensured that anyone wishing to become a waterman would have to serve a one-year apprenticeship, a term substantially increased to seven in 1603. Both trades were later united under one body, becoming the Company of Watermen and Lightermen of the River Thames in 1700.

Boat Race day at Hammersmith. Every square metre of space along the towpath is occupied and as heads are turned upstream to follow the crew's progress, the shore is lashed by waves generated from the wash of the vast flotilla following in the wake of the University Eights.

Unlike the rather low-key Doggett's Coat and Badge Race, the spectacle of Thames Barges being laboriously propelled upstream has become more of a well-promoted tourist attraction, and people follow the progress of the race from the Embankment, road bridges or in river boats offering special packages for the event. However, no amount of marketing or promotion will ever elevate a barge race up to the iconic status achieved by an annual rowing contest between England's two oldest universities.

The **Oxford and Cambridge Boat Race** has become firmly lodged in the nation's psyche as an unmissable sporting occasion and also a world famous event through the medium of radio and television. It is just one of those curiously patriotic phenomena that we English seem so fond of, when people who have no interest whatsoever in a particular sport become aficionados and experts for a day in celebration of being part of something that represents the pinnacle of achievement. The race was first broadcast on radio by the BBC in 1927, covered by television cameras in 1938 and thought to be either seen or heard in over 180 countries. However, regardless of how good the television coverage might be, a quarter of a million people still flock to every available part of the towpath each spring to be part of the event.

Riverside pubs are full to overflowing from the moment their doors open and many of the people lucky enough to live by the river host lavish boat race parties. Some houses are bedecked with both light and dark blue decorations and balloons to support the event rather than one particular crew, but many others nail their colours firmly to the mast and display only the dark blue of Oxford or the light blue of Cambridge. For those lining the Thames who can actually get a glimpse of the river through the seething mass, the Boat Race is a 'blink and you miss it' event. As with almost all other televised sports, the sheer speed of an event is never properly conveyed to armchair viewers and to watch a racing eight in full competition mode is a truly impressive sight. A Mexican wave of sound that soars to a crescendo and then subsides as the boats pass each vantage point alerts spectators further upstream to the race flotilla's impending arrival.

Despite the noise of the cheering crowds, it is still possible hear the frantic urgings of the team's coxes, sometimes drowned by the more strident, amplified tones of the race umpire issuing warnings to any crew veering off a true racing line into the path of its opponent. Of course some coxes will try and intimidate the opposing crew by steering a dangerously close line but even in the heat of battle, all eighteen competitors know full well that a clash of oars at full speed is both physically dangerous and even more importantly, damaging to the ethos of the race as a sporting contest that was first staged in 1829.

The idea for a rowing race between the two universities originated when two close school friends from Harrow, Charles Merivale and Charles Wordsworth (nephew of poet William) ended up at Cambridge and Oxford Universities respectively and thought the notion of friendly rivalry between the two academic institutions would be fun. Although 'Varsity Matches' extend to other sports such as rugby and tennis, most of those other contests did not appear on the calendar until much later in the nineteenth century. Cambridge issued a challenge to Oxford on 12 March 1829 and that first University Boat Race was actually held on the long reach above the bridge at Henley-on-Thames. After a false start and recall, Oxford were the victors, but it would be another seven years until a rematch was organized. Instead of at Henley, they rowed over a 5½-mile course between Westminster and Putney.

An increase in London's river traffic rendered the contest unsafe and, so the race venue was relocated to the riverside 'country' village of Putney during the 1840s and that 4¼-mile course to Mortlake has been the home of the Boat Race ever since. The race was held intermittently until 1856 when it thereafter became a standing annual fixture, broken only by suspension for the duration of both World Wars. Although there are often periods when one university runs up a sequence of wins, the results over the history of the race ebb and flow like the Thames's tide and by 2010 the totals were 80–75 in favour of Cambridge. There was one controversial dead heat in 1877, a result initially called by the race judge, a professional waterman, 'Honest' John Phelps, as 'a dead-heat to Oxford by five feet', a verdict subsequently published minus the five feet!

There have been other minor incidents over the years but not even the crowd-pleasing sinkings have resulted in injuries to anything other than the sodden crew's pride. Rough water is one of the inevitable (but thankfully not too frequent) consequences of staging a race on a tidal river in spring. The emotions displayed at the finish in the shadow of Chiswick Bridge are inevitably extreme – the winning crew's euphoria contrasting sharply with the slumped bodies of despair in the losing boat. Regardless of the outcome, both crews will have taken themselves far beyond the pain barrier but that is when the hundreds of hours of training kick in and rowers switch to automatic pilot and just make every stroke as powerful and as

Right: Crews competing in the Women's Head of the River Race launching their boats from the steps by Chiswick Boat House. With an entry list of around 300, the race could be a logistical nightmare for rowers and officials but it all somehow runs like clockwork.

perfectly executed as every other one of the 600 or so that it takes to cover the course. Under normal river conditions, the race time will generally be somewhere between 17 and 19 minutes, with Cambridge currently holding the record of an impressive 16 minutes 19 seconds set in 1998. Many of the rowers who compete in the Boat Race are likely to have rowed the Championship Course before but in reverse from Mortlake to Putney.

The **Head of the River Races** are processional races run downstream over the Boat Race course with the ebb tide but are essentially time trials in which crews race against the clock rather in a head-to-head contest or similar regatta format. The first event was held in 1926 and was the brainchild of the influential Australian born rowing coach, Steve Fairbairn (1862–1938), who rowed in the Cambridge boat four times during the 1880s and later coached at Cambridge University and on the Tideway at both the Thames and London Rowing Clubs. He ruffled the feathers of many traditionalists with innovations that included longer seat slides to allow the legs to play a greater role in the rowing action. This not only generated more power and drive but also created a more relaxed, smooth flowing style totally at odds with the prevailing rigid posture, causing his detractors to describe his rowing style as sloppy.

Fairbairn was also a great advocate of distance training, and what better way to blow away the cobwebs after winter training than a 4¼-mile breeze down the Thames against the clock? Many of the Tideway rowing clubs were already based around Putney and so had access to that long stretch of river, but creating the Head Races also gave crews from further afield a chance to sample the course. Many clubs outside London simply do not have such long reaches and therefore cannot test the stamina of their rowers over such a long, unbroken stretch of water.

The inaugural Women's Eights Head of the River was held a year later in 1927, but as only two crews entered was run as a proper race and it was not until 1930 that five clubs competed, transforming it into the same processional format already used by the men. It seems entirely appropriate that the winners of that first proper Head race represented the pioneering Furnivall Sculling Club. However, the women's races of today have significantly more than five entries, in fact 295 more but, not content with the challenge of marshalling 300 boats, the organizers of the men's race accept a hundred more! I only attended the women's race, but even the logistics of accommodating their 'reduced' entry were complex to say the least. Three hundred boats and their crews had to get to the river through busy London suburbs, find

A seemingly never-ending flotilla of boats competing in the Women's Head of the River edging their way upstream past Barnes to the start line at Chiswick Bridge. The race is run downstream against the clock over the full Boat Race course to Putney.

Races in Oxford's Summer Eights Week can become quite physical and to the uninitiated might appear to be a floating version of dodgem car racing. Because the Thames is not wide enough for standard racing, competition is based upon overtaking the boat in front and hence the mid-stream kerfuffle.

parking slots to accommodate the long trailers carrying the very long racing boats and find a space somewhere along the course to get onto the water.

Once launched, the boats then have to get into numerical order, harried and shepherded by race marshals armed with loudhailers constantly buzzing up and down the lines of boats extending way downstream and out of sight along each bank. The competitors paddle slowly forward to the start at Chiswick Bridge, passing beneath the outer arches and continuing upstream until turning in for their final approach. Boats are sent off at ten-second intervals and race down the centre channel past their queuing fellow competitors. For many crews it is purely a training run and a chance to maybe harmonize a newly formed crew or put into practice techniques learnt during the winter prior to the spring and summer racing season. However, a substantial number of elite boats are there to race and winning a Head of the River brings great kudos to the victorious crew and their club.

In races of such mixed abilities, and where the starting draw is random rather than seeded, the skill of a cox is really tested. They have to ensure that slower crews about to be overhauled are passed safely and with enough clear water between the two sets of blades, but also without deviating from the straightest line and thereby losing priceless seconds. It was a fascinating experience being able stand midway down the course and observe the boats passing by *en route* to Putney at racing pace. By that stage many had already run out of steam and the rowing technique had become ragged and uncoordinated; others steamed by in perfect harmony and with effortless style. The refreshing thing about the Head of the River Races is that schools teams, veterans, average club rowers and Olympians are all welcomed under the umbrella of that one event. It was just a brilliant concept that Steve Fairbairn devised and he fully deserves the memorial obelisk set exactly 1 mile from the Putney start/finish line, which is used as a formal intermediate timing point for races run on the Championship Course.

Processional races commonly feature on the calendars of most rowing clubs throughout England, as the majority of our rivers are insufficiently wide or straight to accommodate head to head contests. The outcome of such events is usually determined by the stopwatch, but Oxford's main intercollegiate rowing championships are a bit more physical. **Oxford Summer Eights Week** is probably now a shadow of its former glorious self in those halcyon days when the top decks of college barges moored alongside Christ Church Meadow were a colourful crush of parasols and alarmingly striped blazers. However, Eights Week is still an important event in the University calendar, and the viewing platforms of the boathouses are still crowded each May when the event is held. It goes without saying that copious quantities of Pimm's are drunk and, as the four days of competition near their climax, the narrow towpath becomes even more crowded with students lending vociferous support to their particular college crews. The competition is also known as 'Bumps Week' and the clue is in the title. The minutiae of the rules can be difficult to interpret but in essence, the championships are divided into divisions of thirteen boats, and crews progress up through those divisions by catching or 'bumping' the boats ahead of them during a race.

The races are started on the reach extending upstream from Iffley Lock and the eights line up in single file, separated by a distance equivalent to one and a half lengths. The cox maintains his boat's starting position by holding onto one end of a rope secured to a metal ring set into the riverbank and when a starting canon is fired, the mooring is released and boats accelerate away in pursuit of those ahead. A 'bump' is achieved either by actual contact or by the cox of a boat about to be caught accepting the inevitable and raising his hand, thereby avoiding potentially costly damage to a very expensive boat. Both the 'bumper' and 'bumpee' pull over to allow other crews to continue racing and those two boats will then reverse their starting positions for the next heat. Getting all the way down the course is referred to as 'rowing-over'.

Matters are further complicated by the course narrowing into an S-bend called the 'Gut' and if a 'bump' takes place there, the crews involved inadvertently create mayhem by not being able to pull over fast enough to clear the racing channel, and a multi-boat pile up is not uncommon. Back in the pre-War days when Eights Week was covered in depth by *The Times* and the published 'bump charts' and results were earnestly scrutinized by alumni both home and abroad, race reports could have easily included bizarre headlines such as 'Magdalen bumps Jesus in the Gut'.

Having reached the top of a division, that eight becomes the 'sandwich' boat and moves up to become the bottom boat of the next division. Moving up through the ranks can be a long slow process towards the ultimate goal of being crowned Head of the River, especially as an eight's starting position for the following year will be the one on which it ended the preceding competition. To the uninitiated casual observer, the Eights Week bump races may simply appear as a floating version of fairground dodgems but it has been run as a serious competition since first conceived during the early nineteenth century.

The **Henley Royal Regatta** is also held annually on the Thames but its races are all run in the traditional head-to-head manner without bumping. Henley's reputation on the international rowing scene is now firmly established and many of the world's best oarsmen congregate on the banks of the Thames each June to compete in this unique event. The regatta's origins can be traced back to the time of the inaugural Oxford and Cambridge Boat Race staged at Henley, an event that proved extremely lucrative through the influx of thousands of visitors. Other race days had also been judged a success and so a public meeting was convened in the town hall to discuss the possibility of Henley staging its own annual event. The proposer was Captain Edmund Gardiner, who suggested that aside from the obvious benefits to the local economy, an annual regatta would be 'a source of amusement and gratification to the neighbourhood and the public in general'.

The townspeople patently agreed with the idea, staging the first in 1839 and, apart from suspensions during both World Wars, a regatta has been held annually on Henley's naturally straight reach ever since. Although initially run as a one-day event, the regatta proved so popular that it was immediately extended to two and when the Great Railway's branch line was opened in 1857, even more people were able to attend and two days became three in 1886 and a further was added. That status was maintained right through until 1986 when a fifth day was added to the schedule and it retains that format today. The regatta received royal patronage from Prince Albert in 1851 and successive reigning monarchs have always consented to be Patron.

Henley's regatta course is just over 100 metres longer than the standard international distance of 2,000 metres but as its width is just under 25 metres, there is only enough room for two crews to race alongside each other.

Below: Summer Eights Week races are also known as 'Bumps', for obvious reasons, and the rules stipulate that the cox of a boat about to be caught raise their arm in acknowledgement of defeat.

Bottom: Despite its curious format, the racing is deadly serious, although many crews elect to abandon tradition shorts and singlets in favour of something a bit more colourful.

Henley Regatta's championship course is wider than the Thames at Oxford but even so can still only accommodate two boats racing line abreast.

A timber boom divides the course from the main Thames channel, along which the normal day-to-day traffic of motor cruisers and pleasureboats potter gently along, and because of the width restriction, Henley operates a knock-out draw. Consequently, during the early stages of competition, there can be up to ninety races a day until that elimination process whittles down the numbers. As the average time taken to row the course is about 7 minutes, two separate contests can be accommodated on the course at the same time although it must be a nightmare for the official commentator.

Henley was always part of a 'London Season', which included sporting events such as Royal Ascot and Wimbledon, but the finals day at Henley now seems to clash with the climax of the All England Championships – the men's singles final. For those having to make the painful choice between one event or the other, is does at least mean one less wardrobe conundrum! The Stewards Enclosure at Henley remains the Holy Grail for many and there is always a long waiting list for membership. Members are perfectly aware of the strict dress code that applies within the Enclosure but there have been embarrassing occasions when guests have not quite understood the rules and been found wanting in either the hemline or jacket and tie departments.

The Stewards Enclosure is adjacent to the blue-and-white striped temporary boat tents that are in turn close to the Leander Club, set directly next to Henley Bridge. As already mentioned earlier, it is thought to be one of England's oldest rowing clubs, predated only by educational institutions such as Jesus and Brasenose colleges at Oxford and Westminser School in London. Leander was a Tideway-based club until moving to Henley towards the end of the nineteenth century, and its clubhouse is one of the most elegant and comfortable to grace any sporting club. Its members, past and present read like a *Who's Who* of British rowing and include names such as Sir Stephen Redgrave, Sir Matthew Pinsent, James Cracknell OBE, Tim Foster, Ed Coode MBE and many others.

While it is true that some aspects of Henley are associated solely with privilege, much of the regatta does still tick the boxes suggested at that first meeting in the town hall, and it remains 'a source of amusement to the public in general' because access to much of the riverbank is unrestricted and lined with bars, food outlets and a perfect view of the racing. Fawley Meadow is now a mini city of luxurious hospitality tents for companies or individuals to treat favoured clients or friends and family to a special day out, and there will be many who attend the regatta and have little or no interest in the rowing but can at last say they were there. However, there will also be rowing club members from all over England, school pupils and university students who stand by the riverbank as the crews flash past and maybe picture themselves in the bow seat – and why not?

Supreme physical fitness is the key requisite for a competitor at Henley, but just a little further upstream lie two villages who jointly host an event for which fitness does have a part to play but possibly it is less essential than a good sense of balance and an even better sense of humour. The **Wargrave & Shiplake Regatta** is thought to be one of the largest traditional regattas held on the Thames each summer and almost certainly one of the oldest. Local press reports and articles in the *Parish Magazine* from the mid-1860s give details of the event and, although the course has changed over time, the concept of the event remains unchanged. This was during an era when the Victorians were 'discovering' the Thames and flocked to its banks at every opportunity in their skiffs, punts and canoes, even retiring to weekend houseboats whose lavish interiors would eclipse most cruisers currently on the river. The ethos of true amateur sporting tradition so refreshingly maintained downstream at Henley is also reflected here, but although staged for fun, the competition is taken no less seriously. There is also the added frisson that not only will village pride be at stake, but the Thames is also a county boundary at this point – Wargrave is in Berkshire and Shiplake is part of Oxfordshire.

The regatta has become so much a part of the local community that many people who have long since left the villages make an annual pilgrimage back there in early August. Although there are traditional marquees erected to provide under-cover accommodation for the bar, refreshments and officials, the overall aura is not of a tented village but rather a gazebo hamlet. They line the reach along which the regatta is held and, yes, there is a formal enclosure for which badges are required to be purchased, but the dress code is just a little more relaxed than that required by others. However, what really makes the regatta so special is the sheer variety of events, and the impressive array of traditional vessels used to stage them, including the gloriously named dongola.

A dongola is a 3-foot-wide punt, propelled by a team of six kneeling paddlers. With three boats racing line abreast down the 400-metre-long regatta course, the noise generated by eighteen paddlers and their cheering riverside supporters generates a tremendous atmosphere. It is obviously a fun, social event, but also fiercely competitive, and judging by the state of some competitors at the finish, also totally exhausting. People who might pride themselves in being reasonably fit prior to taking part in a dongola race will discover that the action of paddling while kneeling makes demands on entirely new sets of muscles that have hitherto lain happily dormant. The traditional double-scull rowing

Temple Island is the starting point for all races rowed at Henley Regatta, and what better way could there be to spend a gloriously sunny English summer's afternoon than lazing by the Thames with a glass of Pimm's watching others exert themselves?

Top: The punting canoe event at the Wargrave & Shiplake Regatta requires a tricky combination of power, balance and extreme concentration.

Middle: Competitors at the Shepperton Slalom Canoe Club watching how others fare amid the swirling waters below the weir.

Bottom: A practice session prior to competition allows competitors to become acquainted with the strength of water and mid-stream slalom gate placement.

skiffs used at the regatta differ little from the vessels that gently rowed down the river on a nineteenth-century Sunday afternoon, although those on duty at Wargrave are probably travelling a good deal faster and also have a cox in the stern seat shouting encouragement rather than making small talk about the passing flora and fauna.

The Wargrave & Shiplake Regatta is a truly family-run event in the wider sense of the word because, even though the current economic climate makes funding doubly difficult, the communities have just worked harder to make it happen. When one considers that the two-day regatta comprises some 400 events contested by almost 1,000 individual competitors, it patently requires a considerable degree of organization. Such regattas are a timeless slice of Thames life, and this particular event should be doubly celebrated because the regatta owns all its own craft and also helps maintain the tradition by lending them out to others.

The Canadian-style canoes used in the Wargrave & Shiplake Regatta's flat-water events would probably not fare too well if subjected to the rigours of white-water canoeing, an increasingly popular sport taking place beneath the outflow of Thames weirs such as Shepperton. The **Shepperton Slalom Canoe Club** has the only permanent slalom site in the south-east of England, with headquarters, boat store and clubhouse facilities on Shepperton's Lock Island. The site looks directly across the weir pool to the undeveloped tip of Hamhaugh Island, thereby making it possible to string the network of cables, from which the coloured slalom poles are suspended between the trees set on either bank. Immediately downstream from the weir is the natural basin where the Thames is joined by the River Wey, and the far Weybridge bank makes an excellent vantage point from which to view the slalomists in action.

The river downstream from the weir towards Sunbury offers an ideal stretch of water for fitness work, but it is the dangling white and coloured poles, swinging around on the breeze like a disconnected wind chime that are the magnet. Canoe slalom can be one of the most spectacular water-based sports, demanding skill, an abundance of stamina and courage, laced with just a hint of insanity. In much the same way that slalom skiers must negotiate a difficult pattern of gates, canoeists face the same type of challenge but with significant complications.For example, skiers are not penalized for touching the poles of a gate as they pass through but canoeists will incur penalties if they do. Their courses are set with both upstream and downstream gates that are cunningly placed so that tricky and often quite violent cross-currents must be negotiated to reach them. Each run is timed and any

A canoeist competing at a slalom event at Shepperton. The force of water flowing through the weir does depend on river levels and competitions are consequently not normally held in midsummer.

infringements result in a number of seconds being added to the finishing score. It is customary to have two runs in competitions, the best of which will be counted.

As with all sporting and leisure events that are weather related, conditions will never be the same two days running, and that is the frustrating challenge faced by organizers, who must set competition dates months in advance. The phrase 'you should have been here last week, it was fantastic' is one that photographers are quite used to hearing, and the same almost probably applies to white water canoe slaloming.

If anybody watching the activity at Shepperton is inclined towards thinking that canoeists are a quirky bunch, that opinion would almost certainly be ratified if they happened to be on the river sometime during the Easter weekend. The **Devizes to Westminster International Canoe Marathon** sounds like one of those typically crazy ideas hatched by a group of Englishmen in a pub after a few pints of beer and guess what: it was! The pub was The Greyhound in Pewsey, a small Wiltshire village just outside the market town of Devizes, the year was 1947 and the challenge was to take a boat from Devizes to Westminster in under 100 hours. Sadly, the idea's originator, Roy Cooke, was actually unable to undertake the adventure, but the local Devizes Scout Group did pick up the gauntlet. Local townspeople offered generous sponsorship towards Scout funds and in 1948, four seventeen-year-olds successfully completed the 125-mile challenge in a time of 89 hours and 50 minutes. What should be remembered is that first and many subsequent successful completions were done along the largely derelict Kennet and Avon Canal.

As restoration of the waterway progressed, more stretches became unclogged and freed from choking weed, but one aspect of the race that hasn't been affected in any way by improvements to the canal is the issue of locks. Nobody competing in a time trial can afford to sit around and take a breather while locks are filled and drained and so the canoeists pull into the bank on one side of the lock, lift the boat out of the water, run past the lock gates and rejoin the canal. The race has seventy-seven of those portages and towards the latter stages of the journey, when competitors are almost running on automatic pilot, having to constantly break one's metronomic paddling rhythm must be soul destroying. The portage may not be so bad for the various groups taking the whole Easter weekend to complete the course but, for the elite Senior Doubles crews, there is no respite.

The non-stop Senior Doubles event is a colossal achievement, completed in one continuous effort starting on Easter Saturday and finishing on the Tideway near Westminster Bridge on the ebbing tide of Easter Sunday morning (times and dates may vary with the tide tables). Most paddlers will take around twenty-four hours to complete the course, not stopping to eat, sleep or rest and from the early 1950s for almost two decades, the race became the exclusive domain of Britain's Special Forces. The Royal Marines, SAS and Parachute Regiment all vied

Two-man crews negotiating one of the seventy-seven portages required in the Devizes to Westminster International Canoe Marathon. It is a 125-mile test of physical and mental endurance along a course that combines the Kennet & Avon Canal and River Thames.

with each other for supremacy and some of the times they posted were truly remarkable given that many of them were carrying the same heavy Klepper Aerius folding kayaks they would have used on military operations.

The rules were amended in 1971 to enable civilian crews to compete on more level terms. Prior to that change, competitors had been obliged to carry all the food, supplies and equipment they would need for the duration, but it was decided that 'pit crews' would be allowed to service their teams at appropriate access points. Any lock that has a tarmac road nearby will be crowded with family, friends and supporters of the paddlers, anxiously waiting for them to arrive at the next portage point where they can be hastily topped up with easily digestible high-energy food and drinks before setting out on the next leg. The D.W.s, as they are called, make their way across some beautiful landscape but for the elite teams, much of it is lost in the blackness beyond the narrow beam of their head torches as they paddle through the night. The record currently stands at an astounding 15 hours 34 minutes and, as that represents a feat so utterly beyond comprehension, maybe it is time to leave the hardy athletes and indulge in the activity that attracts most people to the Thames.

Messing About on the River can mean different things to different people, but I did find a dictionary definition of 'messing about' that seemed to perfectly sum up a midsummer's day on the Thames – 'spending time doing something in a pleasantly desultory way, with no definite purpose or serious intent'! That phrase could be easily applied to punting on the Cherwell in Oxford but although an activity that appears so graceful and effortless from a distance, the realities can be just a little more taxing. Practice, experience and local knowledge are the keys to successful punting, but a few drinks and the desire to show off to a member of the opposite sex are unlikely to have a happy outcome. Steering a punt is less easy than it looks and most hire boats are equipped with a paddle to cope with any anxious moments should an accident happen.

The Cherwell can be a delightfully tranquil and secluded place to go punting but some of that seclusion is due to overhanging trees that also have low branches. The other thing that all punters dread is the 'pole stuck in mud syndrome', a problem that can happen to anyone unless on a river with a gravel bottom. The secret is to sense the problem immediately and let go of the pole, reach for the paddle and propel the punt back to retrieve it. There used to be a student dining club in Oxford called the Charon Club, membership of which was exclusively reserved for 'punters who have entered the river involuntarily fully clothed'. However, even though today's undergraduates still have a good time, university is now such an expensive and serious investment that few students have the time or money to indulge in the carefree high jinx of their older alumni, who incidentally also did not have a health and safety culture to worry about either!

Left: Punts moored near Magdalene Bridge, Oxford, awaiting yet another day of excitement, potential embarrassment and mishap on the Cherwell.

Below: Gently cruising along the deserted Thames in a converted canal boat on a perfectly still autumn morning highlights why so many people love taking to the river. Unfortunately, they all want do it at the same time and the joy is then lost.

The exploitation of the Thames for pleasure grew spectacularly during the latter decades of the nineteenth century, with people taking to the river in droves – either collectively in large pleasure steamers or in rowing skiffs that gave total freedom because they were also equipped with canvas awnings to transform them into floating tents. Specialist companies still hire out some of those old style boats but the rise and rise of motor cruisers and canal boats on the Thames in recent years can tarnish the experience of rowing the river under one's own steam. Once late autumn arrives and most of the thousands of motor cruisers are safely tucked up for the winter beneath protective tarpaulins, the river reclaims itself and can once again luxuriate in the diesel-free stillness. From a photographer's perspective, autumn, winter and spring are by far the best times to be out and about along the Thames so I am more than happy that the cruisers are hibernating. However, regardless of whether one uses the Thames for sport, leisure or simply a place of quiet inspiration, there really is room for everybody, but we take it for granted at our peril.

CHAPTER SEVEN

The Royal Thames
From Reading to Hampton Court

Opposite: A lone sailor makes his way upstream amid the lonely surroundings of Cliveden Reach, the boats wake appearing to transform the Thames into a glistening sheet of corrugated metal.

Between Reading and Windsor, the Thames charts an almost geometrically configured course resembling three sides of a square but thereafter maintains a predominately south-easterly flow towards the end of this leg of the journey at Hampton Court. There are some stretches of the river where road access can be frustratingly difficult or occasionally impossible, but there are comparatively few key locations where the motorist might be at a serious disadvantage compared to those walking the Thames Path. However, those following the river on foot will discover that their route sometimes happens to be on the opposite side of the river to a place of potential interest, with no viable crossing point close by, so once again the pendulum of fortune swings more or less evenly between the two modes of transport.

After departure from Reading and Caversham, the next destination on the Thames itinerary is Sonning. Motorists who drove across Caversham Bridge to Reading would be advised to recross the bridge and follow the A4155 to Henley-on-Thames for about 3 miles, and thereafter take a right turn to follow a minor road to Sonning. The current incarnation of Caversham Bridge is probably not on exactly the same site as the earliest versions, but few of those making the crossing from the Reading bank will realize that they are following in the footsteps of the countless medieval pilgrims who visited the shrine of Our Lady of Caversham. Housed within the chapel of St Mary at Caversham priory, it was second only to the other great Marian shrine at Walsingham in Norfolk.

The Thames Path continues from the bridge on the Reading side of the river, passing by an assortment of riverside apartments and office blocks, which although not aesthetically offensive, are equally unlikely to elicit enthusiastic nods of approval. Greater visual interest is provided by Fry's Island (also known as De Montfort Island), a quite substantial natural midstream island comprising a couple of boatyards, one private house and a bowling green. The Island Bohemian Club has been in existence for over 100 years and is possibly the only club in the world with its own private ferry to transport members from the adjacent riverside jetty. Competition among bowlers might be fierce, but even the most closely fought contest could not match the ferocity of a duel that took place on the island in 1163 between Robert de Montfort and Henry of Essex.

The latter named knight was Henry II's Standard Bearer, who stood accused of cowardice and treachery at the Battle of Coleshill in 1157 after fleeing the field of battle, having feared that his Sovereign had been slain. Robert de Montfort levelled the charge against him while the Court was sitting at nearby Reading Abbey, and the king decreed that the matter should be settled through a 'trial by combat'. The island's alternative name clearly

indicates who the victor was and although Essex was pronounced dead at the scene and his body carried to the abbey for burial, he was actually only gravely wounded and subsequently recovered. However, upon recovery he wisely elected to remain within the sanctuary of the abbey and took monastic orders.

Reading Bridge lies just a little further downstream from Fry's Island and is virtually an identical twin to its concrete neighbour at Caversham. The noise of traffic crossing the river is left behind once Caversham Lock has been passed, and the footpath enters the wide expanse of King's Meadow. Any sense of rural tranquillity engendered by the surrounding greenery is merely transient because a more industrial environment awaits just a little further downstream where the Kennet flows into the Thames. The site is clearly signalled in advance by the gaunt skeletal framework of a gasholder, a pair of red-brick rail bridges and the old horse bridge once used to carry the towpath over the Kennet (see pages 51–3). There are other traces of old industries and more modern office blocks in the vicinity, but the path soon breaks free from the environs of Reading, encircles a wetlands nature reserve and thereafter progresses uneventfully onwards towards the pristine surroundings of Sonning Lock.

It is here that the river becomes divided when the weir and mill race that serviced the Sonning Mill branch away to the left. The main stream passes through the elegant eighteenth-century arches of Sonning Bridge, its central arch marked with the letters O. & B., signifying that the county boundaries of Oxfordshire and Berkshire run up the middle of the Thames. Three mills were listed at Sonning in the Domesday Book, although the one still standing on its backwater island dates from the eighteenth century and was still in operation as a flour mill as late as 1969. Thankfully it was not left to rot when deemed to be no longer economically viable and has since been restored and transformed into a renowned dinner theatre.

The backwaters of Sonning are tranquil, foliage-draped pools, but the bridges built over them seem to have been a constant source of ire or inconvenience to locals and road-users alike. Although the elegant bridge over the main channel was built from brick in 1775, those over the weir pool and millrace were merely functional structures of slatted timber, and perfectly adequate to safely carry horse-drawn vehicles. The Industrial Revolution brought advances in technology that included steam-driven traction engines, whose huge iron wheels and the heavily laden trucks they hauled wrought havoc upon many rural roads and bridges.

Locals complained about the unacceptable racket generated by the road trains clattering over the wooden bridges; other-road users moaned about the degeneration of the structures; and artists and conservationists were

Houseboats moored along the Thames come in all shapes and sizes but this one moored downstream from Reading appears to be in the throes of an identity crisis and cannot decide whether to be a boat or an allotment.

vociferous in their opposition to the wholesale destruction of England's quaint rural bridges under the guise of progress. Practicalities won the day when stone, brick and iron replaced the old wooden trellises over Sonning Backwaters in 1902, and those 'modern' crossings survived until 1996, when they were again upgraded to cope with the demands of twenty-first-century traffic. Traffic lights control the flow across Sonning Bridge, and as the only road crossing of the Thames between Reading and Henley, morning and evening rush hours create long queues. The name Sonning is derived from 'Sunna's people' and was a place of some significance in Saxon and medieval times. Most communities along the banks of the Thames achieved prominence of one kind or another during their history and in Sonning's case it became established as the episcopal centre of Berkshire. During the early tenth century, its minster was elevated in stature to become one of the twin cathedrals of the newly created diocese of Ramsbury and Sonning, and an episcopal palace was built near the church. Despite the diocese being later transferred to Salisbury, the palace retained its importance and expanded during the medieval and later periods into a lavish crenellated residence, although there are now but fragmentary remains of that building.

Although the river downstream from Sonning makes so many twists and turns that it is easy to lose one's bearing, its direction of flow is predominately northerly, with the Thames Path following what is effectively the river's west bank. From Sonning village, pedestrians cross the eighteenth-century brick bridge over the main channel and then turn right to cross the weir stream via a functional concrete walkway. Drivers are advised to return to the main A4155, following the signs to Shiplake and Henley. The distant horizon comprises the Chiltern Hills, with steep, beech-clad slopes cascading down to the river beyond Henley, but downstream from Sonning the surroundings are distinctly more pastoral, an impression enhanced by the presence of numerous islands set in the middle of the river.

A mile downstream from Sonning, St Patrick's Bridge appears on the right to mark the presence of St Patrick's Stream, which leaves the river at this point and re-enters it at Shiplake. This is yet another example of Thames engineering, as the River Loddon used to enter the river at this point, but now does so by Shiplake Lock.

Sonning is particularly known for its ancient mill, now converted to a theatre and another legacy of the mill is the tranquil pond that now stands alongside the road and main stream of the Thames. The famous French Horn restaurant can just be glimpsed through the trees in centre frame.

Below: The graceful five-arched bridge over the Thames at Henley was built in 1786 to replace an earlier wooden version, the foundations of which can be seen in the basement of the Henley Royal Regatta headquarters.

Opposite: Elegant riverside houses and the tower of St Mary the Virgin dominate the riverbank at Henley-on-Thames. During regatta week they provide the 'best seat in the house' but the view during the other fifty-one isn't too bad either.

The area of land encompassed by St Patrick's Stream and the divided Loddon channels is known as Borough Marsh.

Upon arrival at Shiplake Lock, the Thames Path leaves the river and follows a lane via Lashbrook into Shiplake, passing by the railway station prior to being reunited with the river on its approach to Henley-on-Thames. That section of the path leading from Shiplake station to the open meadows initially runs along Bolney Road, a lane that offers tantalizing glimpses of the lavish houses and gardens that become more of a part of the riverside scenery as London draws closer. Shiplake, Lower Shiplake, Wargrave and Henley are all served by a railway branch line that connects with the Great Western Railway at Twyford. Even though one might appear to be in the heart of rural England, the City of London is little more than an hour away by train and properties in the vicinity of Henley close to the Thames attract a hefty premium and are offered for sale at eye-watering prices.

Wargrave is Shiplake's immediate neigbour on the opposite bank and the two communities combine annually to stage the Wargrave & Shiplake Regatta (see pages 154–6), one of the river's more endearing amateur regattas. Wargrave itself is an attractive village of Georgian and timber-framed houses, seventeenth-century pubs and a Queen Anne vicarage. It climbs up from the Thames onto a hillside set above the Hennerton Backwater, but for those following the river on foot or driving from Sonning, it can only be accessed via either Sonning or Henley Bridges. For those that do make that detour and don't get too waylaid by the excellent pubs, there are a couple of graves worthy of note in the churchyard. Thomas Day was an eighteenth-century author and noted abolitionist, who met his end after having been thrown by an unbroken horse while in the process of demonstrating that animals only be tamed by kindness. Also laid to rest in Wargrave was Madame Marie Tussaud (1760–1850), founder of the famous waxworks exhibition.

However, even though Wargrave itself might be a detour too far, the beauty of that entire stretch of heavily wooded east bank can actually be more fully appreciated from distance, rather than being in its midst. Walkers will inevitably arrive at Marsh Lock just before the outskirts of Henley become visible ahead, and motorists too can easily access the site via a side road shortly after passing the ubiquitous out-of-town supermarket on the right hand side. Despite being largely screened by trees, visitors to Marsh Lock might catch a glimpse of Park Place, an early-eighteenth-century house that was later remodelled in French Renaissance style.

Actually walking into Henley-on-Thames is by far the most pleasurable, and if motorists park near the well-signposted rail station and Rowing Museum, they too can enjoy that last stroll past rows of moored boats before arriving at Henley Bridge. It is refreshing to encounter once again a really well proportioned stone bridge, and the ballustraded, five-arched structure designed by William Hayward in 1786 is a perfect foil for both the Thames and the dignified elegance of Henley itself. The bridge is also remarkable for the relief sculptures of Thames and Isis carved on each side by the Honourable

Mrs Anne Damer, an accomplished eighteenth-century sculptress. She was also responsible for the great marble bust of Admiral Lord Nelson that still graces London's Guildhall today.

The world-famous Henley Regatta was featured on pages 152–5 and it goes without saying that anyone wishing to explore the town and its environs in peace should avoid that week. The Thames Path conveniently arrives at The Angel, an old coaching inn set immediately next to the bridge, whose terrace is a perfect spot to take refreshment and watch the almost non-stop activity taking place on the river just a few feet away. Public pleasureboats, launches and rowing skiffs are constantly on the move, and even in non-competition weeks one is reminded of Henley's status in the rowing world by the equally famous Leander Club's boathouse on the opposite bank to The Angel. The predominance of Georgian architecture in Henley can be attributed to a period from around 1750 when it became a fashionable and prosperous social centre. Many of those buildings are actually much older but were simply dressed with eighteenth-century façades.

Henley had been an important inland port since medieval times, shipping timber, corn and malt, and during the coaching era became an important staging post on the Oxford-to-London route. Hart Street leads from the bridge into the town centre, passing initially beneath Henley's most distinctive landmark, the tall sixteenth-century tower of St Mary's Church, thought to have been built by Henry VIII's confessor, John Longland, Bishop of Lincoln from 1521 until his death in 1547. Hart Street also contains two gabled Tudor houses that escaped the 'Georgianization' inflicted upon many of their peers. One of the dwellings belonged to William Lenthall, Speaker of the House of Commons during the Long Parliament called by Charles I in 1640.

Henley's other distinctive public building is the ornate Queen Anne-style town hall, built around 1900 and occupying a prominent position at the head of the market place. The road steepens noticeably up to the town hall and the gradient increases even more severely thereafter up Gravel Hill and onto the tree-laden hills and open fields that surround the town. After Henley, the next important destination is Marlow, and as there are no interim bridges, road-users will have to decide whether to proceed either north or south of the river. The more direct route is via the Maidenhead road, giving easy access to the historic villages of Hurley and Bisham, whose abbey is now renowned as being the site of England's National Sports Centre. The slightly longer route that follows the long, looping bend in the river after the regatta reach passes by the great mansion of Fawley Court, Hambleden Mill and Medmenham.

Downstream from the bridge, Henley's regatta course runs straight as an arrow for just over a mile to the race start at Temple Island and, having passed by the Leander Club, the Thames Path hugs the river bank in the direction of Remenham, a tiny village whose name is given to a surprisingly big parish. The flint church of St Nicholas is flanked by a handful of cottages, an ensemble set part way up the hillside rising away from the Thames.

The church of St Nicholas at Remenham stands overlooking the Thames to the east of Henley. It is now largely Victorian, restored in flint in an attempt to recapture the style of the Norman original.

The view across the valley is quite magnificent although during regatta week it becomes a sea of striped hospitality marquees and the narrow lanes connecting the village with Henley and Remenham Hill are transformed into a reversible one-way traffic system.

The temple after which Temple Island is named was originally built as a fishing lodge by the owners of nearby Fawley Court in 1771 during the era when the Grand Tour was almost *de rigueur* and wealthy landowners across the length and breadth of England returned home to grace their carefully laid out parks with follies styled upon the classical temples and statuary of ancient Greece and Rome. Many of these structures were carefully located to create an arresting visual feature at the end of an avenue of trees or other landscape feature, and Temple Island was no exception. Although Fawley Court has a history that dates back to the eleventh century, the current house was designed by Sir Christopher Wren in the 1680s for Colonel William Freeman as a magnificent family home and with landscaping by Lancelot 'Capability' Brown and a carved drawing room ceiling by Grinling Gibbons, it could not have failed to impress.

Having passed Temple Island, the Thames executes a sharp bend and then straightens out as it runs down to Hambleden Lock and Mill. Access to either side of the mill, lock and weir complex is easy for both walkers and motorists as the weir is crossed by a long pedestrian footbridge. Drivers arriving at the hamlet of Mill End on the A4155 from Henley should turn left towards Hambleden village and park in the public car park just 100 metres or so from the road junction and walk back to the river.

The sixteenth-century, white weatherboarded mill was driven by a water-powered turbine and remained in operation until 1955 but has since been converted for residential use and is now probably one of the most photographed apartment blocks on the River Thames. The original towing path changes banks again at Hambleden leaving the Thames Path to continue along the south side of the river, passing through the village of Aston and running past Culham Court, another of the area's historic eighteenth-century mansions. A little further downstream lies Medmenham Abbey, although precious little of its medieval Cistercian origins have survived the numerous restorations and alterations inflicted upon it by a succession of occupants. The most influential of those was Sir Francis Dashwood (1708–81), who leased the building from its owner, Francis Duffield, and remodelled the complex in the eighteenth-century Gothick style.

It thereafter became one of the meeting places of the intimate circle of friends gathered together by Sir Francis named 'The Knights of St Francis of Wycombe'. The other, and arguably more sinister location, was the labyrinth of caves dug in the grounds of the Dashwood ancestral home, West Wycombe Park. The entrance was a full size replica of a gothic church's west front, designed as a prominent landscape feature to be admired from the house. There is little doubt that 'hanky panky' occurred at both locations, especially in the caves, where courtesans and other women were regular visitors to enhance and enrich the meetings.

There were probably pseudo-religious ceremonies at Medmenham, but the stories of Black Masses and Satanism performed by the 'Monks of Medmenham' were probably a bit wide of the mark. Sir Francis's *côterie* was largely a men's drinking club, an excuse to gather on dull Sundays and generally let their hair down without reproach from more staid members of society. Sir Francis is generally credited with being the founder of the infamous Hellfire Club in the 1740s, but it was actually Philip Wharton, 1st Duke of Wharton, who created the first Hellfire Club in 1719. It was disbanded just a couple of years later upon a royal edict from George I following a smear campaign by Wharton's political opponents.

The Hellfire Club 'brand' was subsequently adopted by numerous other groups of like-minded people drawn from politics and the upper echelons of society during the eighteenth century, and whose activities ranged from bawdy, drunken behaviour to significantly darker practices. It is not easy to determine how high the 'Monks of Medmenham' ever went up the scale of depravity, but it was rumoured that in addition to copious quantities of wine, serious works of literature and backgammon sets were discovered at the abbey!

As the old towing path changed sides at Medmenham ferry, it is once again reunited with the Thames Path for the next leg down to Hurley and Temple locks *en route* to Marlow. During the summer months in particular, walkers approaching Hurley will have to run the gauntlet of car-borne picnickers hugging the riverbank and a seemingly never-ending line of caravans and mobile homes occupying a leisure park just a few metres inland. Any inconvenience caused by noise and clutter is soon forgotten as one enters the comparative tranquillity of Hurley village, where the footpath emerges close by a village green flanked by ancient tithe barns and a medieval church of St Mary.

St Mary's has been fashioned from the nave of Hurley Priory's church, an eleventh-century Benedictine monastery built on the site of an early Anglo-Saxon church, and it is reputed that Edith, sister of Edward the Confessor, is buried here. The priory was consecrated in 1086 by St Osmund, Bishop of Sarum (forerunner of modern Salisbury), and although few traces of the original

Below: The willow-fringed lawns of Medmenham Abbey were once allegedly associated with the infamous Hellfire Club.

Bottom: Henley Reach extends way downstream beyond the regatta course and Temple Island, thereby giving rowers an good long stretch of water on which to train before having to turn around at Hambleden Lock.

Left: The Norman door of St Mary's, Hurley, a parish church fashioned from the nave of a twelfth-century Benedictine priory, founded on the site of an earlier Saxon church destroyed by the Danes.

Below: The sixteenth-century brick tower of Bisham Abbey is clearly visible from the Thames Path running along the opposite bank. The church buildings were lost after the Dissolution, but the refashioned manor house acquired by the Hoby family remains intact and now forms part of the National Sports Centre.

buildings remain, a refectory wall has been incorporated into a later house and one of the priory's two tithe barns has also been converted into a private residence complete with fourteenth-century dovecote. A little way up the village street from the church and green is The Olde Bell, a coaching inn whose legacy of hospitality extends back to the twelfth century when originally used as the priory's guest house. Although significantly modernized over time and now an award-winning hotel and restaurant, the building still contains part of the original walls and in places is delightfully topsy-turvy with countless nooks, crannies and undulating, creaking floorboards.

In the great post-Conquest census of England's people, property and landholdings entered in the Domesday Book, Hurley (then called Herlei) was noted as possessing a church, a mill, two fisheries, twenty-five villagers, twelve cottagers and ten slaves, although it is unclear who actually owned the slaves. Hurley's name is thankfully shorter than its original Old English translation – 'wooded clearing in a recess by the trees', but they described the place absolutely perfectly as trees abound both on the sloping land leading away from the village and on the complex of islands amid which Hurley Lock and weir are located. The Thames Path actually uses the lock cut island to progress downstream, accessed at one end via a rustic bridge, and at the far tip of the island a similar structure leads back to the riverbank, where a short walk of less than half a mile brings one surprisingly quickly to Temple Lock and shortly thereafter to Bisham Abbey.

Temple Lock derives its name from the presence of the Knights Templar, who owned significant amounts of land in the vicinity and also ran numerous mills along the Thames. The Templars held the nearby manor of Bisham, but it was taken over by Edward II and used as a comfortable place of confinement for important prisoners when he suppressed the Order in 1307. One such 'inmate' was Elizabeth of Scotland, wife of Robert the Bruce, who was captured and imprisoned by the English for several years until released in exchange for the Earl of Hereford after Bruce's defeat of the English at the Battle of Bannockburn in 1314.

In 1335, Bisham was granted to the Barons Montacute (later the Earls of Salisbury), who founded a priory alongside the house that remained as their main residence for two centuries, and one particularly notable member of the family to live there was Richard Neville (the Kingmaker), whose son-in-law was Richard III. The priory was handed over to Henry VIII's Commissioners during the Dissolution of 1536, but later briefly re-established as an abbey. That re-incarnation was short-lived, however, and the abbey buildings were pulled down, although the house itself was passed on to Henry's fourth wife, Anne of Cleves, as part of her divorce settlement. She in turn sold it to the powerful Hoby family, and it was from the latter decades of the sixteenth century onwards that the existing buildings expanded into a significantly larger residence – the distinctive and imposing brick tower clearly visible from the Thames Path on the opposite bank being added in 1567. The abbey's name will, of course, be familiar to people with even just a passing interest in sport, as it is now one of the UK's National Sports Centres used by England's football, rugby and hockey teams for high-level training.

Thames Path walkers will have to content themselves with a tree-shrouded view of the abbey complex, but in consolation will be rewarded with a totally unhindered of Bisham's parish church of All Saints, standing perilously

Above: Bisham's parish church of All Saints' lies just a short distance downstream from the abbey. Its twelfth-century tower and elongated churchyard crammed with memorials and gravestones in a hotchpotch of styles is one of the visual highlights on the Upper Thames.

Above: Almost immediately after leaving Bisham, another All Saints' looms large on the horizon, and although arguably less atmospheric, Marlow's is certainly better known and the combination of the church's 170-foot spire and William Tierney Clark's suspension bridge is instantly recognisable.

Opposite: In the depths of winter, when weekend sailors seem unwilling to venture out on the river, the moorings at Bourne End Marina resemble an aquatic car park. Surely that is the best time to be on the Thames, rather than having to endure bouts of 'lock rage' on a busy August Sunday?

close to the river's edge just a few metres downstream from the abbey. Although the church's setting is unparalleled and it retains most of its twelfth-century tower and the sixteenth-century Hoby chapel, it was heavily over-restored in the 1850s. That aesthetically pleasing setting of Bisham's riverside church is quickly replaced by one of the Thames's classic views, heralding one's arrival into Marlow – William Tierney Clark's suspension bridge of 1832 and the pinnacled spire of All Saints' Church. As there is ample car parking at the Court Garden Leisure Complex set by the river within the Higginson Park, drivers should leave their vehicles and walk back up the Thames Path for a couple of hundred metres towards Bisham to savour that same panorama.

William Tierney Clark (1783–1852) was particularly renowned for his pioneering work on suspension bridges, Marlow being the sole extant survivor of an impressive body of work that included Hammersmith Bridge (opened in 1827 and the first suspension bridge to span the Thames) and the Szechenyi Chain Bridge over the Danube in Budapest, which was completed in 1849 but rebuilt to Clark's original design exactly a century later after serious damage inflicted upon it during the Second World War. Marlow Bridge was an almost identical but smaller prototype for bridge over the Danube, whose longest single span is over 200 metres, compared to Marlow's 72 metres. The major challenge to suspension bridges is whether they can withstand the demands placed upon them by the sheer weight of modern-day traffic. Even the finest and most perceptive Victorian engineer could never have predicted that our society would become so utterly dependent on motorized transport. Hammersmith Bridge was replaced after just sixty years and so Marlow did very well to survive until the 1950s. At that time a concrete replacement was proposed, but a preservation committee, set up specifically to save the suspension bridge, immediately opposed the plan.

A compromise solution evolved when, in 1965, the bridge was faithfully reconstructed by Buckinghamshire County Council and now carries a weight restriction of just 3 tonnes. Ample walkways run either side of the single carriageway, giving not only a detailed insight into how the bridge functions, but also wonderful views of the Thames and Marlow's riverside environs. The

most obvious structure is the 170-foot-high spire of All Saints, the rebuilt version of an earlier church that was demolished in 1832, at around the same time that the suspension bridge was being completed. The spire was a later addition towards the end of the nineteenth century and, although substantially higher than its predecessor, the current versions of both church and spire are not dissimilar to their predecessors. Numerous atmospheric eighteenth-century engravings of Marlow clearly show the church in its current position but the foreground is occupied by the town's original wooden bridge, itself a victim of the growing traffic generated by the Reading and Hatfield turnpike road as it collapsed in 1828.

Facing the church from across the rives is the famous Compleat Angler, a hotel whose name was inspired by the English writer, Izaak Walton (1593–1683), whose treatise on fishing, *The Compleat Angler*, is still regarded by many enthusiasts as one of the seminal works on the sport, despite its antiquity. Speaking of antiquity: Walton lived to the not inconsiderable age of ninety, thereby suggesting that decades spent outdoors in the company of nature and in the hours of quiet contemplation that are inevitably part of a fisherman's day are good for longevity.

Marlow flourished as a river port in medieval and later times but its real growth has been during the post-war era of the twentieth century, and although several older buildings from the sixteenth, seveneteenth and eighteenth centuries have survived intact during the town's expansion and modernization, others have been transformed into shops. Both High Street and West Street are worth exploring on foot, the latter being associated with Percy Bysshe Shelley, who lived there between 1817–18 with his wife, Mary. During their stay in Marlow, Mary was working on her immortal classic *Frankenstein* while Percy was in the throes of reworking one of his long, visionary poems, *Laon and Cythna* – later published as *The Revolt of Islam*.

Marlow weir cascades noisily past The Compleat Angler, while the navigation channel is located closer to the bank occupied by All Saints' Church. Thames Path walkers (and other visitors) wishing to stroll along to the lock will discover that there is no towpath immediately downstream from the bridge and the footpath follows a

tortuous route (well signposted) known by local residents as Seven Corner Alley. This is obviously not a problem for twenty-first-century pedestrians but spare a thought for bargees charged with somehow hauling or manhandling their heavily laden vessels from bridge to lock while the horses were led round the adjoining streets to bypass the churchyard and adjacent waterside properties.

The Thames Path remains on tarmac before rejoining the towpath downstream from the lock. As it is but a very short walk from the road, it is worthwhile making the detour to savour a different perspective on the suspension bridge. The extensive group of mills that once occupied land adjacent to the lock were demolished and the site transformed into a housing complex in which the spirit of the mills has been retained through their white boarding and steeply pitched roofs. For the onward walk to Bourne End and Cookham, much of the visual interest is on the opposite side of the river, where Quarry Wood and Winter Hill make an imposing backdrop to the Thames.

Road users can either follow the main road to the north of Marlow that virtually mirrors the river's course round to Bourne End and Cookham, but it is much more rewarding to head south over the bridge and make for Cookham via the complex network of lanes that sprawl up and over Winter Hill. From the highest elevations there are wonderful glimpses down into the river valley around Cookham, and a first sighting of the steep, wooded bluff upon which the Astor family's old home, Cliveden House, is situated.

Imminent arrival at Bourne End is signalled by a rapid increase in signs of river activity, of both wind- and motor-powered types. The Upper Thames Sailing Club is based here, taking advantage of a long curving reach that generates ideal conditions for sailing. The path continues past row after row of moored motor cruisers of all sizes and degrees of sophistication before crossing the river via a walkway incorporated into the railway bridge. The riverside path then enters the National Trust-owned Cock Marsh, one of the best lowland wetland sites held by the Trust, and of great importance for both its flora and breeding waders. Unfortunately, this traditionally grazed and managed habitat is under increasing risk from drainage and the abstraction of water on the adjacent land.

As the Thames progresses past the more built-up part of Bourne End it passes a succession of exclusive riverside properties that appear to become even more salubrious as the river draws closer to Cookham. Fortunately for those residents, the river is sufficiently wide along Cookham reach to ensure that their privacy is not too seriously compromised. It would be galling to spend millions on

Left: As one walks along the Thames Path opposite Cookham Reach, it is hard to resist feeling just a small twinge of envy at the smart motor cruisers moored in front of the even smarter houses. It was the Thames and surrounding landscape around Cookham that provided the inspiration for Kenneth Grahame's characters and settings in *The Wind in the Willows*.

Right: The annual Swan Upping ceremony is a harmonious blend of pageantry and wildlife conservation, its origins dating back to the time when swans were a highly prized commodity and those on the Thames belonged to the Crown.

Opposite: Despite having to maintain a fairly demanding schedule during the five days in July when the census takes place, rowing a heavy skiff and chasing swans is thirsty work and riverside pubs such as the Barley Mow at Clifton Hampden come in very handy around lunchtime.

a secluded riverside mansion equipped with state-of-the-art security gates and closed-circuit security cameras, yet still not dare to venture out into the garden when the footpath opposite is busier than Oxford Street Circus in the rush hour.

After the architectural excesses of Cookham Reach, the bridge over the Thames is a major surprise, appearing in the distance as a strip of blue ribbon stretched across the river. It is a simple metal structure dating from 1867, but despite being aesthetically soulless, the bridge still does its job and also provides an excellent vantage point from which to admire the point near Cookham Lock where the Thames suddenly divides into four streams. Of the three islands created by those channels, Formosa is the largest, and comprises some 50 acres of woodland. The Thames Path actually enters Cookham before the bridge via a footpath that runs through the graveyard of Holy Trinity, a stone and flint church of Norman origins but with a late-Perpendicular sixteenth-century tower.

The big village green, Cookham Moor, provides an insight into what the village might have been like before expanding towards its current form, and houses named Malting and Forge remember trades and businesses that once formed the lifeblood of such rural communities. Cookham's High Street is flanked by numerous houses from the seventeenth and eighteenth centuries, but there are examples from earlier periods, such as the Tudor building housing The Bel & the Dragon restaurant. Although it is common knowledge that several high-profile celebrities from the world of entertainment live in and around Cookham, two of its most famous past residents were renowned for their contributions to the more traditional genres of art and literature.

Kenneth Grahame lived in the village of Cookham Dean, set midway along the cross-country route from Marlow, and although easily incorporated into a road itinerary, making a pilgrimage on foot from the Thames Path might be a few thousand steps too far. When exploring the variety of landscape types incorporated into riverbank, heath and woodland areas surrounding Cookham, one quickly appreciates what a rich source of material Grahame had to draw upon when creating his characters and the settings in which they lived.

Cookham was also the birthplace and home of the painter Sir Stanley Spencer (1891–1959), whose life and work are celebrated in the Spencer Gallery, housed in what was the village's Methodist Chapel. One of the more curious exhibits is a black and battered old pram, used by the artist to trundle his materials around the village that he used as a background for many of his works. Although much in demand as a landscape painter for a large part of his working life, he was also deeply affected by his service as a medic in the Great War, experiences that were movingly manifested set of murals he painted in the Sandham Memorial Chapel at Burghclere in Berkshire. Spencer also worked as a war artist in the Second World War, graphically documenting the lives of Clyde shipbuilders and their families.

However, it was Spencer's unique interpretation of religious themes that endure as his greatest legacy, using Cookham village as a substitute location for the Holy Land, and its real life residents as biblical characters. One of his most famous works on that theme, *The Resurrection, Cookham* hangs in London's Tate Britain, but one of my favourite pieces is *Christ Preaching at Cookham Regatta*, which, although incomplete due to being a work in progress at the time of Spencer's death, still receives the accolade for being one of the best titles ever bestowed upon a work of art. Significantly more straightforward in both title and content is another 'Cookham' painting in the Tate's collection – *Swan Upping at Cookham*.

Swan Upping is the annual census of the Thames's mute swan population, a centuries-old ceremony conducted between Sunbury and Abingdon during the third week in July, when the parent adult birds are generally in moult and the cygnets still too young to fly.

This historic event dates back to the early medieval period when the birds were a highly-prized foodstuff (before turkeys arrived) and the reigning monarch claimed ownership of all unmarked mute swans or assigned it to others. During the fifteenth century, rights were granted to two of London's historic Livery Companies, the Vintners and Dyers, and they too participate in the event, being the only two bodies to have retained those ancient rights of swan marking.

The three groups of Swan Uppers take five days to cover the 79 miles, travelling in a flotilla of six traditional rowing skiffs, accompanied by one or two motor launches as support vessels and to offer a tow when required. The Queen's Swan Marker, David Barber, wears a scarlet uniform, while his opposite number from the Dyers (the Bargemaster) is in navy blue and the Vintners' representative in dark green. Swans belonging to the Crown have traditionally been unmarked; all others bore identifying nicks painlessly cut into a cygnet's beak. The brood was divided up according to the marks found on the pen and cob (female and male), although that practice now been abolished and the birds are ringed instead. The Dyers' mark was a single nick and the Vinters made two marks on their birds – hence the quite common pub or inn name, The Swan with Two Necks ('necks' = 'nicks').

Modern-day Swan Upping is more about conservation and education rather than establishing entitlement, and although the census does not include the river's swan population upriver beyond Abingdon, that monitored segment of the Thames provides a clear indication of whether numbers are on the increase or in decline. From a low point during the early twentieth century, the numbers briefly declined during the Second World War, climbing to a record high of 1,300 birds in the mid-1960s to a startling low point of just seven breeding pairs two decades later. Anglers were the chief culprits, causing the death of many birds through poisoning when inadvertently swallowing lead weights either attached to bait or entangled in places where swans were grazing.

Since the abolition of lead weights, the population has begun to steadily increase again, although there will always be years when adverse natural conditions such as floods or protracted periods of fast-running water will kill many cygnets. However, even though things are looking better, man is still making life difficult for swans to continue thriving. A marked increase in the numbers of leisure craft moored along the riverbanks frequently blocks access to the swan's customary feeding and grazing sites, as do the sections where metal or concrete have been used to arrest erosion caused by the motor cruisers and large pleasureboats when not moored.

Swan Upping is conducted with the precision of a military operation and, once sighted, a family of swans has no chance of escape. The skiffs are quickly manoeuvred to form a solid rectangle around the birds, whereupon they are secured and taken ashore to be recorded, weighed, ringed and given a thorough health check. Despite the reduction in deaths from ingesting lead, fishermen's lines and hooks are still discovered tangled up in the beaks of many swans. Riverside first aid is often sufficient to rectify such problems, but for those needing more serious treatment or even surgery, rescue centres funded by the two Livery Companies are available for ongoing care and recuperation until the birds can be safely repatriated to the river. Yes, Swan Upping is a slice of historic pageantry, but behind the façade of brightly coloured livery and peaked caps adorned with feathers are serious conservationists, dedicated to ensuring the continued well-being of the swans that form such an integral part of the Thames.

The broad riverside meadows and public footpaths flanking the eastern banks of Cookham are perfect vantage points from which to watch the Swan Uppers glide past, but the complexion of the river changes dramatically on the downstream side of the lock. Unlike motorists following the river, those walking the Thames Path will probably have to content themselves with occasional glimpses of the grand Italianate mansion of Cliveden House perched high above its heavily wooded cliff. The first house to occupy the site was built for George Villiers, 2nd Duke of Buckingham. There were later additions to the house during the eighteenth century, and a variety of occupants, including Frederick, Prince of Wales (George

Above: The Italianate mansion of Cliveden House was once the home of Waldorf and Nancy Astor and became the glittering hub of early-twentieth-century society. The 376-acre country estate is now in the care of the National Trust and the house itself leased and run as a luxury hotel.

Right: The 100-foot-high clock tower is actually a cunningly disguised water tower that stands to the west of the house.

III's father). Unfortunately, the place was all but destroyed by fire in 1795 and its replacement suffered the same fate half a century later in 1849, shortly after the 2nd Duke of Sutherland had paid £30,000 for the house.

The new owner of that rather expensive smouldering pile of rubble commissioned Sir Charles Barry (1795–1860) to design the nine-bayed and balustraded mansion that has survived to the twenty-first century without further mishap. By the time Barry arrived to tackle the Cliveden problem, he was already an architectural designer of considerable standing, whose reputation rocketed even higher when selected to design and rebuild parts of the fire-damaged Palace of Westminster. Although the lavish Italianate styling of the exterior is not to everyone's taste, the architect actually based some of his designs for the interior on that of the old house. Some features of Cliveden, such as John Clutton's clock tower, may be perceived as a trifle ostentatious, but the formal parterre laid out in 1855 by John Fleming, extending away from the house for hundreds of yards, is quite breathtaking.

Queen Victoria was a regular visitor to Cliveden during the ownership of the Sutherlands, and also when later purchased by the Duke of Westminster upon the Duchess's death in 1868. However, it would appear from curt correspondence to the Duke that she was less than amused to discover that he felt obliged to sell the house. In 1893, it became the property of a wealthy American entrepreneur, William Waldorf Astor (later 1st Viscount Astor). Some dramatic interior remodelling took place, including the insertion of a huge, Renaissance French fireplace and a complete dining room of Rococo French panelling from the Château d'Asnières near Paris, which was occupied for some time by Madame de Pompadour.

Cliveden was gifted to Astor's son, Waldorf, upon his marriage to Nancy Langhorne in 1906, and whereas his father collected artifacts, he was more interested in people, and so began the legendary era when Cliveden became one of the great social hubs of England, whose weekend parties became the stuff of legend. Politicians, statesmen, writers and artists mingled together in an eclectic blend that continued for decades, especially after Nancy Astor had made history in 1919, becoming the first female Member of Parliament to take her seat at Westminster.

Waldorf Astor was a great conservationist and, perhaps mindful of the future, donated the house and estate to the National Trust in 1942, but upon condition that they retained the right to still live in the house. It was during the time of the 3rd Viscount Astor in the early 1960s that the name of Cliveden became irrevocably linked to the infamous Profumo Affair, a scandal that not only pierced the heart of government and posed a potential threat to national security during the Cold War, but also provoked a sense of moral indignation in an England that had yet to encounter the 'swinging sixties' or become accustomed to a daily diet of gossip and titillation from as yet unborn tabloid newspapers.

The drama's cast list included Stephen Ward (a society osteopath), John Profumo (British Secretary of State for War), Captain Yevgeny Ivanov (assistant naval attaché and Russian spy) and Christine Keeler (model and showgirl). Ward rented a cottage from his friend, Bill Astor, and Keeler was one of his weekend houseguests who met Profumo around the swimming pool of the main house, a brief encounter that led to an affair. It later transpired that Keeler had been sleeping with the Russian while seeing Profumo and the consequent fall-out from the affair was far reaching and tragic. John Profumo lied to the House of Commons over his involvement and his political career collapsed, Stephen Ward committed suicide while on trial for a pathetically trumped-up charge relating to living off immoral earnings (essentially calling him a brothel keeper) and Harold MacMillan's Conservative government failed to be re-elected at the following year's General Election.

The Cliveden Estate is wonderfully managed and presented by the National Trust, and even though the house itself is leased out as a luxury hotel, the grounds and gardens are open to the public and there is also occasional limited access to some parts of the interior. The views from Cliveden are magnificent, especially from the vantage point of Giacomo Leoni's eighteenth-century gazebo, later converted into a chapel by the 1st Viscount Astor, who is buried there. Despite being deprived of the delights of Cliveden, as the My Lady Ferry no longer runs across from Cookham, walkers progressing along the dark, almost sinister section of footpath along Cliveden Reach (also known as Cliveden Deep) will get an intimate view of Spring Cottage, the place rented by Stephen Ward during what turned out to be an ill-fated hot summer's weekend that, for some, was to get considerably hotter.

As the gradient of the Cliveden bluff moderates, the route of the path is transformed from wooded wilderness to a more tranquil environment of moored boats and the villas, with immaculate lawns on the outskirts of Maidenhead. However, in much the same way that the Thames bypassed Reading, the same applies here, and the riverside 'resort' atmosphere still prevailing in the vicinity of Boulter's Lock is a throwback to the times when this stretch of river was *the* place to promenade

on a Sunday afternoon. Faded sepia photographs from the 1920s show pleasureboats disgorging crowds of day-trippers up from London, the men in fine suits and ladies resplendent in full-length dresses and with hats and parasols. Times and fashions have changed but the allure of a riverside car park, café, ice cream stalls and children's playground still attract countless visitors to the Maidenhead 'riviera'.

Maidenhead town centre is typical of many, and while its shops and pedestrian precincts are all perfectly fine, there are no historic sites to make the lengthy detour worthwhile, and perhaps of more interest are the means by which people cross the Thames to get in and out of Maidenhead. As one continues downstream from Boulter's Lock, the first bridge encountered carries what was once the main Great West Road from London to Bath and Bristol, now superceded by the nearby M4 motorway. The thirteen-arched bridge with elegant balustrades was the work of Sir Robert Taylor and opened in 1777; drivers making their way down from Cliveden will emerge just to the east of the river crossing, having passed through Taplow village, which lies near Boulter's Lock on the opposite bank to the Thames Path.

Significantly more famous than Taylor's structure is Maidenhead Railway Bridge, built by Isambard Kingdom Brunel to carry his Great Western Railway across the Thames. Because the structure had to leave the river's navigation channels and towpath unobstructed, Brunel defied gravity and precedence by creating the widest brick arches in the world (spanning 39 metres), but in order to maintain the level gradient of the railway, the arches could be only just over 7 metres high. Critics predicted disaster but the genius of Brunel prevailed yet again and although strengthened and widened in the interim, it still carries the main line from London Paddington to Bristol and South Wales.

The Thames Path crosses to the Taplow side of Maidenhead road bridge and continues through surprisingly open countryside towards Eton and Windsor via Dorney Reach, passing the village of Bray on the opposite bank. Although currently renowned for its stellar collection of restaurants, Bray's longer-standing claim to fame is as the home of the 'Vicar of Bray', subject of a much-loved eighteenth-century song that told the insightful tale of the spiritually flexible Vicar of Bray, who prided himself in his ability to adapt his religious beliefs to the ever-changing political climate that marked the tumultuous sixty-seven years from the opening of the reign of Charles II to the death of George I.

Although motorists have the option of proceeding on either side of the river (and could opt for the 'lunch in Bray' route), I recommend heading east from the Taplow junction near the bridge, passing the large lake known as Amersham Ponds and then taking a turn right down Marsh Lane, a minor road signed to Dorney. The waterway seen snaking across open fields near this point is the Jubilee River, a man-made flood relief channel devised to alleviate the threat of flooding to the Maidenhead, Windsor and Eton areas. It extends for some 12 kilometres, beginning near Boulter's Lock and re-entering the Thames below Romney Lock near Windsor.

Another artificial stretch of water glimpsed further down the road is Dorney Lake, the world-class Eton College rowing lake chosen to host the rowing and kayak events for London's 2012 Olympic and Paralympic Games. Impressive though that site may be, the visual appeal of a flat sheet of water pales into insignificance when compared to Dorney Court – the nearby magnificent Tudor mansion set directly on the route by road, and easily accessible via a footpath leading from the Thames Path.

From Dorney Court, the road to Eton arrives at the western tip of Dorney Common, where it bifurcates, offering a right fork back towards the river near Boveney Lock and weir, although goes no further and is effectively a cul de sac. The direct route is the B3026, which passes through the suburb of Eton Wick before arriving in the very heart of Eton close by the magnificent Tudor buildings of Eton College. The Thames Path runs almost parallel to the Eton Rowing Course, and as it passes close by the lake's southern tip, a mill stream branches off from the Thames, creating an island large enough to accommodate the Royal Windsor Racecourse, a figure-of-eight track whose regular Monday evening fixtures attract massive crowds. Although accessible by road, racegoers travelling from Windsor can also make the 10-minute journey by river taxi on board vessels equipped with one of the essentials for any trip to the races: a fully stocked bar.

Walkers passing by Boveney Lock will by now be getting more frequent glimpses of Windsor Castle, although those sightings can be fewer during months when the trees are in full leaf. Almost immediately after passing under a road bridge and the river crossing of one of the two railways feeding into Windsor, and rounding another foliage-clad curve in the river, the royal castle is revealed in full view. As one draws ever closer along the towpath, its sheer scale becomes even more impressive, but the Eton side of the river also has its own distinctive landmarks – the tower and chapel of Eton College.

Eton was founded by Henry VI in 1440, and although a largely undistinguished king, he was nevertheless an

Opposite: Maidenhead Bridge is a Grade I Listed structure built in 1777 by Robert Taylor.

Above: The North Terrace State Apartments and Great Round Tower of Windsor Castle at sunset. The tower was built by Henry II on the site first occupied by William the Conqueror's wooden motte and bailey castle, and from that initial military garrison, Windsor has been added to by successive reigning monarchs and transformed from a dour fortress to a sumptuous royal palace.

Opposite: The tree-lined Long Walk leads away from the castle into the 5,000 acres of Windsor Great Park, which once served as the royal hunting grounds.

inspired educationalist. He had been impressed by the success of the partnership established between Winchester School and New College, Oxford (both founded by William Wykeham, Bishop of Winchester), in which the school acted as a dedicated feeder to provide undergraduates for the University college. Henry therefore decided to mirror that system for his newly founded college at Cambridge (King's) and established a school for seventy scholars at Eton, set just across the river from Windsor Castle. The king took a close personal interest in the school, often visiting the scholars and taking note of their progress but was apparently angry when the boys visited in return, fearful that 'his young lambs should come to relish the corrupt deeds and habits of his courtiers'.

Eton's cobbled School Yard is flanked by a remarkable ensemble of buildings that include Lower School and College, the first classroom and accommodation to be built back in the fifteenth century, and still in use today. The seventeenth-century Upper School was added when Lower School ran out of capacity. Eton's College Chapel, a glorious example of Perpendicular gothic architecture, is an almost identical, but slightly smaller version of King's College Chapel in Cambridge. Eton's was originally planned to be significantly larger, but when Edward IV usurped the throne in 1461, he diverted the lavish endowments bestowed upon Eton by Henry to St George's Chapel at Windsor Castle.

Eton is by far the best starting point for a visit to Windsor, especially now that Windsor Bridge is barred to traffic, enabling an opportunity to savour one's surroundings in peace and comparative safety. Car drivers will find more than ample car parking facilities on the Windsor side and, as a result of privately owned rail companies vying with each other to secure royal patronage, the town is blessed with two termini, the Central and Windsor & Eton Riverside stations. Whichever mode of transport is used to arrive in Windsor, the castle is invariably one's ultimate destination, although there other noteworthy buildings, such as the pillared seveneenth-century Guildhall designed by Sir Thomas Fiddes and completed by Sir Christopher Wren due to Sir Thomas's premature demise before the building was finished.

The open ground floor originally served as a covered corn market, and civic business was conducted on the floor above, a venue that is now a particularly sought-after venue for wedding ceremonies and was chosen by

H.R.H. the Prince of Wales for his marriage to Camilla Parker-Bowles in 2005. The Guildhall is but a few steps away from Castle Hill and Henry VII's Gateway to Windsor Castle. This is the main public entrance to the largest inhabited castle in the world and the official residence of Her Majesty Queen Elizabeth II. The castle was first founded in the eleventh century by William the Conqueror as one link in a chain of fortresses erected around London's perimeter to consolidate his conquest. As with all early Norman castles, Windsor would originally have been a motte-and-bailey type, comprising a wooden fortification set upon a mound of earth resembling an upturned pudding basin.

As the current line of Windsor's outer wall is remarkably little changed from the original layout devised by William in the 1070s, one can readily appreciate that this was a serious military base. It was one of medieval England's great castle builders, Henry II, who began the task of replacing wood with stone, and he was responsible for upgrading the round tower on top of the mound, the outer walls of the Upper and most of the Lower Ward and also the royal apartments in the Upper Ward. It was not until well after the English Civil War that Windsor began its serious transformation from a military-based stronghold into a sumptuous royal palace that also happened to be fortified. Charles II began that process in earnest following the Restoration, creating elegant new State Apartments, featuring mural and ceiling paintings by the Italian artist, Antonio Verrio and woodcarving by the legendary Grinling Gibbons. Charles was also responsible for creating the Long Walk, a magnificent avenue extending due south from the castle into Windsor Great Park.

However, even though the Stuart monarch had left his mark upon the royal palace, the most influential contributor to Windsor's current appearance belonged to the following ruling dynasty of the House of Hanover. George IV worked closely with architect Sir Jeffry Wyatville, refashioning many of the buildings in mock-gothic style, adding turrets, towers and crenellations to create just a hint of Rhineland fantasy castle overlooking the Thames. The castle's interior was also remodelled, and many of the formal rooms used for State Occasions are little changed from when designed and furnished under George IV. One of his most dramatic contributions was the Waterloo Room, created during the 1820s to commemorate Wellington's victory over Napoleon at the Battle of Waterloo in 1815. The walls are adorned with a specially commissioned series of portraits by the artist, Sir Thomas Lawrence, depicting the monarchs, statesmen and generals from both the victorious and vanquished sides.

One of the more glittering formal occasions held in the Waterloo Room is the annual Garter Luncheon hosted by the Queen each June for the Knights and Ladies of the Garter, the oldest British Order of Chivalry originally founded by Edward III in 1348. After lunch

St George's Chapel, Windsor Castle, is the spiritual home of the Order of the Garter, founded by Edward III in 1348. The present chapel was begun by Edward IV in 1475 to be his place of burial and completed by Henry VIII. The Perpendicular vaulting in the choir is just sublime and to stand amid the banners and coats of arms of the Garter Knights is an experience to savour.

the knights process in full regalia to a service held in St George's Chapel, whose choir surely represents the apogee of Perpendicular gothic architecture.

The chapel was built at the instigation of Edward IV to serve as a royal mausoleum and to be the spiritual home of the Order of the Garter. Within the chapel are the tombs of ten monarchs, but it is the glorious fan-vaulted choir, resplendent with banners and other forms of heraldry, that is the building's most arresting feature. Every knight is required to display a banner of his arms in the chapel, together with a helmet, crest and sword and also an enamelled stall plate. The insignia are taken down and returned to the sovereign upon a knight's death, but the plaques above the choir stalls remain as an enduring and extremely moving memorial.

Although a saunter down the glorious elm-tree-lined avenue of Long Walk is a tempting proposition, every stride out into the 5,000 acres of Windsor Great Park has to be retraced if one is to rejoin the river. The Thames Path crosses to the south bank at Windsor Bridge, snaking its way around the fringes of the vast Home Park and its playing field, past Romney Lock, before briefly changing sides again over Victoria Bridge, passing alongside Datchet village and then re-crossing via Albert Bridge at the southern end of Home Park, from where there are excellent retrospective views of Windsor Castle. Motorists can take the same route via the two bridges or take the A308 from Windsor towards Egham and Staines. Road and towpath are united at Old Windsor, a disappointingly bland, modern village for one with such a historic past.

Old Windsor was originally the site of an important ninth-century Saxon settlement, with a royal palace particularly favoured by Edward the Confessor and although William the Conqueror was responsible for effectively establishing 'new' Windsor by building his castle there, he always opted to actually stay in the one established by his Saxon predecessors. The road leading away from Old Windsor runs close to the river as they jointly arrive at Runnymede, the riverside location where the Magna Carta was signed by King John in June 1215. The charter is traditionally seen as guaranteeing basic human rights (especially relating to maladministration of justice) against the excessive use of royal power, and King John finally acceded to the Barons' demands by placing both himself and future sovereigns within the rule of law.

Many of the clauses contained within the document specifically related to aspects of feudal law, but as feudalism declined, Magna Carta lost its significance and under the Tudors was almost forgotten. However, during the seventeenth century it was rediscovered and reinterpreted as a democratic document and, as that was also the time when the Pilgrim Fathers and first settlers headed across the Atlantic, many of its basic premises also became incorporated into the American Constitution. Runnymede itself probably had no particular significance in the process. It just happened to be an easily accessible flat area able to accommodate the vast retinues of all the participants, and was conveniently set midway between the Barons' base at Staines and Windsor Castle.

Inappropriate development of any kind on or near this historic site was thwarted by Lady Fairhaven's gift of the land to the National Trust in 1931, thereby ensuring no Magna Carta catering outlets selling 'Beefy Baron Burgers' (or worse). The entire site is marked by little more than elegant brick lodges designed by Sir Edwin Lutyens

Left: The Magna Carta Memorial at Runnymede was erected amid woodland and meadows near the banks of the Thames in 1957.

Below: The Kennedy Memorial at Runnymede is a simple and dignified tribute to the assassinated American President.

(one housing a National Trust tea room – no burgers), a discretely sited car park and low-key information boards. Three important memorials erected during the twentieth century are set upon the lower, middle and upper slopes of Cooper's Hill: the Commonwealth Air Forces Memorial (1953), the Magna Carta Memorial (1957) and the John F. Kennedy Memorial (1965).

Appropriately enough, the highest-located memorial is to the Air Force, commemorating the 20,000 airmen and airwomen of the Commonwealth Air Forces who died over Europe during the Second World War and have no known grave. Part of the inscription at the entrance to the memorial's cloister states that 'they died for freedom in raid and sortie over the British Isles and the land and seas of northern and western Europe'. The Air Force Memorial is accessible by road, has a dedicated car park and is well signposted for both motorists and walkers.

Legs are the only mode of transport to the other two sites, a factor that ensures they are seldom uncomfortably crowded. During my first visits to the sites some years ago, I was surprised to discover that those two memorials, on a site of such significance to English history, democracy and law, were either erected by, or dedicated to Americans. However, upon further consideration over time it seems less important who actually paid for the stones but just good that at least somebody did. The Magna Carta Memorial is in the form of a domed classical temple containing a pillar of English granite on which is inscribed: 'To commemorate Magna Carta, symbol of Freedom Under Law'. It was erected by the American Bar Association and funded through voluntary donations by some 9,000 American lawyers.

The Kennedy Memorial, unveiled by the Queen in 1965, lies midway up Cooper's Hill and the final steep part of the ascent is via a set of forty-six irregular granite steps, one for each year of the President's life. The memorial itself is moving in its simplicity – a block of white Portland stone – but it is the poignancy of the inscriptions that sends one away from Runnymede in perhaps more reflective mood. The wording on the top part of the stone simply states the fact that 'This acre of English ground was given to the United States of America by the people of Britain in memory of John F. Kennedy, born 19th May, 1917: President of the United States 1961–63: died by an assassin's hand 22nd November, 1963'. However, it is the extract from the President's inaugural address in 1961, now almost half a century ago, that is perhaps the most chilling and sombre aspect of the memorial. 'Let every Nation know, whether it wishes us well or ill, that we shall pay any price, bear any burden, meet any hardship, support any friend or oppose any foe, in order to assure the survival and success of liberty.'

Right: The Thames at Runnymede near Magna Carta Island. It might be a bit of romantic wishful thinking to imagine that the famous document was actually signed there.

Below: The non-tidal Thames has plenty of marinas, where motor launches may be stored, repaired and serviced, but traditional boat builders, with sheds stacked with seasoning timber, are becoming less common.

Despite the pleasure of pottering alongside the Thames in a car being proportionately diminished with each mile travelled towards London, the roads are perfectly bearable, so long as leisure drivers remember to avoid the teeth-bared, white-knuckle ride of the combined rush hour and school run. Walkers on the Thames Path face fewer hazards, but there are some sections of towpath where pedestrians and cyclists are obliged to share the same public right of way and must co-exist in harmony.

Soon after leaving the green meadows of Runnymede, both road (A308) and footpath maintain their identical courses, passing under the noisy M25 motorway bridge and onwards to Staines. Midway between the motorway and Staines Bridge, walkers might catch sight of the London Stone, set under trees on the opposite bank. This is actually a replica of the original that marked the upstream limit of the City of London's jurisdiction over the Thames, a power that had existed from 1285 right through to 1857, when the Thames Conservators took over that responsibility. Staines was an important river crossing to the Romans, carrying their main road from London (Londinium) to Bath (Aquae Sulis), but apart from a quiet corner of the old town near St Mary's Church and the park containing the London Stone, Staines should not detain visitors too long. Having crossed Staines Bridge, the Thames Path continues along the north bank, and a minor road, the B376 signed for Laleham and Shepperton, will not only keep drivers off the main roads but also in close touch with the river.

Although not really apparent from either the road or footpath, Staines is reservoir country and almost every square acre not covered by houses or roads seems to be a man-made sheet of water, some of which are named after royal family members, including the Queen Mother, George VI and, south-east from Staines, the largest of them all: the Queen Mary Reservoir. The Queen Mary covers 700 acres and is kept supplied with millions of gallons of Thames water extracted via an inlet near Laleham, a small village set slightly back from the river and almost directly opposite Penton Hook Lock and Island. Penton Hook is a curious phenomenon: a place where the Thames has virtually carved itself over time into a teardrop shaped loop, a bend that has now been bypassed by Penton Hook Lock and weirs, and the resulting island is managed by the Environment Agency as a nature reserve. There is an enchanting path running around its perimeter and in the quiet backwater shrouded in dense foliage is pure *Swallows and Amazons* territory.

The next river crossing is a little further downstream at the late-eighteenth-century Chertsey Bridge, with the town centre set about a mile to the west. Detailed maps of the immediate area show many references to the Benedictine Abbey of Chertsey, a legacy sadly surviving in name only. A monastic foundation on the site had existed since the seventh century, but after the Norman Conquest, when it was reconstructed in stone, the abbey flourished as one of the most important and richly endowed in the south. It was here that Henry VI's body was brought for burial following his murder at the Tower of London in 1471, and Chertsey grew rich upon the proceeds of pilgrimage. However, Richard III removed the body to St George's at Windsor in 1484 to put a stop to the pilgrimages and the talk of miracles happening in Chertsey.

Drivers arriving from Laleham could park by Chertsey Bridge and join the Thames Path on its way through Dumsey Meadow, an SSSI (Site of Special Scientific Interest). Dumsey is the only unimproved grazed water meadow in Surrey, and one of only a few in the Thames Valley not lost to agricultural improvement, development or converted into a more formal recreational area. The most remarkable thing about the meadow is that to the uninformed eye, it appears as just a field with a few old willow trees in the middle, rather than a priceless species-rich area of natural grassland.

Even for those exploring the Thames for the first time, the name of Shepperton will probably have a familiar ring, as it is home to one of Britain's most famous film studios, now incorporated into the Pinewood Group. However, the heart of Shepperton village remains untouched by the glamour of the movie industry, and the old square down by the river still comprises the church of St Nicholas, the rectory, a couple of pubs and some old houses. The approach from Chertsey to Shepperton along the river is full of interest and worth a slight detour from the main road. Secluded amid trees after leaving Dumsey Meadow are

Chertsey Bridge was built from white stone towards the end of the eighteenth century.

Sunrise over Dumsey Meadow Nature Reserve on the banks of the Thames at Chertsey.

Top: The upstream tip of Pharaoh's Island and the south bank of the Thames near Shepperton, photographed at dusk.

Above: The Shepperton Ferry provides an invaluable service to both local residents and those walking the Thames Path, and in the case of the latter, saves a long a rather tedious detour.

probably the first real houseboats encountered thus far. Although people do live in their narrow boats, it tends to be for protracted holidays rather than as dwellings, but these boats are converted for comfortable living and small colonies become quite a common sight as London draws closer.

Another common sight along this part of the Thames are the riverside chalet-bungalows in a variety of shapes, sizes and colours. They line the riverbank up to Shepperton Lock and a number also share Pharaoh's Island with a few more sumptuous houses, one of which just happens to be called The Sphinx, and has appropriate statues set either side of its landing steps. The occupants of the houses on the island all have to travel by boat to get to the 'mainland', an idyllic proposition in summertime, but on a dark winter's night with a week's shopping from the supermarket to carry? The island is reputedly so named having been gifted to Admiral Lord Nelson in 1798 after his victory at the Battle of the Nile.

The downstream tip of Pharaoh's Island heralds the start of a confusing and convoluted stretch of river – 'rivers', actually, because it is here that the River Wey (see pages 53–5) flows into the Thames from nearby Weybridge. The Thames Path transfers from north to south banks here via one of the very few passenger ferries operating on a regular basis along the non-tidal river. If the ferry is not running, walkers are obliged to take an alternative footpath to Walton Bridge, following the river's original course around several alarmingly sharp serpentine loops. They patently made navigation difficult and potentially hazardous and so were bypassed by the Desborough Cut, a channel dug in 1930s and named after the chairman of the Thames Conservancy, Lord Desborough.

The Shepperton ferry operates at 15-minute intervals during 'office hours', with slightly later starting times at weekends. Passengers travelling from the south bank must ring a ship's bell to summon the ferry – but only on the quarter hour. Those lucky enough to have been able to secure a passage across the river have a straightforward walk along a well-laid track downstream to Walton Bridge. Shortly after setting out on this segment, one's eye is almost immediately drawn to a rather ornate villa set on a small island in midstream, connected to the towpath by an arched footbridge. This is known as D'Oyly Carte Island and was named after the theatrical impresario and hotelier (famed for his association with Gilbert and Sullivan), who bought it in 1887 and built Eyot House there. He later thought of establishing it as a summer riverside annex to London's Savoy Hotel that he had built in 1889, but abandoned the scheme as he was unable to secure a liquor licence, and a 'dry' bar in the middle of the Thames was a definite non-starter.

Walton Bridge is on the verge of yet another reincarnation, as all necessary permissions were finally granted by the various Secretaries of State in December

Below: D'Oyly Carte Island and Eyot House, built by the theatrical impresario in the late-nineteenth century.

Right: The river bank around Walton is sadly blighted by a continuous line of ugly chalets and bungalows that probably still command eye-watering price tags.

Below: The reach above Molesey Lock is lined with assorted houseboats, some of which seem little more than floating portacabins, but there is nevertheless an endearing quality to this rather motley crew and they create an interesting visual juxtaposition with Garrick's domed temple.

2009 to enable the building of bridge number six. Curiously enough, the first version (1750–83) seemed to have been the most elegant of the quintet, to judge by a 1754 painting by Canaletto – its wooden lattice structure being a work of considerable complexity. Bridge number two was an attractive arched crossing of stone and brick, surviving from 1788 until 1859, but that version's successors have alternated between functional or downright ugly, so the twenty-first-century model will be a welcome addition to the Thames landscape. Although the river views downstream will be enriched by the new structure, those back upstream are unlikely to be improved, as the Shepperton bank is crowded with timber framed chalets or bungalows.

The majority of these simple one-storey dwellings were designed as holiday homes, rather than permanent residences, during the late-Victorian and early-Edwardian period of the nineteenth and twentieth centuries, largely as a result of the runaway success of Jerome K. Jerome's book *Three Men in a Boat*. People just could not wait to emulate the lifestyle and adventures of the three companions, and riverside living soon ceased to be the exclusive domain of the privileged and wealthy, although few of those Sunday adventurers would have ever dreamed that their picnic huts would one day become permanent homes.

In terms of onward progress for the final stage to Hampton Court Palace, walkers maintain their association with the river's southern bank, passing a succession of attractive eyots, aits and islands exhibiting varying degrees of habitation. Most island dwellings are huddled together on *terra firma*, others attached to it courtesy of a houseboat's gangplank, although some of the alleged houseboats seem significantly more house than boat and might not fare too well if required to actually get under way. Navigating this section by road from Walton Bridge can be either via the more direct southern route along the A3050 or north over the bridge and thereafter turning right for Sunbury. The latter option is more favourable because it keeps close contact with the Thames and also affords the opportunity to savour several good pubs around the older part of Sunbury set close by the Thames.

The Thames Path also passes some riverside pubs on the approach to Sunbury Locks, unusual in that the original pound lock dating back to 1812 still sits alongside its successor built over a century later in 1925. The far bank and intervening islands are sufficiently wooded in places to sustain the illusion of still being in a more rural environment, but the landscape on the towpath side downstream from the locks becomes singularly dreary as it encounters another area of gravel extraction and the Molesey Reservoirs and water treatment plants, a scene also soon replicated on the far bank. Surroundings improve rapidly with the path's arrival at Hurst Park, once the home of one of two famous racecourses set on either side of the Thames, the other being Kempton Park located between Sunbury and Hampton. Hurst Park was established in 1890, hosting both flat and national hunt racing until its closure in 1962 when sold off for residential development.

Fortunately there is still plenty of open parkland to savour and there are delightful views across to Hampton and the slender church tower of St Mary's. The midstream island set directly opposite the heart of Hampton village is Garrick's Ait, named after the famous eighteenth-century actor and theatre manager, David Garrick (1717–79), who made Hampton his home when buying a riverside villa, subsequently remodelled by the Adam brothers and the gardens laid out by Lancelot 'Capability' Brown. Garrick also indulged in an act of pure theatrical excess by building a domed temple with Ionic portico on his front lawn to celebrate the genius of Shakespeare. He commissioned the sculptor, Roubiliac to create a life-size statue of the playwright for which Garrick himself was the model.

In today's terms Garrick was a real superstar, and his reputation and standing within the theatrical world

The church of St Mary stands close by the domed temple erected by the famous eighteenth-century actor David Garrick in celebration of the genius of Shakespeare.

Above: Hampton Court Palace is a magnificent collection of buildings from different periods but one of its most photogenic and endearing features is the twisted and convoluted network of Tudor brick chimneys.

Below: Jean Tijou's glorious ironwork screen of 1701 for William and Mary divides the Thames Path from Hampton Court's Privy Garden.

Opposite: A historical re-enactment of Henry VIII's procession up the Thames from the Tower of London to Hampton Court.

and beyond can be measured by the fact that he was the first of only two actors to be afforded the accolade of being buried in Westminster Abbey (Lord Olivier was the second). Although Garrick's ego contributed to the raising of a little riverside folly, far greater architectural manifestations of over-inflated self worth lie just a little further downstream at Hampton Court Palace.

The road bridge at Hampton Court is perhaps surprisingly only the fourth river crossing there, and prior to the building of the first bridge in 1753, the site had been served by a ferry. Paintings depicting that first bridge suggest that the designer was in the throes of a nervous breakdown when trying to create a structure

of sufficient stature to stand next to a royal palace but without appearing too grandiose. The result was described rather vaguely as 'rococo' and consisted of seven arches, undulating like a sheet of corrugated iron embellished with twin, pagoda styled turrets over the central arch. The renowned architect, Sir Edwin Lutyens (1869–1944) was responsible for the current bridge, built from Portland stone and red brick in a style that simply echoes those parts of Hampton Court designed by Sir Christopher Wren during the late-seventeenth century. The bridge was sited some 30 metres downstream from its predecessor so that the river crossing would be unaffected during construction of Lutyens' version. It was officially opened in 1933 by the Prince of Wales (the future Edward VIII).

The origins of Hampton Court date back to the thirteenth century, when acquired as a grange by the Knights Hospitallers of St John of Jerusalem, a religious order founded in the eleventh century during the Crusades. When it became surplus to their needs, they rented out the property, and following on from notable tenants such as Giles Daubeney, Lord Chamberlain to Henry VII, the lease was assigned to Thomas Wolsey in 1514. Wolsey was an astute, ambitious man who was made a cardinal by the Pope in 1515 and subsequently rose rapidly up the rungs of power in Tudor England until, as Lord Chancellor to Henry VIII, he appeared almost as powerful as the monarch he had been appointed to serve.

Wolsey set about building a majestic residence that was a palace in all but name, evolving into one of the largest houses in northern Europe in its day but, as so often happened in those fickle times, the cardinal's fall was as spectacular and rapid as his ascent. Having failed to secure Henry's divorce from Catherine of Aragon, Wolsey gifted Hampton Court to the king in 1528, hoping the gesture might appease Henry's wrath and avoid a terminal encounter with an executioner's axe. He did survive, albeit temporarily, dying in 1530 while *en route* from Yorkshire to London to answer charges of treason. Hampton Court was further enlarged and embellished by Henry into the most sumptuous of all his houses, creating a mini township by the Thames capable of hosting lavish events for hundreds of guests and their retinues. Leisure pursuits were amply catered for and included 1,100 acres of deer park for hunting, bowling alleys and, of course, Henry's famous tennis courts.

The royal household and guests were fed from a range of kitchens covering over 3,000 square metres in total, and having eaten under the mighty hammerbeam roof of the Great Hall, a visit to the Great House of Easement might have been welcomed. The G.H. of E. was actually a communal *garderobe* (toilet), capable of accommodating twenty-eight people in a single seating. Yes, it does conjure up a myriad array of questions and mental images, but perhaps it is best not to dwell on them.

Fortunately, Henry left Wolsey's entrance façade and gatehouse more or less untouched during his reworking of the palace and that most famous of entrances has become one of Hampton's Court's 'signature' images. It provides such an extraordinary contrast to the architectural style that comprises such a dominant proportion of the palace – the south and east Baroque façades from the rebuilding ordered by William III and Mary II shortly after their accession to the throne in 1689. Sir Christopher Wren was commissioned to undertake the redesign and, had it not been for a shortage of time and money, almost the entire Tudor palace (except for the Great Hall) would have been demolished.

Although it is not possible to 'do' Hampton Court Palace in a hurry, advance research can be a huge benefit to ensure that none of the key elements of the palace is missed and also that precious time is not spent going round in circles, unless of course one is in the maze where it is expected. In essence, the 'Royal River' extends onwards to the Tower of London and Greenwich, but for the purposes of this particular journey, Windsor Castle, Hampton Court and the monarch's swans that glide along this stretch of the Thames make it a most royal river.

CHAPTER EIGHT

Urban Elegance
From Hampton Court to Westminster

LONDON
Westminister Bridge
Lambeth Palace
Chelsea
Battersea Park
Chiswick House
Syon Park
Kew Gardens
Putney Bridge
Richmond
Eel Pie Island
Twickenham
Teddington Lock
Kingston Upon Thames
Hampton Court

Hampton Court Palace provides not only an excellent conclusion to a walk, but also an appropriate starting point for the journey to the Tower of London – that royal fortress, arsenal and prison that played such a significant role in the life of Henry VIII. However, the distinctive outline of Tower Bridge is still some distance away and so the journey begins alongside Hampton Court, where red brick gives way to the flamboyant ironwork screen at the riverside end of the restored Privy Garden. It was created in 1701 by Jean Tijou, a master blacksmith who arrived in England as part of William III and Mary II's entourage following the 'Glorious Revolution' of 1688. The landing stages immediately in front of the palace, once used by the royal barges to transport the king and his retinue to and from London, are now used by modern ferry services.

The Thames Path thereafter follows a long curving arc alongside the 700 acres of Hampton Court Park, also referred to as the Home Park, that was used by the Tudors and later royal dynasties for hunting. The even greater expanse of Bushy Park lies on the other side of the A308 Hampton Court to Kingston upon Thames road, and is freely accessible to the public. One of Bushy's most famous landmarks is the magnificent seventeenth-century Diana Fountain, used by Sir Christopher Wren as a focal point for the chestnut and lime tree avenue planted as a grand approach to Hampton Court Palace.

Regardless of what detours may have been taken into the royal parks, all roads and paths lead to Kingston upon Thames, although drivers visiting for the first time should note that trying to navigate around the town centre's one-way system may result in a nervous breakdown. There is car parking on the Hampton side of the Thames and by far the best (and sanest) option is to follow the minor road to Teddington that branches off just before Kingston Bridge. Walkers on the Thames Path are directed across the elegant early-nineteenth-century bridge, as their route continues on the opposite bank and onwards to Teddington and the start of the tidal river.

The name Kingston is derived from 'Kinges Tun', meaning royal manor, and the town's formal title is actually the Royal Borough of Kingston upon Thames, one of only three Royal Boroughs in England. The other two are 'Kensington and Chelsea' and 'Windsor and Maidenhead'. According to Kingston's Coronation Stone set outside the Guildhall, seven Saxon kings were crowned here, the most notable being Alfred the Great's grandson, Aethelstan (r. 924–39). He was cited as having proclaimed himself to be 'King of all England', and his task was to weld together a nation made up of different Saxon kingdoms and even settled Danes and Norsemen. He largely succeeded through being an active law maker and also by introducing the simple unifying device of a single currency for the entire realm.

Although Kingston's importance dwindled after the Conquest, there is little doubt that it was a place of considerable stature and an important communications

Twilight descends over Westminster and the Albert Embankment.

hub, being the next viable upstream river crossing after London Bridge. The approach and departure on foot from Kingston is likely to be accompanied by plenty of activity upon the Thames itself, as Kingston is a great rowing centre blessed with good long reaches both upstream and downstream of the bridge. Apart from watching extremely fit people glide past in needle-thin boats, there are few salient points of interest to warrant breaking stride until the steady rumble of the as yet unseen Teddington Weir heralds arrival at the mighty lock complex where fresh water from the Cotwolds finally gets to mingle with salt from the North Sea, and the Thames thereafter becomes a tidal river which, for the next few miles, is generally referred to as the Tideway.

Those arriving on foot are able to easily able to transfer to the north bank via two footbridges, one of which is an elegant suspension bridge affording mesmerizing views of the weir. Motorists who have happily meandered their way from the source will probably be able to find somewhere nearby to leave their vehicles and approach the river from the opposite side to the Thames Path. Unfortunately, the end of the non-tidal Thames also signals the point at which continuous exploration of the river by car does involve more inconvenience, stress and expense than can be reasonably tolerated, as we have now crossed the border into a land of yellow lines, parking meters and entire streets of 'residents only' parking bays. Consequently, I shall make no further suggestions as to which particular route might be the best option to see the river at its best, as the bus, tube and train network is now the only viable option for protracted sightseeing.

Another route-finding landmark is reached on arrival at Teddington because up to this point, the Thames Path has fluctuated from north to south banks of the river in much the same manner as the original towpath was obliged to constantly fluctuate. However, from Teddington onwards downstream to the National Trail's end at the Thames Barrier, there are continuous paths on both sides of the Thames but for the purposes of this narrative, the south bank will remain as the default, but with occasional sorties across the nearest convenient bridges to visit particular points of interest on the other side.

The Thames Path continues from Teddington alongside an attractive and surprisingly large area of scrub and grassland known as Ham Lands, and just about 400 metres downstream from the lock is an obelisk erected in 1909 to establish the boundary where the jurisdiction of the Port of London Authroity ended and the Thames Conservancy began. The green surroundings are in marked contrast to the more built-up nature across the river where Teddington has seamlessly merged into Twickenham. Although now world famous

Above: Teddington has the largest weir on the Thames, and consequently a considerable weir pool. Pedestrian access to the lock complex is via two footbridges, one of which is an elegant suspension bridge. It was here that a flotilla of small boats from the non-tidal Thames assembled in 1940, prior to making the hazardous journey across the Channel to aid the evacuation of Dunkirk.

Right: Eel Pie Island near Twickenham was legendary during the 'swinging sixties' for being one of London's great music venues, but it now exudes a singularly more tranquil atmosphere.

for being the home of English rugby, Twickenham was once a fashionable 'place in the country', where affluent people built villas overlooking the Thames. One such was Horace Walpole (1717–97), fourth son of Britain's first Prime Minister, Robert Walpole, who bought an existing modest house there and transformed it into the gothic fantasy of Strawberry Hill, a project Walpole referred to as 'a little Gothic castle', and that turned out to be the forerunner of the popular nineteenth-century gothic so popular with many Victorians.

As the river executes a sharp curve after Twickenham, it broadens slightly as though to accommodate Eel Pie Island, the only inhabited island on the Tideway and whose hotel, The White Cross, was a popular venue in the nineteenth century for boating parties. Although originally known as Twickenham Ait, both island and hotel were renamed in honour of the popular dish served there. During the 1920s and 1930s it hosted tea dances, later evolving into jazz dances until becoming synonymous with the 'rhythm and blues' music imported from America that kicked off the 'swinging sixties'. Famous bands such as The Who and The Rolling Stones played there and the island somewhat incongruously evolved into one London's premier venues until forced to close in 1967 because the management could not afford the repairs and safety measures insisted upon by the police. All seems a little more serene upon the island now, and there is not an eel pie to be found anywhere.

The next few miles along the Thames are an absolute delight, comprising gracious mansions, Richmond and its royal deer park and at Kew, one of the world's most important botanic gardens and research centres. The first noble building on 'our side' of the river is Ham House, a Stuart period mansion built in 1610 for Sir Thomas Vavasour, Knight Marshal to James I. Upon his death in 1620, the house was acquired by William Murray, who undertook the first of several remodellings by successive owners, all keen to stamp their own tastes and authority upon a building that was as much a reflection of their status at court or within the hierarchy of society. For his loyalty to the Royalist cause of his close friend, Charles I, Murray was created 1st Earl of Dysart, and when he died in 1655 his titles were conferred upon his daughter, Elizabeth, who then became the Countess of Dysart.

It was during her time at Ham House that the most significant changes took place, although not with the same partner. Elizabeth was regarded as something of an ambitious political schemer and, having borne her first husband, Sir Lionel Tollemache, eleven children – of whom five survived to adulthood – she was seemingly also a person of considerable stamina and fortitude. As a staunch Loyalist, she was alleged to have been a member of the Sealed Knot (a secret Royalist society formed to bring the exiled Charles II back to the throne during the English Interregnum), and following the Restoration in 1660, formed a liaison with the King's Secretary of State

Ham House lies within a stone's throw of the Thames Path, but even if one happens to be passing outside opening hours, there is plenty to see from outside the railings. The house was built in 1610 for Sir Thomas Vavasour, Knight Marshal to James I, and despite being extended later that century, it remains one of the nation's outstanding Stuart houses from that period.

for Scotland, John Maitland, 1st Duke of Lauderdale. They married in 1672, three years after her first husband's death, and it was the following decade that was the most influential at Ham House. It was extended and refurbished in palatial style to reflect the Duke's status as a member of Charles II's inner circle of advisers, a cabal that held many of its meetings at Ham House.

It is indeed fortunate that one of the mere handful of ferries surviving on the Thames operates just a few metres downstream from Ham House, thereby facilitating a quick trip across to the idyllically set riverside villa of Marble Hill House. In terms of river crossings, Hammerton's is unusual because it does not maintain a centuries-old tradition, having only come into operation during the early twentieth century, and it was named after its founder, Walter Hammerton, rather than the customary place name. The current ferry runs on weekdays between February and October and all year round at weekends.

Were it not for the availability of a ferry, walkers might otherwise be restricted to simply admiring the perfect symmetry of Marble Hill House from across the river. It was built in its secluded riverside setting in 1724–9 by George II's mistress, Henrietta Howard (later Countess of Suffolk), as a summer retreat and a place where she might make provision for life outside Court. The house was set in an enviable location within sight of Richmond Hill, and featured prominently in one of Turner's finest versions of Richmond Terrace, painted in 1836. Marble Hill House derives its impact from the perfect proportions inspired by the works of Italian architect Andrea Palladio (1508–80) and the design of the house was by Colen Campbell, originator of the Palladio–Inigo Jones architectural revival.

Upon the Countess's death in 1767, the house remained in her family for a time, before passing into other ownerships, the most enduring of which was that of Jonathan Peel (brother of British Prime Minister, Robert Peel). Peel died in 1879 but his widow remained in the house until she passed away in 1887, and their sixty-two years there was significantly longer than Henrietta's residence. The house and grounds deteriorated and by the turn of the twentieth century had been purchased by members of the Cunard shipping family, who were on the very brink of developing the site until the London County Council and others stepped in at the eleventh hour and managed to buy back Marble Hill, thereby preserving the famous view from Richmond Hill. Over the intervening years of the twentieth century, the house evolved from run-down tearoom into a perfectly restored historic house museum, complete with many of the original pieces of furniture and paintings from its heyday, which have been tracked down from all corners of the globe and reunited with Marble Hill.

As one traverses back across the river via Hammerton's ferry, the view ahead is almost entirely taken with the great bluff of Richmond Hill, with its distinctive terrace of Georgian houses running across the skyline. However, all are dwarfed by the vast Neo-Georgian façade of the Royal Star & Garter Home, opened in 1924 by King George V and Queen Mary as a home for severely disabled servicemen wounded in the First World War. It was Queen Mary who instigated the formation of the Star & Garter Charity in 1916 under the auspices of the Red Cross, concerned for the future of the many young men whose bodies and minds had been mutilated in the trenches. The original care facility was created from the

The symmetry of Marble Hill House is simply awesome, and because the proportions of the Palladian villa are so perfect it has been rather insultingly likened to a doll's house. It was built in the early 1700s for Henrietta Howard, mistress of the future King George III while he was still Prince of Wales, and rather like Cliveden some two centuries later, it became the focal point of London's literati and just about 'everybody who was anybody' in eighteenth-century society.

Old Star & Garter Hotel, but its layout and facilities proved wholly inadequate and so the new building designed by Sir Edwin Cooper was the one opened by the King and Queen just six years after the guns had fallen silent.

Complete panoramic views downstream to Richmond from the towpath are fleeting at best due to a pronounced bend in the Thames after Hammerton's Ferry and the dense tree cover on both Glover's Island and the riverbank beneath Richmond Hill itself. Beautifully presented footpaths lead directly from the Thames Path up through Terrace Garden and onto the terrace and its viewpoints, or one can continue on towards Richmond Bridge and double back via a slightly kinder incline. Whichever way it is approached, a visit to Richmond Hill is compulsory and still the only view in England preserved by a Parliamentary Preservation order – the Richmond, Ham and Petersham Open Spaces Act (1902).

Richmond is doubly blessed with natural assets because it is also the location of London's largest royal park, comprising almost 2,500 acres of woodlands, grasslands, ponds and gardens, set amid a landscape of ancient trees that is home to around 600 free-roaming deer. Although the area was used as a hunting ground by earlier monarchs, it was Charles I who first established the park in the form that largely survives today when relocating his Court from the heart of the capital in 1625. His decision to completely enclose the park with an 8-mile wall to contain the herds of deer he introduced there angered locals, as it rode roughshod over some existing rights of access, blocked off common grazing land and also prevented the gathering of wood, although that right was grudgingly later facilitated by the placing of ladders against the walls.

Above and below: The approach to Richmond along the riverside path from Ham House is full of interest because the perspective of houses, trees and river changes with every passing step, and on my own first visit I was quite taken aback by its beauty. That sense of amazement increased with the retrospective view from Richmond Hill and one can readily appreciate why that vista was deemed worthy of protection through an Act of Parliament.

When confronted by the expanses of the former royal hunting ground of Richmond Deer Park, it is difficult to believe that it still lies within a London Borough and must surely rank as one of the greatest natural assets and open spaces of any European capital city.

The park's highest point is known as Henry's Mound, from which a planned vista to St Paul's Cathedral was created early in the eighteenth century. That view to London's most iconic landmark is still protected today through planning laws that prevent any new buildings in the intervening 12-mile corridor exceeding a specified height.

Richmond was first established as a major royal residence during the reign of Edward III (1327–77), who embellished and extended the existing Shene (Sheen) Manor into the royal palace where he died. However, it was Henry VII who not only created the magnificent brick and stone palace much loved and favoured by his Tudor successors (Elizabeth I also died there in 1603), but also renamed it Richmond in honour of his family's title as Earls of Richmond (in Yorkshire). Fragments such as the original gatehouse have survived and incorporated into more modern dwellings on the fringe of Richmond Green, and it was perhaps as well that Henry did effect the name change because Sheen somehow does have quite the same cachet as Richmond.

From Richmond Green there are various roads leading back towards the town and river but by far the most atmospheric are Old Palace Lane and Hill Street, thoroughfares whose houses leave one in no doubt that Richmond has been one of the most sought-after places to live within reach of London. Some of the older houses flanking the Green were originally built using materials from the royal palace, and Hill Street is a fine example of the more appealing end of the Victorian architectural spectrum. The river frontage in the vicinity of Richmond Bridge has been extremely well restored in a manner that recognizes the needs of tourists and day visitors but without compromising the legacy of its past.

The town's bridge is an elegant five-arch structure of gleaming Portland stone, designed by James Paine and described in a local magazine as being 'one of the most beautiful ornaments of the river and the country adjacent'. It was completed in 1777 and not a moment too soon, according to letters written three years earlier by Horace Walpole to his cousin, Henry Seymour Conway, complaining of nightmare crossings while the Thames was in flood. 'Lady Browne and I, coming last Sunday night from Lady Blandford's, were in a piteous plight and the ferry to Twickenham was turned round by the current and carried to Isleworth.' (Intended destination: upstream; actual destination: downstream.)

The Thames Path leaves the Richmond waterfront area, passing close by other eighteenth- and nineteenth-century houses and villas built within the curtilage of

Henry VII's palace. The aura of elegant riverside retreat is soon dispelled on arrival at the Richmond rail and Twickenham road bridges. Although set close together in terms of distance, their construction dates were almost a century apart, being 1846 and 1933 respectively. Both structures were patently designed for their respective functions rather than any kind of visual appeal, although the painted metal girders of the nineteenth-century rail crossing are less abrasive to the eye than the dour concrete of the road bridge.

Another bridge bearing distinct similarities to the one recently passed carrying the rail line appears a little further downstream, but this is simply an elaborate footbridge over Richmond Lock. This is the furthest downstream lock on the Thames and, being located on the Tideway, is owned and managed by the Port of London Authority. It is readily apparent that this is unlike any of the locks encountered thus far on the journey, and is described as a 'half-tide lock', designed to maintain a sufficient body of water between Richmond and Teddington to allow continuous safe navigation. Vertical sluice gates are suspended from the footbridge and lowered two hours after the passing of the tide to effectively block the river. During that time of channel restriction, a conventional barge lock takes any traffic, but when the gates are again raised, boats may pass through the centre arch of the bridge as normal.

The rather flat, green expanse to the right of the towpath is Old Deer Park, a hunting ground established by James I after his accession in 1603 to provide a recreational area close to the palace but subsequently demoted upon the creation and enclosure of the much larger Richmond Park by Charles II in 1637. The Hanovarians also enjoyed the Old Deer Park, transforming the hunting lodge originally built by James I into a fabulous country residence renamed Richmond Lodge and embarking upon an ambitious programme of landscaping and building that extended beyond the Deer Park and into Kew.

The long, tree-clad Isleworth Ait blocks out the river's far bank but beyond the island's downstream tip when visual contact is restored, the grouping of Old Isleworth's colour-washed houses Georgian houses and church above a gently sloping jetty is the kind of tranquil scene one normally associates with a West Country river estuary

Opposite: The understated elegance of Richmond Bridge acts as a perfect foil for the Georgian buildings that predominate around the town's central waterfront. It was built from pale Portland stone by James Paine Thames during the mid-1770s.

Above: Richmond Half Lock is the lowest lock on the Thames and was deemed necessary to maintain adequate water levels upstream to Teddington.

Below: The gentle atmosphere of Old Isleworth is perhaps reminiscent of bygone days when such places were rural villages, rather than just one picturesque fragment of a vast built-up metropolis.

rather than Greater London. Isleworth was already an established settlement by the time of the Conquest, (recorded in the Domesday Book as Gisteleswordc) and the manor there was subsequently held by generations of Norman barons from the de Valeri family, until confiscated by Henry III during the thirteenth century.

Richmond was already renowned for its royal connections, and much of this area bordering the Thames up to and including Kew was later established by some of the Hanovarian monarchs as a royal riverside playground. Consequently, it was inevitable that the upper echelons of eighteenth-century society would gravitate there too, thereby establishing an Arcadian corridor of country houses between Kew and Twickenham, styled and landscaped by the very best architects and gardeners of the period such as Robert Adam and Lancelot 'Capability' Brown. Although many of those houses have long since been demolished, the work of Adam and Brown remains very much extant in Syon House and Park, for centuries the London home of the Dukes of Northumberland, whose boundaries extend almost to the shadow cast by Isleworth's fourteenth-century church tower.

The origins of Syon House date back to its foundation as a Brigittine monastery (its name derived from Mount Zion in the Holy Land) by Henry V in 1415. It flourished as a place of spirituality and learning, but despite being particularly favoured by Henry VIII's first wife, Catherine of Aragon, the abbey suffered the same fate as all other monastic foundations in the country and was dissolved by her husband in 1539. In the post-Dissolution era, the estate passed to the 1st Duke of Somerset (Lord Protector to the young Edward VI), who built a house in an Italian Renaissance style on the site of the ruined west end of the great abbey church.

After Somerset was executed for alleged treason, the house experienced several owners before being acquired in 1594 by Henry Percy, 9th Earl of Northumberland, through his marriage to Dorothy Devereux, and the Percy family has lived at Syon House since that date. The Syon House that visitors see today can be largely attributed to the mid-eighteenth century, when Sir Hugh Smithson married the Percy heiress, Elizabeth Seymour, was created Earl and then 1st Duke of Northumberland in 1766. It was he who commissioned Robert Adam to transform the interior of Syon but instructed that the exterior remain largely untouched. Consequently, those walking along the Thames Path on the opposite side of the river see only a plain, crenellated building adorned with a statue of the famous Percy Lion, which was removed from the old Northumberland House in The Strand on its demolition in 1894.

Lancelot Brown laid the landscape foundations for the gardens that would evolve into the magnificent collection of rare plants and trees that are now registered as Grade I in the English Heritage Register of Parks and Gardens of Historic Importance. However, regardless of how many rare botanical specimens the gardens hold, Syon's crowning glory is the Great Conservatory, commissioned by the 3rd Duke in 1826 as a show house for his exotic plant and cactus collection. The vastness of its central pavilion with glass and metal dome rather transcends the perceived concept of a greenhouse, presenting such a daunting atmosphere it is difficult to envisage anyone actually enjoying a quiet Sunday morning potter around one's plants before lunch. The architect was Charles Fowler (also responsible for the main building at the heart of Covent Garden), and his work on the great metal and glass conservatory dome at Syon later served as an inspiration to Joseph Paxton when designing the Crystal Palace to house the Great Exhibition of 1851 in Hyde Park.

Below: Syon House and park has been the London home of the Dukes of Northumberland for over four centuries, but the river frontage betrays little of the grandeur beyond and the interiors contain some of Robert Adams' finest work.

Opposite: It seems somehow ironic that such a historic building set almost directly across the Thames from Kew Gardens should be able to boast that one of its finest architectural features is a Great Conservatory, constructed from gunmetal, Bath stone and glass in 1826.

Although the environment here is one of almost pastoral tranquillity, the view downstream is dominated by the distinctive outline of the Brentford Tower Blocks, confirming that the Thames is rapidly drawing closer to the heart of London. Syon Park is replaced on the far bank by Brentford Marina and almost immediately thereafter by the river's junction with the Grand Union Canal (see page 55). Along the Brentford/Kew Reach, between the mouth of the canal and Kew Bridge, there is a marked difference between the two banks. The Brentford river frontage is gradually being developed and restored, but still retains elements of its dockland and industrial past, whereas a history of royal ownership has safeguarded the green spaces of Kew Green and the vast Botanic Gardens.

The Brentford Tower Blocks were built on the vast site once occupied by the water filtration beds of the Grand Junction Water Works Company, formed in 1811 to take domestic drinking water from the Thames. Their initial works were at Chelsea, but through an Act of Parliament granted in 1835, were allowed to build a new extraction and treatment plant at Kew. However, just two decades later the Thames was so polluted that all extraction below Teddington was banned and Kew became a filtration and distribution centre for water drawn from Hampton. All privately owned water companies were taken over by the Metropolitan Water Board in 1902, and when the more modern Ashford Common Works adjacent to the Queen Mary Reservoir at Staines became operational, Kew's filter beds became redundant and given over to housing.

The six blocks of flats were actually named to commemorate some of the engines and engineers associated with the Kew site, and included 'Boulton,' after Matthew Boulton (1728–1809), who, together with his partner, James Watt, was a pioneer in the development of steam engines for use in pumping. Another block was simply named 'Cornish', in recognition of the fact that most of the engines used on the Thames were of the same type as those developed to pump water out of Cornwall's tin mines in the early nineteenth century. A more tangible legacy of that era, and a notable river landmark, is the distinctive Kew Bridge Standpipe Tower, built in the 1860s by Alexander Fraser to act as a giant safety valve for the massive beam engine steam pumps. It housed a

The octagonal tower of the now redundant St George's Church survives as a rather forlorn but proud survivor from centuries past amid Brentford's revamped river frontage. It comprises a medley of styles that have no style at all, and residents of the moored houseboats may have fared better than their neighbours on dry land.

Above: The Palm House of the Royal Botanic Gardens, Kew, is just one of several iconic buildings, both old and new, set within the 300 acres of the UNESCO-designated World Heritage Site.

Opposite: Kew Palace was built in 1631 and became the home of the Hanovarian Royal family during the eighteenth century. It was once known as the Dutch House, after its distinctive gabling style.

pipe almost 200 feet long and replaced an earlier one encased in a steel lattice casing that was damaged by frost. The brick built tower provided greater insulation and during periods of extreme cold, lighting fires around its base provided additional protection.

The tower's design is not dissimilar to an Italian *campanile*, and its architect may have been influenced by those distinctive Italian bell towers, but Kew's other landmark tower, set in the heart of Kew Gardens – the Pagoda – is unmistakably of the Orient. The replica of a Chinese pagoda built by Sir William Chambers in 1762 was one of the first structures erected in the garden established in 1759 by the Dowager Princess Augusta, mother of King George III. Chambers also designed the classical Orangery, which, for a time, was the largest glasshouse in England. The Orangery was later complemented by two further glass houses: the iconic Palm House of 1848 and the even larger Temperate House that was begun in 1859 but, due to funding issues, was not completed until 1898. Both those structures were designed by the prolific English architect, Decimus Burton (1800–81), whose body of work also included the Triumphal Screen and Wellington Arch at Hyde Park Corner.

The Royal Botanic Gardens were awarded the accolade of World Heritage Site status by UNESCO in 2003, although not merely for the 300 acres of outstandingly diverse gardens and the remarkable collection of buildings housed within them, but also for Kew's outstanding contribution to scientific advances in botany, ecology and conservation. That process of transforming Kew from a garden, simply devoted to plant collection and showing, into somewhere that also seriously engaged in the science of botany, began when George III inherited Kew upon the death of Princes Augusta in 1772. During the following year the king met the wealthy entrepreneur and natural history enthusiast Sir Joseph Banks (1743–1820), who had recently accompanied

Captain James Cook on his round-the-world expedition aboard the *Endeavour*. Banks and his self-funded party of botanists and scientists gathered considerable scientific, botanical and anthropological material and returned home to wide acclaim.

George III was hugely impressed by this work, and Sir Joseph Banks became established at Kew almost immediately, working closely with the monarch to develop economic uses for both native and imported exotic plants and, without his guidance, it is unlikely that Kew would have grown into the world's most respected botanical research centre. The two major glasshouses of Kew epitomize the 'anything and everything is possible' attitude prevalent during the Victorian age of industrial, scientific and technological advancement. Although the Palm House was Decimus Burton's design, it was the Irish ironmaster Richard Turner (1798–1881) who transformed one-dimensional drawings into the three-dimensional reality of wrought-iron, glass and an elaborate heating system to generate sufficient heat and humidity to enable the tropical palms and other plants to survive. The main body of the Palm House actually resembles the upturned hull of a ship and, by using the shipbuilding technology of light but strong wrought-iron ribs, Turner was able to create the great open space needed to accommodate the tall palms and other specimen plants.

Even on the sunniest summer days, Kew could never be described as 'tropical' and so even though the glass of the Palm House amplified the sun's rays, additional heating was required. Coal-fired boilers were installed in a basement and refuelled by a small railway that ran through an underground tunnel also used to carry the boilers' flues, and whose smoke was discharged through yet another 'Kew Campanile' located 150 metres from the Palm House. As might be expected from an iron-based structure having had to endure so many decades of extreme humidity, the Palm House has needed substantial renovation with the passage of time. There was a partial restoration in the mid-1950s, during which the plants were simply shuffled around the floor in a game of botanical chess, but then completely removed into temporary care when the building was completely dismantled and rebuilt using stainless steel and toughened safety glass three decades later.

The Temperate House is twice the size of the Palm House and in the historical context of Kew's rapidly expanding collection of tender woody plants from the world's more temperate zones, was actually needed more than a tropical glasshouse. Its construction was bedevilled by delays through lack of funding, taking almost forty years to complete. Fortunately, its modular nature enabled partial opening well in advance of absolute completion. The Temperate House underwent a total restoration in 1977, using neoprene glazing and the latest high-efficiency heating equipment. Both those Grade I Listed structures have been brought up to date through restoration, but Kew's other great glasshouse, the Princess of Wales Conservatory, opened in 1987, represents ten different climate zones individually controlled by computer programs.

Kew Bridge may not be the most aesthetically pleasing Thames crossing, but does have rather elegant lamps and I wanted to photograph when they were illuminated but before the sky went too dark, so that the scrollwork would be accentuated in silhouette against the coloured sky at dusk.

The Royal Botanic Garden's oldest building, dating back to 1631, is Kew Palace, originally built by the wealthy Flemish merchant, Samuel Fortrey. It was also known as the Dutch House, because of its origins and the distinctive gabling. It was used intermittently as a royal residence from 1728 when leased by Queen Caroline while her husband George II was extending Richmond Lodge and Gardens. Their son, Prince Frederick, married Princess Augusta in 1736, and although he had begun plans for the gardens, his untimely death in 1751 resulted in Princess Augusta continuing that work. After Queen Charlotte died at Kew Palace in 1818, it was closed until, in December 1896, Queen Victoria agreed to Kew's acquisition of the Palace, providing there was no alteration to the room in which Queen Charlotte died. In 1898, the palace passed to the Department of Works and opened to the public.

The main entrance to the Royal Botanic Gardens is through Victoria Gate on Kew Green, a surprisingly large expanse lined by trees and elegant houses from both the Georgian and Victorian periods. Unfortunately, it also happens to be bisected by the main A205 South Circular Road that crosses the river at Kew, but despite an almost constant flow of traffic, parts of the Green are sufficiently secluded to provide a sense of how London's Thames-side communities might have appeared prior to the rampant development that has blighted so many other similar enclaves. Indeed, had it not been for the passing of an Act of Parliament in 1824 providing significant planning protection to Kew Green, its current appearance might be very different. The temporary illusion of being in the heart of rural England is furthered by presence of a small village pond in one corner and a carefully nurtured and well-guarded cricket square, sharing the larger part of the green with St Anne's Church. A formal cricket match was recorded as having taken place as early as 1737, but Kew Cricket Club itself was not formed until the 1870s.

Although first established as a simple chapel to serve the sparse local communities, the origins of the current church dedicated to St Anne began with a grant from Queen Anne in 1714. The close proximity of the royal residences resulted in further patronage, most notably when enlarged by George III in 1770 and again in 1805, at which time he arranged for the erection of a special gallery to accommodate his increasingly large family at Sunday worship. (George and Charlotte had fifteen children, of whom only two did not survive through to adulthood.)

The current Kew Bridge is a functionally elegant Grade II Listed structure of Cornish granite, designed by John Wolfe-Barry and opened in 1903. It replaced an earlier stone bridge that had endured since being officially opened by George III in 1789 amid great pomp and ceremony but, as the twentieth century approached, was deemed inadequate to handle the substantial increase in the weight of traffic, and also required substantial modification to provide better access from the Brentford side. The first bridge had been built to replace an existing ferry just thirty years earlier in 1759, more or less coinciding with the period when Kew increasingly became the focus of royal attention.

For those generally following the Thames on foot, I had earlier suggested that the south bank path was the better of the two options and thus far from Teddington, that theory has held well. However, the view from Kew Bridge downstream to the attractive riverside village of Strand-on-the-Green strongly suggests that a switch to the north bank might be beneficial, especially when taking into account the three outstanding eighteenth-century waterside pubs set directly on the river's edge. The Bell & Crown, The City Barge and The Bull's Head all share the same narrow stretch of pathway running past the waterfront houses, whose frontages are draped in spring with clematis and wisteria.

At low tide, the Thames recedes a considerable distance, exposing the wide gravel shore from which 'Strand' derives its name, but for both visitors and residents alike, any beach-front illusion is regularly shattered by sound of trains clattering over the adjacent Kew Rail Bridge. It was designed by W.R. Galbraith and completed in 1869, and although its lattice girders are aesthetically pleasing, from the perspective of Strand-on-the-Green, it would have been an even greater visual and aural delight if placed anywhere but there. Flooding is another potential hazard for waterfront dwellers, most notably when protracted spells of bad weather over the watersheds of the Thames and its tributaries coincides with excessively high tides. Protective walls and steps leading up to the raised doorways on some houses repel all but the worst floods, but the riverside pubs have to be more accessible at ground level and consequently tend to suffer more.

Regardless of which side of the river walkers elect to follow from Kew Bridge, the surroundings contain little of interest, and as there are no great riverscapes to admire, one might just as well stay on the north bank route to Chiswick Bridge and thereafter continue along past the vast expanses of the Dukes Meadows sports ground. It is extraordinary to note that, having once been an area of flourishing market gardens and orchards, much of the land to the east of Chiswick Bridge was excavated for gravel between the First and Second World Wars, creating an environment of excavated pits and spoil heaps. It was later filled in and re-landscaped using rubble from demolition sites. As the Thames Path passes by Chiswick Bridge, the distinctive shape of the old Mortlake Brewery looms across the river. Its name will also be familiar to watchers of the Boat Race as it is virtually the final landmark seen on television coverage or mentioned in commentary.

The large Chiswick Boathouse stands in the shadow of the bridge and just a few yards further downstream is the University Stone, marking the official finish of the 4-mile course from Putney (see pages 147–9). Another sight familiar to Boat Race viewers is the Barnes Railway Bridge, set a little further round the sharp loop of Dukes Meadows. The bridge also carries a useful pedestrian crossing, but that is closed for safety reasons during the passage of the Boat Race flotilla. Back in the 'good old days', trains would actually stop on the bridge to afford passengers a bird's-eye view of the race.

One of the architectural highlights of London's western suburbs is Chiswick House, which although not actually adjacent to the Thames Path, is easily accessed on foot from Chiswick village, and really well the effort of a detour. Built in 1727–9 by Lord Burlington, it revived interest in the architectural style of Andrea Palladio (1508–80), which had been introduced into England by Inigo Jones (1573–1652) a century earlier.

As a keen enthusiast of the Italian architect's work, a style that reflected power and wealth but on a human scale, Lord Burlington sought to emulate the glory of ancient Rome by creating the kind of house and garden that might have been found in the suburbs there and built it adjacent to his older, Elizabethan House, which was subsequently demolished in 1788. Lord Burlington drew his inspiration from several sources, including Palladio's own Villa Rotundo near Vicenza.

The columns of Chiswick's portico were based upon the Roman temple of Jupiter Stator, the shallow dome on Rome's Pantheon and the semi-circular windows directly below it on the ancient Roman baths of Diocletian. Burlington's creative debt to Inigo Jones and Palladio is acknowledged in their statues flanking the main entrance. The principal rooms within Chiswick are located on the first floor, where the octagonal hall at its heart is sparsely furnished, with room for functions or entertainment. Radiating from the central octagon, the colourful and opulently decorated rooms were more intimate – venues for affable encounters between like-minded connoisseurs and specifically designed to house some of Burlington's art collection, each also adorned with finely detailed allegorical ceiling paintings.

Although some of these paintings were probably attributable to William Kent (1685–1748), his major contribution to Chiswick House was to the house and gardens, and through the patronage of Lord Burlington, is remembered as a major contributor to the Palladian revival. However, Kent was also an innovative landscape designer who was described by Horace Walpole as being

Above and below: Chiswick House is a magnificent neo-Palladian villa built by the 3rd Earl of Burlington in 1720 as a homage to the great renaissance architect, Palladio. It very much reflects the architecture of ancient Rome and sixteenth-century Italy that so inspired wealthy English landowners when they returned from their 'grand tours' to Europe. The ongoing care and management of the house and gardens is now in the hands of the Chiswick House & Gardens Trust, a joint body established in 2005 between English Heritage and the London Borough of Hounslow.

'the first to leap the fence and see that all nature was a garden'. The natural contents of a garden or segment of the landscape were allowed to remain, but were also carefully manipulated to create a variety of interwoven vistas punctuated by water features, classical temples, obelisks and statues.

The fragment of Chiswick clustered around Church Street and along the riverside is an unexpected delight, assuming one survives an encounter with the notorious Hogarth Roundabout to make it that far. The road junction is named after the great satirist, painter and engraver, William Hogarth (1697–1764), whose house stands but a few metres away from the junction. It served as Hogarth's country home from 1749 until his death, providing a quiet summer retreat from the bustle of city life around his main residence and studio in what is now Leicester Square in London. The house is currently undergoing restoration following a fire in August 2009, but is normally open to the public. Hogarth's House stands on one of London's main arterial roads and consequently hardly endowed with any vestiges of the tranquillity afforded to its original owner, but a corner of Chiswick where such serenity still prevails is the churchyard of St Nicholas.

Set almost on the banks of the Thames at the foot of Church Street, the leafy graveyard is the final resting place for an eclectic mix of famous names associated with Chiswick, including, most notably, William Hogarth, Lord Burlington and William Kent, the artist James McNeill Whistler, Private William Hitch VC (awarded at the Battle of Rorke's Drift, famously recreated in the film *Zulu*), Barbara Villiers (1st Duchess of Cleveland and Charles II's mistress), two of Oliver Cromwell's daughters – Lady Mary Fauconberg and Lady Frances Russell – and also Sir Charles Tilston Bright, knighted at the age of twenty-six by Queen Victoria in recognition of his achievement in laying the first trans-Atlantic cable to America in 1858. The church is dedicated to the patron saint of sailors and fishermen, although the Thames at low tide seems to offer little in the way of peril, and twenty-first-century riverbank anglers are more likely to risk death by boredom than by drowning.

The Thames Path progresses downstream along the pavement of Chiswick Mall, a narrow street lined with supremely elegant houses from the eighteenth century, where Chiswick merges almost imperceptibly into Hammersmith, with the Mall continuing as Upper and then Lower Mall right up to Hammersmith's suspension bridge. Although Chiswick arguably has more beauty, Hammersmith has plenty to offer the visitor, especially close by the surprisingly quiet riverside, for those arriving

The tomb of William Hogarth, the eighteenth-century painter, satirist and cartoonist, lies in the churchyard of St Nicholas, Chiswick.
overleaf: Chiswick House Gardens.

on foot along the Thames Path. The route temporarily parts company with the Thames to enter and progress along Hammersmith Terrace, a row of almost identical Georgian houses overlooking the Thames at the west end of Hammersmith's Upper Mall, three of which are adorned with English Heritage 'Blue Plaques'.

The distinctive plaques indicate that a remarkable person either lived or worked there at some point during the building's existence. The fascination of the system is that although the person honoured had significantly enriched the nation through contributions to the arts, sciences or politics, not all were necessarily household names. At No. 3 is a plaque to Edward Johnston, a calligrapher renowned as the creator of the emblematic font and red roundel design for the London Undergound. The distinctive style of sans serif lettering (named after its originator) was first introduced in 1916 and, despite being modified and redesigned to enable it to work with modern printing technology, nevertheless remains the typeface of Transport for London.

No. 7 Hammersmith Terrace is an internationally important Arts & Crafts showpiece which, from 1903 until his death thirty years later, was the home of Emery Walker, the great printer and antiquary, who was also friend and mentor to William Morris. The house and its contents of William Morris treasures were preserved virtually unchanged by Walker's daughter and her successors and are now in the care of the Emery Walker Trust, who open the house to the public (by prior appointment only). It is but a short stroll down further along Upper Mall to No. 26, Kelmscott House, William Morris's London home from 1871 until his death in 1896, and although now a private house, the basement and coach house serve as both a museum and the headquarters of the William Morris Society.

It is not known whether Morris frequented The Dove, a historic riverside pub. Its origins date back to a seventeenth-century coffee house and its terrace

affords an excellent view of the soaring green towers of Hammersmith Bridge, the second suspension bridge to cross the Thames at this point. The first bridge (opened in 1825), was the work of William Tierney Clark (also responsible for the suspension bridge upstream at Marlow), but, in common with several other eighteenth- and nineteenth-century bridges over the Thames, was deemed unable to cope with the stresses placed upon the structures by the increased volume and weight of road traffic (even before the arrival of motorized transport). That original bridge's structural integrity was further put to the test in 1870 when an estimated 12,000 people crowded onto it to watch the University Boat Race.

A replacement bridge was designed and built by Sir Joseph Bazalgette (1819–91), a remarkable civil engineer whose work on London's Embankment and sewage system will feature a little further downstream. He used the bridge's original piers, creating a structure not dissimilar to its predecessor, and although decorated by over elaborate scroll-work and ornate pavilion tops, the effect just about manages to tilt in favour of being endearing rather than ridiculous, especially now that the colour scheme has reverted back to the original green and gilt in which it was painted upon completion in 1887.

The flamboyant architecture and rather genteel ambiance of the bridge are in marked contrast to the noise and mayhem of the nearby Hammersmith flyover and gyratory system, although the view ahead to the Barnes side of the river does suggest a more tranquil scene. The Thames is not particularly visually appealing at this point, apart from the world-famous outline of the late-nineteenth-century Harrods Furniture Depository, but by crossing Hammersmith Bridge and continuing along the south bank, one is able to observe the Harrods fortress at closer quarters and thereafter either visit, or simply view *en passant*, the London Wetland Centre. This is a vast nature reserve created from the old Barnes Elms reservoirs that were made redundant in 1986 and later transformed into a mosaic of important wetland habitats by the Wildfowl and Wetlands Trust.

The final approach to Putney Bridge also signals the end of the original Thames towpath that has criss-crossed its way from bank to bank all the way downstream from Lechlade. The Thames Path now runs alongside a collection of boathouses stacked with sleek-looking racing shells, and house gyms equipped with state-of-the-art fitness equipment – Putney is a serious rowing centre and also the location for the Oxford Cambridge Boat Race start marker.

The current Putney Bridge is another of Sir Joseph Bazalgette's river crossings, and its rather plain five spans of stone and Cornish granite offer a considerable contrast to the extravagances of Hammersmith. However, Putney Bridge was not designed simply as a functional road crossing; it was also cleverly used as a vehicle for carrying concealed water pipes across the Thames as part of Bazalgette's new sewerage and drainage system for London. As one walks across the seldom-quiet bridge towards the Fulham bank, it is difficult to imagine that Fulham was one of the riverside villages whose market gardens supplied the capital with fruit and vegetables. A left turn leads to the park surrounding the grand Tudor mansion and associated buildings of Fulham Palace, used for centuries as a residence by the Bishops of London until finally relinquishing it in 1975. It is owned by the Church Commissioners and jointly leased to Hammersmith and Fulham Council and the Fulham

Below: St Mary's, Battersea, stands by the foreshore of the Thames, but its immediate environment has changed dramatically since it rebuilt in its present form in 1776.

Opposite: Albert Bridge's current livery of candy pink and white can look just a bit too 'Disney' on bright days.

Palace Trust, who are undertaking a meticulous long-term restoration programme, but the Palace Museum and gardens remain open to the public.

As neither of the Thames Path options between Putney and Battersea have any sites of notable historical, architectural or visual interest, the south bank liaison could be maintained. Having crossed the River Wandle, from which Wandsworth derives its name, the official path detours around a couple of industrial sites and a heliport before arriving at the distinctive mid-eighteenth-century parish church of St Mary, Battersea.

The church once stood proudly alone on the water's edge, set apart from the old flourmill and rather ugly high-rise tower blocks that were its nearest neighbours, but the unquenchable thirst for riverside living has resulted in the flour mill being replaced by yet another high-tech edifice of glass and steel that now completely dwarfs the church. It is absolutely right that redundant and decaying industrial sites should be developed in some way, but one wonders whether the modern apartments will be standing as proud as St Mary's when they too have been there for over 250 years? The poet William Blake was married here in 1782 and the artist J.M.W. Turner was regularly ferried across the Thames from his Chelsea home to paint atmospheric river scenes from the comfortable vantage point of a chair set by the vestry window.

St Mary's is set almost at the end of Battersea Reach, one of the few straight segments of the Thames since it passed alongside Hampton Park, and as the river prepares to execute a sharp turn to the right, we pass by the inlet that is Chelsea Harbour. Although the name might suggest a river port bustling with commercial traffic, the days of coal barges discharging tons of coal for the nearby Lots Road power station are long gone, and the old wharf is now a marina for the luxury hotels and apartments that emerged from the desolate wasteland of railway sidings and industrial waste. Although the river has executed far tighter turns along its length thus far, the particular angle at which Battersea Bridge is set does seem to have presented navigational problems to river traffic and it has suffered more than its fair share of collisions. Fortunately, the current five-arched Grade II Listed structure is another Bazalgette bridge of cast iron and granite, and sufficiently robust to withstand most impacts, although it did have to be closed to most road traffic during repairs necessitated by an altercation with a 200-ton barge in 2005.

The current bridge was opened in 1890, replacing an increasingly rickety wooden bridge comprising nineteen narrow spans that had provided a river crossing at the site since 1771. Because the old Battersea Bridge had been the last of London's wooden bridges, and therefore something of a notable landmark, it was painted by many of the period's leading artists, including the American-born James McNeill Whistler (1834–1903), whose famous study of the old bridge *Nocturne: Blue and Gold – Old Battersea Bridge* was painted in the early 1870s and now hangs in Tate Britain at Millbank. That particular work was just one of a series set around the river at Battersea, and a more romanticized interpretation than some of Whistler's other tonal portraits of the Thames.

From the second-floor window of his riverside home in Cheyne Walk, Whistler looked directly out over Battersea Bridge and a river backed by smoking factory chimneys. Some of his portrayals of Victorian grime and smoke-laden skies offer a chilling insight into just how polluted parts of London must have been during that part of the nineteenth century, when Britain was establishing itself

Opposite: The great four-chimneyed bulk of Battersea Power Station is one of the Thames's most familiar landmarks, and although it could not ranked alongside St Paul's or Tower Bridge, the river's landscape would be bereft without it. However, the time-bomb of decay and dereliction has been ticking for some time, and it needs rescuing soon.

Below: Designed by Sir Christopher Wren and opened in 1692, the Royal Hospital Chelsea has changed little over time since first commissioned by Charles II to care for the nation's war veterans in their retirement.

as the 'workshop of the world'. Immediately after Battersea Bridge, Cheyne Walk becomes the southern boundary of the original old Chelsea village, an atmospheric quadrant whose streets and squares are lined by elegant town houses, many of which bear the blue plaques denoting a famous past resident, others currently being lived in by the famous names of today that will sport the blue plaques of tomorrow.

At the heart of the village is Chelsea Old Church, badly damaged by a Second World War bomb, but both the fabric and most of its historic monuments have been restored to their pre-1941 splendour. The South Chapel was originally built as his private chapel by Henry VIII's Chancellor, Sir Thomas More, having taken up residence in Chelsea, which was then a countryside location offering easy access by river to both Westminster and Hampton Court. Chelsea and Battersea are linked by two bridges, the second of which, Albert Bridge, must surely rank as one of the most elegant of the Thames crossings, and when illuminated at night has more of the appearance of a Victorian seaside pier than a bridge in England's capital city. The cable-stayed toll bridge was built to his own patented design by Rowland Ordish and opened in 1873, but was deemed structurally unsound when inspected less than a decade later by Sir Joseph Bazalgette. To preserve the bridge's integrity, he added some of the more conventional design elements associated with suspension bridges, but despite those modifications, its frailty persisted and has been on the critical list for most of its life. The Greater London Council proposed demolition in 1973 but were forced to back down in the face of a vociferous protest campaign led by the Poet Laureate, Sir John Betjeman. The compromise solution was the provision of additional support by new concrete piers, but dear old Albert was scheduled for an 18-month period of restorative surgery that commenced in February 2010. The bridge will remain open to dismounted cyclists, pedestrians (and their dogs) heading across the river to Battersea Park, but one does wonder for how much longer the bridge can go on supporting a mode of transport for which it was never intended.

Although originally laid out in the 1850s using spoil excavated from the vast Royal Victoria Dock, Battersea Park really came to public prominence when transformed into the Festival Gardens for the 1951 Festival of Britain, and will always be remembered for its funfair and American-style roller-coaster, the Big Dipper. The fair finally closed in 1977 and the park's newest distinctive landmark is the Peace Pagoda, a Buddhist stupa erected in 1985 as one of a worldwide network of similar structures whose origins date back to 1947, when the first were built in Hiroshima and Nagasaki.

The eastern most segment of Cheyne Walk leads into Royal Hospital Road and an opportunity to pause and visit the Chelsea Physic Garden, whose main entrance is just round the corner in Swan Walk. The gardens were founded in 1673 by the Worshipful Society of Apothacaries for the purpose of training apprentices in identifying plants, and to promote the study of botany in relation to medicine. On a warm English summer's day, the atmosphere within the gardens can be quite soporific and the Chelsea Physic Garden remains one of London's hidden treasures.

Chelsea's other great treasure, the Royal Hospital, is no secret at all and although maybe not quite so architecturally spectacular as his Royal Naval College at Greenwich (see pages 243–5), Sir Christopher Wren's retirement and nursing home for retired and wounded soldiers is appropriately stately and dignified. Its residents are known as the 'Chelsea Pensioners' and famous for their distinctive scarlet coats and tricorne hats worn at all official ceremonies. The Hospital was founded by Charles II in 1681 and work began the following year on a site that had housed a partially built, but abandoned, theological college from the reign of James I.

The long-term care and welfare of soldiers wounded on active service has for many years been the responsibility of the State, but it was not always so, and when establishing the Chelsea Hospital, it is thought that Charles II was inspired to follow the example of his French counterpart, Louis XIV, who had already made provision for his own disabled servicemen when founding the famous Hôtel des Invalides. The main building is flanked by two wings to form an open court, Figure Court, with two further quadrangles being created on either side to provide additional space. The main entrance is graced by white Tuscan columns and at the centre of the courtyard stands a statue of Charles II by Grinling Gibbons in which the monarch is portrayed as a Roman general. All the pomp and ceremony of a royal occasion occurs every year in late May on Founder's Day, which is also referred to as Oak Apple Day in remembrance of the time when the future king hid in an oak tree to escape capture by the Parliamentary forces after defeat at the Battle of Worcester in 1651. As 29 May was the birthday of Charles II and also the date of his Restoration, all

three anniversaries are rolled into one parade at which his statue is draped with garlands of oak leaves.

After visiting the formalized symmetry of the Chelsea Hospital, access back to the river can be found through the less structured form of the adjacent Ranelagh Gardens. The quiet, tree-lined space that survives today stands in marked contrast to the scene that would have greeted visitors 250 years ago in 1742, when it was established as pleasure gardens that became the focal point of eighteenth-century London society. The centrepiece of the gardens was a great, covered rotunda (featured in a well-known painting by Canaletto), in which concerts were staged and even featured a guest appearance by an eight-year-old Mozart. The gardens were legendary for their masked balls and also as a place where matches were made and many illicit affairs conducted within the anonymous sanctuary of their darker recesses. Ranelagh Gardens flourished for half a century and then suddenly fell out fashion, closing in 1804.

Any lingering thoughts of glittering candelabra and swirling dancers are quickly dispelled, upon arrival back at the Embankment by Chelsea Bridge, by the looming, iconic shell and four pale chimneys of the Grade II* Listed Battersea Power Station, which ironically is also on the English Heritage Buildings at Risk Register. All it needs now is a Blue Plaque, and Sir Giles Gilbert Scott's red-brick industrial cathedral giant will have a full set. Battersea is actually two power stations, the first of which became operational in 1933 and its identical twin some fifteen years later. It seems extraordinary to think that the control room and other parts of the interior of the 1930s model were embellished with Art Deco fixtures and fittings, polished parquet floors and elaborate wrought-iron staircases. The post-war version had to settle for stainless steel throughout.

The stations were decommissioned in 1983 and have since been the subject of numerous failed planning proposals for regeneration but at the time of writing, another complex submission is in the pipeline – or perhaps one should say chimney? The power station has featured in numerous films, but the image that gave it worldwide fame was when used on a Pink Floyd album cover in 1977, complete with a giant inflatable pink pig tethered to one of the chimneys. On that particular day, pigs certainly did fly as it broke free from its mooring and floated off into the flight path for Heathrow airport, no doubt causing palpitations among both passengers and the crews of approaching jets.

As one stands on the perfectly clean and neat Chelsea Embankment facing directly onto the untidy industrial shore on which the power station stands, a brief insight may be had into what London and the Thames might have been like back in the nineteenth century, when the sky was thick with the clouds of polluting smoke that feature so prominently in the some of the river's portrayals by Turner and Whistler. However, the worst pollution suffered by the capital by the mid-1850s was not borne on the wind, although the stench created by tons of raw sewage certainly was. London's drainage was either by cesspit or by direct discharge into the Thames or its tributaries, cholera epidemics were all too frequent and sewage management was in the hands of self-contained Commissioners of Sewers, each dealing with their own district rather than addressing the needs of the city as a whole.

This changed in 1856 on the foundation of the Metropolitan Board of Works and the appointment of

Sir Joseph Bazalgette as its Chief Engineer. Bazalgette was empowered to design and execute 'a system of sewerage to prevent any part of the sewage within the Metropolis from passing into the River Thames in or near the Metropolis'. Prior to this project being instigated, the banks of the Thames in central London were not protected by an embankment, consisting solely of mud, shingle and sewage, onto which these various drains, outlets and ditches had discharged.

Bazalgette's solution comprised the construction of intercepting sewers both north and south of the Thames and running parallel to the river. These were to receive sewage from the sewers and drains that had previously discharged directly into the Thames and were built behind and below the stone embankments that are such a distinctive feature of London's riverside. From Chelsea to the Victoria Embankment at Westminster on the north bank and the Albert Embankment to the south, all the roads, paths and small riverside gardens that now separate the nearest buildings from the water's edge were all built over Bazalgette's vast underground network. Victorian engineers were renowned for their resourcefulness, doggedness and ingenuity but even so, the construction of the sewers alone represented a major civil engineering project and between 1856 and 1859, 82 miles of interconnecting sewers were built below London's streets, all flowing eastwards by natural gravity. These were in turn connected to hundreds of miles of main and lesser sewers and their combined contents gravitated towards the more sparsely inhabited marshes well to the east of London to be discharged into the river by the Crossness and Abbey Mills pumping stations.

Any doubts about the costs and complexities of such an operation were immediately dispelled by the 'Great Stink' of 1858, when an exceptionally hot summer combined with low water levels to render central London almost uninhabitable from the stench. The other benefit derived from Bazalgette's London Embankments was that they considerably narrowed the width of the Thames, thereby ensuring a faster flow of water, and any sewage or industrial waste that did find its way into the river would be more efficiently and speedily flushed downstream towards the estuary. It would be some years later before actual sewage treatment plants would become part of the human waste disposal solution, but in the meantime, it was decided that to keep the effluent away from a burgeoning population was the most crucial thing.

As the river approaches Vauxhall Bridge it swings north into Lambeth Reach. Grosvenor Road becomes Millbank and, downstream from the bridge, the start of the Albert Embankment along the south bank of the Thames ensures its passage through the heart of London brings a greater sense of symmetry to the waterfront. Unlike its northern counterpart, the Albert Embankment was not created to carry interceptor sewers, but by embanking the reclaimed foreshore, Bazalgette not only reduced the risk of flooding to low lying areas of Lambeth but also alleviated congestion by creating a new riverside road to bypass the existing network of narrow streets. The current Vauxhall Bridge was opened in 1906 and is a quietly unassuming gem built of steel and granite, with monumental bronze statues weighing approximately 2 tons each set above the piers. The figures were created by Alfred Drury and Frederick Pomeroy and apparently symbolize themes such as Agriculture, Education, Local Government, Pottery and Engineering.

The environs of Vauxhall Bridge could be deemed representative of how London's architectural evolution has progressed throughout the latter decades of the twentieth century and into the present, although many traditionalists see it as a regression and opinions remain firmly polarized. The upstream south bank side of the bridge is dominated by the serried ranks of the St George Wharf residential development, whose green glass towers soar above the complex like green glass flower vases. The green-and-cream theme is continued on the upstream side by the Vauxhall Cross Building, a futuristic interpretation of an ancient Mesopotamian ziggurat, the headquarters of MI6, Britain's Secret Intelligence Service.

The unmistakable skyline feature of the north bank between Vauxhall and Lambeth Bridges is the 118-metre-high Millbank Tower, built in 1963, and although clearly regarded as 'cutting edge' fifty years ago, it now appears as a rather bland monolith compared to some of its more flamboyant neighbours. However, it probably will not be too far into the future before it is regarded as fashionably 'retro' and its Listed Building status will ensure it survives to receive that accolade.

Tradition also plays a significant role on the riverside's architecture and there is no better place to find it than the Tate Gallery, now re-branded as Tate Britain since

The main entrance to Lambeth Palace, the London residence of the Archbishops of Canterbury, with the Palace of Westminster standing in the background on the Thames' north bank.

The Palace of Westminster is dominated by the glorious Perpendicular-style Victoria Tower, although it is the clock tower, commonly known as 'Big Ben' that attracts most attention.

Tate Modern was established within the Bankside Power Station, opposite St Paul's Cathedral. The collection of British art from 1500 to the present is housed in the neo-Classical building erected in 1897 and funded by the sugar magnate Sir Henry Tate (1818–99). For much of the nineteenth century, Millbank was dominated by the dour fortress of Millbank Prison, used both as a penitentiary and as a holding place for those awaiting deportation to Australia. The prison was demolished in 1890 and the Tate building erected in its place. Tate Britain houses the major part of the Turner bequest comprising around 300 oil paintings and thousands of sketches and watercolours in the custom-built Clore Gallery.

As the Thames flows along the latter sector of Millbank Reach towards Lambeth Bridge and Westminster, a series of rather staid concrete buildings predominates on both sides of the river, including the grim Portland Stone façade of Thames House, built in 1930 for ICI but now the headquarters of the Britain's other Security Service, MI5. Horseferry Road runs past Thames House onto Lambeth Bridge and prior to the erection of the first bridge, opened in 1869 by Queen Victoria, the ferry that operated there was one of the few capable of actually transporting a coach and horses across the river as one unit. The ferry closed down when Westminster Bridge was built in 1750 but only after compensation terms had been agreed with the Archbishops of Canterbury, whose official London residence, Lambeth Palace sits immediately next to the river crossing.

The setting of Lambeth House, or Manor as it was originally known, might have been convenient in terms of its proximity to Westminster, but thirteenth-century Lambeth was a bleak area of marshland, and even engravings from hundreds of years later still depict the Bishop's residence as an isolated building. The first Archbishop to live there was Stephen Langton, who held office between 1207 until his death in 1228. Langton was one of the driving forces behind the barons' campaign against King John, heading a council of churchmen and barons at Westminster in 1213, at which he called for the renewal of Henry I's Charter of Liberties. That document formed the basis for Magna Carta, drawn up and signed two years later at Runnymede. The Early English-style chapel and crypt survive from Bishop Langton's tenure, and the palace has been added to and remodelled since the thirteenth century. Public access is limited to heavily over-subscribed guided tours although the imposing red-brick Tudor gatehouse and tower built in 1490 by Cardinal John Morton stand close by the Lambeth Bridge roundabout and can be inspected at close quarters.

Glimpses of the Palace's other buildings can be seen from either across the river or the adjoining public space of Archbishop's Park but, having got as far as Lambeth Bridge, the eyes and camera lenses of both long-distance walkers and day visitors will probably be directed more towards Westminster and the world-famous face of Big Ben. Many tourists will probably note the predominately red paint of Lambeth Bridge and the contrasting green of its Westminster counterpart, but not all will be aware of the significance of those colour schemes. Red denotes the colour of the benches within the House of Lords and the House of Commons are fitted out in green.

There can be few more instantly recognized world views than the honey-coloured, neo-gothic Houses of Parliament framed by Victoria Tower at one end and the clock tower of Big Ben at the other. However, had it not been for the disastrous fire of 1834 that gutted most of the buildings, the panorama extending away from Lambeth Bridge today might have been considerably different. The great blaze was so extensive and protracted that it became a tourist attraction and even featured in two dramatic canvases by J.M.W. Turner. The English Parliament is housed in the Palace of Westminster, first established on the site by Edward the Confessor in 1042 so that he could oversee construction of the adjacent Westminster Abbey. The new Norman rulers rebuilt it in stone after the Conquest of 1066 and the palace remained a royal residence used by successive monarchs until another fire in 1512, at which point Henry VIII abandoned the palace in favour of the nearby Palace of Whitehall.

A Royal Commission was established to determine how the palace should be rebuilt and, after much deliberation, decided that it should be in either gothic or Elizabethan style. They held a public competition for which ninety-seven entries (identified only by a symbol or pseudonym) were received. It was the designs and drawings submitted by Charles Barry and Augustus Pugin that were selected. One notable and most precious survivor of the fire was the Great Hall (now Westminster Hall), built by William the Conqueror's son, William Rufus, in 1097, and that historic heart of the original palace was retained as an integral part of the reconstruction plans. The hall's great hammerbeam roof is the largest medieval timber roof in northern Europe and dates back to a remodelling by Richard II towards the end of the fourteenth century.

The palace's great landmark tower, the 98-metre-high Victoria Tower, was for many years the largest square stone tower in the world, designed originally as a royal entrance and repository for Parliamentary records. The Sovereign's Entrance is at the base of the tower and was built wide enough to accommodate the royal coach during State Openings of Parliament. The stairs leading up into the building are known as the Royal Staircase and by tradition the only permitted route when a reigning monarch visits the House of Lords. The symmetry of the building is enhanced by its two other towers, the octagonal central tower and of course, the clock tower commonly referred to as Big Ben, despite that simply being the name of the clock's main bell.

Looking out over the magnificent ensemble of buildings and bridges it is hard to believe that Westminster evolved

from a small community of twelve Benedictine monks established on Thorney Island, a dry piece of land in the marshland that once bordered the Thames. The East Saxons had already built a church there, and the 'west' in Westminster merely indicates that this monastery and its church were located to the west of London's cathedral at St Paul's. From those humble origins arose the great Westminster Abbey that has been the coronation church since William I was crowned there on Christmas Day in 1066. The shrine of the Abbey's founder, Edward the Confessor, sixteen other monarchs and some of the most significant people in the nation's history are buried or commemorated in the Abbey to form one of the finest and most diverse collections of monumental sculpture assembled under one roof.

The present abbey church was begun by in 1245 by Henry III, taking inspiration from such French gothic masterpieces as the cathedrals at Rheims and Amiens, and as with so many other great churches, Westminster evolved over time to incorporate the different phases of gothic architecture. It culminated in the most sublime manifestation of the Perpendicular style used by Henry VII to build a magnificent new Lady Chapel between 1503 and 1519. Its fan-vaulted roof, dripping with stone pendants, is a work of pure genius.

It is an extraordinary experience to stand in Parliament Square flanked by the Palace and Abbey of Westminster and contemplate how much of our national history, sense of identity and the foundations of our laws and the democratic process we take so much for granted is tied up in those two buildings. Although the Thames has still to flow past so much more of London's history and architecture, Westminster nevertheless seems an appropriate place to pause before continuing onwards to the sea.

A detail of the main entrance portal of the Victoria Tower in the Palace of Westminster. Because it was designed as a ceremonial royal entrance, the architect Charles Barry ensured that it was particularly rich in carvings and sculpture. The aura of antiquity achieved in that work is so effective that it hard to believe that it only dates back to the post-fire rebuilding of the mid-nineteenth century.

CHAPTER NINE

England's Tidal Artery
From London to the Sea

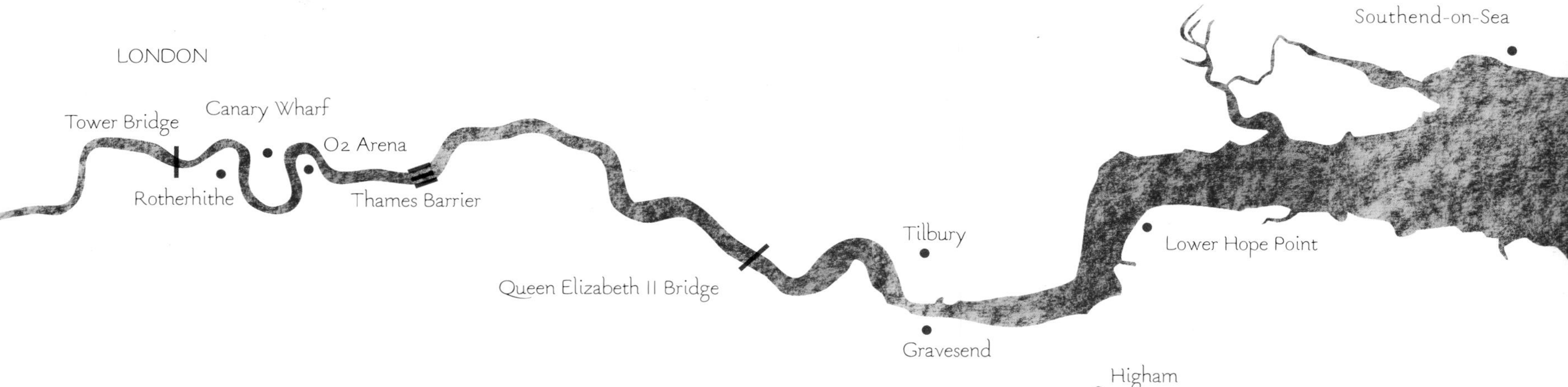

Canaletto's evocative paintings of the newly built Westminster Bridge during the late 1740s serve as an eloquent reminder that the grandest approach to Westminster was by river. However, regardless of the fact that his inimitable style transposes the atmosphere of his native Venice and the Grand Canal to the Thames, it was the elegant marvel of engineering that would have most impressed the contemporary viewer. The palaces of Lambeth and Westminster, centres of ecclesiastical and political power, dominate the skyline, but even during the mid-eighteenth century, their medieval architecture was of only antiquarian interest. The new Westminster Bridge not only opened up the western part of London, but also stood as a symbol for the shift of the capital away from the commercially focused City (with its ancient crowded bridge inhabited by shopkeepers) to a new identity as the home of political power on a global scale.

Symbols of political power lie on both sides of the bridge: national government represented by the Palace of Westminster and the vast complex of ministries and Offices of State centred around Whitehall, whereas London's own administrative body, the Greater London Council, formerly the London County Council, was housed directly across the river in County Hall, a dignified 'Edwardian Baroque' building begun in 1911 and eventually opened by King George V in 1922. The GLC was abolished amid much political acrimony in 1986, with many of its former powers being devolved back to the individual boroughs. The former council was re-organized to become the GLA (Greater London Authority) and is now housed further downstream by Tower Bridge.

County Hall is now very much a tourist attraction, tenanted to hotels, restaurants and is also the home of London's Film Museum, the Sea Life Aquarium and a rather large ferris wheel, the London Eye. The 135-metre-high structure was originally designed as a showpiece to celebrate the Millennium and had been granted planning consent for just five years but has now become a permanent fixture by the Thames. Although entirely different in concept and design, the Eye has done for London what the Eiffel Tower did for Paris, created a publicly accessible symbol that enabled people to enjoy a unique view down into the heart of one of the world's great cities. The glory of the London Eye is its location – set directly opposite the Palace of Westminster and the other historic buildings and streets that radiate away from the Thames and clearly highlight much of London's architectural evolution.

When initially erected alongside Jubilee Gardens, having been assembled on the giant flat barges that brought it up the Thames, the London Eye (or Millennium Wheel as it was then known) had countless detractors and no doubt always will. Architects and planners charged

Originally known as the Millennium Wheel, the London Eye celebrated its tenth birthday in 2010 and appears to have graduated from being a temporary attraction into a permanent fixture. It is an impressive piece of engineering and it is alleged that the view from the summit extends for some 25 miles, but in England, such claims always have to include the phrase, 'on a clear day'.

MOVIEUM
MOVIEUM
DALI
DALI
AQUARIUM

The City of London skyline from Waterloo Bridge presents a constantly changing panorama, as new, state-of-the-art skyscrapers vie with each other to become the tallest or most iconic in the Square Mile. However, no twenty-first-century architectural miracle of concrete, steel and glass will ever diminish the majesty of St Paul's Cathedral.

Opposite top: London's Inner and Middle Temple, divided by Middle Temple Lane, feel like a university, with squares, courts, passages and gardens extending almost down to the river.

Opposite below: The Royal Courts of Justice in The Strand were opened by Queen Victoria in 1882 and are the permanent home of the Supreme Court, a title encompassing the High Court of Justice and the Court of Appeal.

with taking a historic city like London onwards into a new century face a thankless and near-impossible task in attempting to create a harmonious blend between old and new, traditional and cutting edge. The centre of Waterloo Bridge provides the perfect vantage point from which to assimilate London's changing skyline, a panorama studded with prominent office and apartment blocks, but despite their respective individual stature, all are subservient to the big three – St Paul's Cathedral, Tower 42 and 30 St Mary Axe, although Heron Tower will soon be the tallest of all the City skyscrapers.

Despite the claims of many 'young pretenders', the great dome of St Paul's Cathedral has always been *the* image of London. The photograph of it towering unscathed above the smoke and flames after a bombing raid during the Blitz of 1940 became an iconic symbol of Britain's indomitable spirit in the face of seemingly overwhelming odds during the Second World War. The other two dominant buildings are important symbols of London's acceptance that, despite a historical legacy that can be traced back through associated buildings, there is no point in trying to mirror the past through further pastiche and replication. When Tower 42 began its 183-metre climb above the City in 1971, it was known as the NatWest Tower but is now simply named after its number of floors. St Mary Axe is better known as the 'Gherkin' and was built on the former site of the Baltic Exchange, irreparably damaged by a Provisional IRA bomb in 1992.

In the more immediate vicinity of Waterloo Bridge is the South Bank complex, comprising most notably the Royal Festival Hall, Hayward Gallery, Queen Elizabeth Hall, the BFI South Bank (formerly the National Film Theatre) and the Royal National Theatre. The latter is a harsh, geometric building dating from 1976, whose concrete bunker style is not really easy on the eye. However, it does maintain the continuity of the other South Bank buildings that evolved from the 1951 Festival of Britain site and is very much architecture of its time and consequently equally deserving of its place on any list of London's most important buildings. As it has done since Teddington, the Thames Path continues to offer the choice of walking along either bank of the Thames but regardless of whether one is a long-distance walker or just a visitor, I strongly suggest that the northern option from Waterloo Bridge is by far the most rewarding.

As one leaves the exposed, windy plateau of the bridge, the great edifice of Somerset House appears on the right. The choices are to either walk down a flight of steps and continue along the Victoria Embankment beneath its imposing frontage or continue round to the building's main entrance on The Strand. Today's version of Somerset House dates from the 1770s when opened as Britain's first custom-built government office block, whose early occupants included the Navy Board, the Stamp Office (later the Inland Revenue), the Royal Society and the Royal Academy of Arts. For many people, Somerset House will always be associated with the registration of births, marriages and deaths administered there by the General Register Office between 1836 and 1970. The original Somerset House was a mid-sixteenth-century palace built by Edward Seymour, 1st Duke of Somerset (1506–52), who was Lord Protector to the young King Edward VI. Unfortunately, he managed but a couple of years in the palatial residence 'suitable to his high rank' before losing his head on a charge of treason in 1552.

Above: The elaborately carved Norman portal of the circular, twelfth-century Temple Church, built by the Knights Templar.

Below: The Temple's association with the Knight's Templar and the Crusades are marked in several places by 'agnus dei' symbols, including this one on the outer door of the Middle Temple Hall.

A substantial part of Somerset House is now given over to the wonderfully endowed Courtauld galleries and its courtyard is the scene of music events in summer and the home of London's largest artificial ice rink each winter. The original river terrace has now been restored and opened as a café overlooking the Embankment and river beyond. It is extraordinary to think that before Sir Joseph Bazalgette's monumental restructuring of the waterfront to accommodate the great sewer, the Thames (and all its foul-smelling debris) would have lapped right up to the walls of Somerset House. Regardless of whether one continues east along The Strand towards Fleet Street or along the Victoria Embankment, the next important objective is easily overlooked but is a small corner of London that dates back to its earliest medieval period.

Middle Temple Lane or Temple Gardens lead right into the heart of the Middle and Inner Temple, first established as a monastery by the Knights Templar during the twelfth century. Their original round church, consecrated in 1185 by Heraclius, Patriarch of Jerusalem, remains at its heart, although most of the other buildings within the Temple's precincts were destroyed in the Blitz and have been remodelled in Victorian style. One fortunate exception is the Great Hall of the Middle Temple, an almost untouched example of an Elizabethan hall dating from the 1560s. By the mid-fourteenth century, when the royal courts became permanently sited in Westminster, the Temple had become a home for lawyers, who formed two societies there, the Inner and the Middle Temple, which along with Lincoln's Inn and Gray's Inn form the four Inns of Court that have the exclusive right to call men and women to the Bar. The prevailing ambiance within the Temple may be gentle Victorian but there are plenty of reminders of its past through the *agnus dei* (Lamb of God) symbols of the Crusaders that are incorporated into gates, doors and statuary set within the gardens and narrow lanes.

Although the Thames lies just below Temple Gardens, I would still advocate taking one of the Temple exits back onto Fleet Street, because its descent to Ludgate Circus opens up the final approach to St Paul's Cathedral. In reality, it really does not matter how one gets to St Paul's as long as Sir Christopher Wren's great church is not ignored. However, magnificent though the cathedral might be, its architect and his younger colleague, Nicholas Hawksmoor, were also responsible for rebuilding many of the City's eighty-nine parish churches destroyed in the Great Fire of 1666. Despite twentieth-century war damage, Hawksmoor's six churches and fifteen of Wren's original fifty survive to this day, although a keen eye and a degree of patience

will be needed to track some of them down amid the soaring glass, steel and concrete of the City.

One of the most distinctive features of Wren's churches were their elegant spires, and none more so than the famous five-tiered 'wedding cake' of St Brides in Fleet Street. The church is actually invisible from the main road but the tiny alley of Bride's Lane, located immediately before Ludgate Circus, opens out into the smallest of squares into which the church is squeezed. The church that stands today is a faithful recreation of Wren's design, because although St Paul's may have survived the incendiary bomb attack on 29 December 1940, St Bride's was not so lucky. The only gothic church Wren built was St Mary Aldermary, tucked away to the east of St Paul's. Although the architect had essentially been given *carte blanche* by Charles II in the choice of design for his restoration programme, some parishes were more assertive than others in expressing how their place of worship should be restored. A combination of local opinion and the influence of a wealthy benefactor resulted

Opposite: Sir Christopher Wren's glorious five-tiered spire of St Bride's, Fleet Street.

Left: Wren's only gothic-style church in the City was St Mary, Aldermary, justifiably renowned for its glorious vaulted roof.

in a recreation of the original Perpendicular gothic style of the original. Wren adhered to those stipulations in shape and form, but nevertheless introduced his own contribution subtly though the magnificent vaulting. He used plaster instead of stone and created delightful little saucer domes between the fans.

Sir Christopher Wren's knowledge of geometry enabled him to create sensations of depth, space and light that one would have thought impossible from a basic rectangle. St Stephen Walbrook is an outstanding example of his skill in dealing with a restricted ground area. The interior is a perfect rectangle, divided into bays, aisles and a sanctuary by the introduction of sixteen Corinthian columns. The central space is covered by a large lantern-illuminated dome, creating as effect more associated with the Byzantine tradition than that of western Europe. The design, planning and erection of St Stephen's dome were all used as a rehearsal for the ultimate challenge of St Paul's, where the result is so perfectly placed that the acoustics of the church are considered by many to be the finest in London.

Unless time really is of the essence, it really is worth exploring the byways of the City and East End in pursuit of Wren's illusive masterpieces, but no detection work will be required to track down St Paul's Cathedral. Ferris wheels may or may not become permanent features of London's skyline, but St Paul's highly protected status as an iconic symbol of London ensures that it will always be clearly visible through carefully preserved planning corridors. The achievement of designing and building St Paul's is all the more remarkable when one considers just how many other works were attributed to Wren. His energy and enthusiasm would surely have put most of us to shame.

Wren's first model for the cathedral was approved by the king in 1672, but later rejected in the face of public opinion that suggested it was too modest, thereby obliging the king to request a more elaborate design. The revision was presented in the form of an elaborate wooden model, the Great Model (both versions are now displayed in St Paul's) but that was in turn rejected by the clergy as being excessively flamboyant in the manner of European Catholic cathedrals. The resemblance was deemed inappropriate for a staunchly Protestant England anxious to preserve the legacy of the Reformation under its newly restored monarchy. If Wren had a cat, it would surely have been severely bruised by that stage. He redrafted

Right: The choir of St Paul's Cathedral. The elaborate coloured mosaics of the ceiling act as a perfect foil for the dark wood of the Grinling Gibbons carved choir stalls.

Opposite: The dome of St Paul's Cathedral.

the plans and came up with a compromise acceptable to all parties except the architect himself, who thought it lacked the vital inspiration that sets great buildings apart. A royal warrant for the work was issued in May 1675 and the king included a vital clause permitting variation on the approved design that might be 'rather ornamental than essential'.

Because Wren determined to build the cathedral as a whole and not in traditional sections, it would have been difficult to assess the building's form during those early stages when screened by so much scaffolding. The structure that rose from the foundations actually bore an uncanny resemblance to Wren's own favoured design, the rejected 'Great Model' version, including hundreds of modifications to enhance the monumental nature of the building. Much of the work was carried out using 50,000 tonnes of gleaming white Portland stone. Great blocks of it were hauled up from the Thames and then pulled with great difficulty through the narrow streets. In addition, almost 37,000 tonnes of other stone were required and the cathedral accounts detail many compensation payments to those whose buildings were damaged by the cumbersome materials.

Progress became so painfully slow that eventually Wren's salary was halved in an attempt to spur the work on at greater speed. By the time his son placed the last stone on the lantern in 1710, Wren was seventy-nine years old. His magnificent creation distilled key elements from the palaces, châteaux and churches of France. This is most notable in the two tiers of paired Corinthian columns that grace the façade, reminiscent of the Louvre Palace, which Wren saw on a visit to Paris shortly before the Great Fire of London. Wren's other sources included the Italian Baroque architect Borromini, whose work inspired the twin-towers flanking St Paul's west front, and he overcame the complexities of supporting the vast dome by studying Ely Cathedral's 'gravity defying' fourteenth-century lantern tower. In St Paul's, a huge outer drum is constructed above an inner, lower dome. This contains a tall cone of bricks, reinforced by iron chains upon which rests the lightweight timber dome covered in lead sheeting.

The choir of St Paul's Cathedral is probably the nearest that Protestant England has ever come to the Baroque. Its ornate gilded mosaics and saucer domes are extravagant features not normally associated with a rather restrained Anglican church and, perhaps even more surprisingly, were instigated by Queen Victoria's mid-nineteenth-century complaint that the interior was 'most dreary, dingy and undevotional'. It would be safe to say that the work later carried out by Sir William Richmond following extensive field research in Italy certainly eliminated any lingering aura of dreariness. A reasonable degree of physical fitness could be a pre-requisite for being able to fully savour St Paul's as access to the Whispering Gallery around the dome requires the climbing (and descent) of 259 steps and the Golden Gallery located at the top of the dome is 530.

St Paul's is the final resting place of many notable figures such as Nelson and Wellington and whose elaborate monuments adorn the glorious chapels, aisles and transepts of the cathedral. However, one of the most moving memorials is the marble effigy of the poet John Donne, also a dean of the cathedral, who died in 1631 and whose memorial was one the few to survive the Great Fire – scorch marks can still be seen round its base. St Paul's has been undergoing its first ever major cleaning and restoration programme to mark the cathedral's 300th anniversary in 2010 and the results should be astounding. Anyone who has had an old oil painting professionally cleaned will know just how its colour and luminosity are enhanced beyond all expectation, and St Paul's too might reveal something rather special. Sir Christopher Wren is buried in St Paul's but is celebrated by no elaborate funerary sculture – a simple inscription on his tombstone (translated from the Latin) reads 'Reader, if it is a monument you seek, look around you'.

The Great Fire, which burned for several days and destroyed thousands of houses but killed little more than about twenty Londoners, is celebrated by The Monument, built by Wren in 1671–77 and at 61 metres high is still

Left: The Monument stands in the heart of the City and was built by Sir Christopher to commemorate the Great Fire of London and to celebrate the rebuilding of London.

Below: The Millennium Footbridge provides a pedestrian crossing of the Thames between St Paul's and Bankside, the old power station that is now the home of Tate Modern.

Opposite: The faithful recreation of Shakespeare's Globe Theatre was opened in 1997.

the world's tallest free-standing stone column. Its height is exactly the same as the distance between where it stands and the source of the fire. The massive Doric column is surmounted by a flaming urn but it seems this had not been Wren's original intention. He had wanted to place a statue of Charles II on its summit as a celebration of the monarch who restored London, but the king decided that it could equally be interpreted as being to 'Charles II, the king who burnt London'. For those with a head for heights and who have not already scaled the heights of St Paul's, a cantilevered stone staircase of over 300 steps winds up inside The Monument.

However, as The Monument is further east near London Bridge, it may be a detour too far for those exploring the immediate environs of the river, as the south bank of the Thames opposite St Paul's is the next objective and the upper section of the Monument can be seen from a distance on the approach to London Bridge.

Peter's Hill is almost an extension of the cathedral's south transept and runs dead straight down to the Thames and the silver sliver of the Millennium Footbridge. However, both are dwarfed by the massive dark bulk of the old Bankside Power Station, now reincarnated as Tate Modern. This whole segment of the Thames set between Blackfriars and Southwark Bridges is an inspiration because not only does it now contain one of the world's leading galleries of modern art, but also houses the faithful recreation of Shakespeare's Globe Theatre.

Britain's nationwide celebration and marking of the Millennium resulted in numerous grandiose, ill-conceived and wastefully expensive projects, but the Millennium Footbridge and the Bankside conversion were not two of them. Yes, it was more than unfortunate and embarrassing that the bridge had to close almost immediately after it had been opened, but after two years of structural modification, the technical gremlins have been eliminated.

The unexpected oscillations set in motion by the natural sway of people as they walked caused the bridge to sway uncomfortably and quickly became known as the 'Wobbly Bridge'. The design ethos of the bridge was to make it as low profile as possible so that there was minimal visual impairment to the retrospective view of St Paul's, a requirement that necessitated running suspension cables beneath the deck rather than in the customary manner exhibited on some of the river's suspension bridges further upstream. Attempts were made to moderate the problem by limiting the number of pedestrians on the bridge at any one time but the horrendous queues and frayed tempers led to the bridge's complete closure for two years while the problems were rectified.

Bankside was quite a late addition to London's electricity-generating capabilities, the oil-fired power station not coming into operation until 1952. It was commissioned in 1947 as a direct response to serious power shortages, and responsibility for its design was given to Sir Giles Gilbert Scott, an architect and designer with an impressive portfolio that already included Liverpool's Anglican Cathedral, Battersea Power Station and the ubiquitous red telephone kiosk. Bankside closed in 1981 when forced into redundancy by the rapidly escalating price of oil and thereafter spent a dozen years being fought over by various developers and defended by campaigners who wanted it retained as a London landmark. The demolition teams were on the verge of starting to dismantle the building in 1993 when the Tate organization suddenly announced that the Bankside Power Station would be saved, restored and converted into Tate Modern.

The juxtaposition of Bankside and the black-and-white thatched recreation of the Globe Theatre should create an uncomfortable contrast, but the power station is so big and dark that it serves as visual foil to the late-sixteenth-century building. The driving force behind the project was American actor and director Sam Wanamaker, who had apparently visited London in 1949 and been surprised and disappointed to discover no kind of lasting memorial existed to Shakespeare and his riverside theatre. He later founded the organization that would evolve into the Shakespeare Globe Trust,

work began on the site in 1987 and the theatre was opened exactly a decade later. Sadly, Wanamaker died in 1993 but as twelve of the fifteen bays that made up the polygonal building were in place, he could at have had the satisfaction that his dream would be fulfilled.

The original Globe Theatre actually had its origins across the other side of the Thames in Shoreditch and had been the first purpose-built playhouse in London. Prior to the existence of such permanent theatres, playing companies were peripatetic, performing in a variety of locations that included inn yards, college halls or even private houses. The company with which Shakespeare was associated was run by actor-manager James Burbage, but, following an insurmountable problem over the lease, the company moved across to Bankside where they had secured the lease on a plot of land near a rival theatre called the Rose (also scheduled for a future recreation project). Thatch and plaster were comparatively cheap commodities, but building timbers were not and so the original theatre was shipped across the Thames and re-erected. The Globe was burned to the ground following a careless accident during a performance of *Henry VIII* in 1613 when stray wadding from a stage cannon ignited the thatched roof. The theatre was quickly rebuilt with a tiled roof that might well have been more fireproof, but was sadly had no defence against England's Puritan regime when it came to power in 1642 and abolished all such forms of entertainment.

The Globe is thriving once again and plays are performed much as they always were in Shakespeare's day; a three-tiered gallery runs around the theatre's perimeter and an open-air standing area forms the major part of the auditorium in front of the stage – a set-up not dissimilar to the Last Night of the Proms at the Royal Albert Hall. The theatre has obviously been built with flame-retardant materials and the illuminated emergency exits did not feature in the sixteenth-century version, but apart from those concessions to public safety, Shakespeare's work lives on by the Thames.

London Bridge is steeped in the very essence of London's history, and so its current manifestation of pre-stressed concrete is about as visually stimulating as a three-week-old cabbage. This was where London began, almost the very spot where the Romans first stretched a pontoon bridge across the Thames around AD 50, following that temporary structure with a solid pile version some five years later. It was that river crossing and the burgeoning town of Londinium that Boudicca, Queen of the Iceni, razed to the ground in the ferocious, blood-letting revolt by her native tribe in AD 60. The legacy of that devastation recurs in excavations in the capital today, as layers of soot, ash, burned pottery and the possessions of those killed and tortured by the rebellious tribes are unearthed by archaeologists.

The Romans rebuilt both the bridge and Londinium but took the precaution of throwing a wall up around the capital of their new province. London Bridge fell into disrepair when they left, and although there were Saxon crossings there, perhaps the most famous version was the thirteenth-century one with nineteen arches that also had shops and houses built on it. Fortunately, the prospect from the South Bank route of the Thames Path is not all concrete as The Monument pokes its gilded flames above the riverside buildings and the elegant neo-classical façade of Fishmonger's Hall stands as a reminder of the era when the medieval guilds controlled just about every aspect of trade and business in London.

St Katherine's Pier and Tower Bridge with the curiously lopsided glass punctuation mark of City Hall between the bridge's twin towers.

London Bridge marked the upstream boundary of the Pool of London, the segment as far as Tower Bridge referred to as the Upper Pool. Barges, water buses and police launches are now the only traffic ploughing up and down a section of the Thames that was once a mass of shipping. The riverside wharves and warehouses are now offices and luxury apartments, and the only large vessel occupying the Pool is the cruiser HMS *Belfast*, now permanently moored opposite the Tower of London as a floating museum. The Tower itself was also an important component of the expanding English navy under Henry VIII, when it served as the royal armoury. Ships built at the dockyards of Deptford, Greenwich and even on the Channel coast at Portsmouth would sail up to the Tower to be armed.

The Tower of London is the oldest palace, prison and fortress in Europe. Its mighty four-turreted castle keep, the White Tower, was built by William I in 1078. Much of it was the work of Gundulf, the king's master builder from the Abbey of Bec in Normandy, who went on to become both the builder and Bishop of Rochester. Deep in the heart of the White Tower survives one of the purest and most moving examples of the Roman architecture imported by the Normans. The style generally referred to as Romanesque features in many of England's twelfth-century cathedrals and parish churches, where the typical rounded arches and solid pillars were often embellished with elaborate decoration such as the dogtooth or beak head patterns. However, no such adornment clutters the austere chapel of St John, and it really was intended as a humble place of worship and prayer for a devout Christian.

Subsequent monarchs added two rows of curtain walls and a moat, and the Tower served both as a fortress and a prison from the medieval era right up until the Second World War. Some prisoners were just held for a matter of weeks 'while helping the Tudors with their enquiries', others spent the remainder of their lives there and some were executed on Tower Green. As public executions were commonplace, a private appointment with the executioner within the secluded confines of the Green was a privilege of rank afforded to just a handful of prisoners, most notably two of Henry VIII's wives, Anne Boleyn and Catherine Howard.

In medieval times, the majority of prisoners arrived by water, stepping reluctantly ashore at the watergate by the riverside, and so many entered this way it has been known as Traitor's Gate ever since. Once inside the Tower, prisoners were accommodated according to their rank – royalty in the royal apartments, the rest in the small outlying towers linking the curtain walls. As with prisons elsewhere, occupants were allowed creature comforts if they could pay for them and during his time in the Tower, Sir Walter Raleigh even managed to get conjugal visits from his wife.

Contrary to popular belief or Hollywood portrayals, the Tower was not a place where torture was widely practised, and if it was deemed necessary in exceptional circumstances, a royal warrant was required. It appears that obtaining confessions from Catholics during the reign of Elizabeth I was a valid application, although the torturers were at pains to point out it was treason rather than religion they were investigating. Guy Fawkes was brought to the Tower after the failed Gunpowder Plot against James I in 1605 and, having declined to name his co-conspirators, was introduced to the only rack held in England. When his bones began to crack Guy Fawkes' memory suddenly improved and he confessed everything.

Architectural purists might regard torture as simply being incarcerated in the Tower with just one small window looking directly out of the river towards City Hall, the lopsided glass sphere its architects describe as 'geometrically modified'. The home of the Greater London Authority actually 'ticks all the boxes' in terms of environmental considerations, accessibility and landscaping, but it just feels like the wrong building to be facing the Tower of London and immediately adjacent to Tower Bridge. However, as architecture has now become art, and all art is subjective, I can only voice my personal opinion.

Tower Bridge is another of London's iconic buildings, and before the Queen Elizabeth Bridge was opened downstream at the Dartford Crossing, was the most easterly crossing point over the Thames. It was built in 1894 to alleviate the pressure placed upon London Bridge by the rapid rise of goods flowing in and out of the City by road and river. In order to facilitate the passage of shipping through into the Upper Pool, the engineer, John Wolfe-Barry, proposed it should function as a type of drawbridge and its architect, Sir Horace Jones, encased it in a gothic shell to harmonize with the Tower of London alongside. At the time of its construction it was the largest, most advanced bascule bridge in the world, whose arms were raised by steam powered hydraulic pumping engines. Notwithstanding the innovative scientific achievement the bridge works represented, many Victorians castigated it for being an expensive sham.

Above: St Katherine's Dock was one of the earliest casualties of London's commercial docks but has now been successfully redeveloped and rebranded, but with the original Ivory House being retained as a link with the dock's heritage.

Overleaf: The onboard view from a vessel about to pass through the raised bascules of Tower Bridge.

In its early days the bridge was opened up to fifty times a day but now that most of the Port of London's business is conducted way downstream, it might manage just two or three times a week at best. Smaller cruise ships occasionally pass through and berth alongside HMS *Belfast* but most day-to-day river traffic now does not have sufficiently high superstructure to warrant raising the drawbridge. It is perhaps as well that Tower Bridge is so little used because even during the relatively short time it takes to allow one vessel to pass through, a massive traffic jam builds up on the approach roads, and if that was repeated several times a day, the City would become gridlocked.

Almost immediately downstream from Tower Bridge lies the entrance to St Katharine's Dock, a reminder of how the Pool of London might have looked before containerization and an increase in the size of cargo vessels rendered such docks redundant. Prior to the St

Opposite, top: Globe Wharf, Rotherhithe, was a originally a rice warehouse but has now been restored and converted to private apartments.

Below: St Mary's, Rotherhithe. Rotherhithe lies on the south bank, sandwiched between Deptford and Cherry Garden Pier. Despite modern development, it is one of several riverside communities that have managed to retain much of their original character and identity.

Katharine's Docks Bill being passed by Parliament in 1825, the area was a maze of narrow lanes and slum housing located near the hospital of St Katharine from which the dock derived its name. Over 1,200 houses were demolished and 11,000 people displaced when work got under way. The architect, Thomas Telford, had insisted that the warehouses be set as close to the quaysides as possible so that goods might be unloaded directly into them. As the docks handled high-value commodities – such as spices, perfumes, ivory, indigo, sugar and rum – rather than bulk cargoes, the fact that the dock entrance was difficult to access did not matter as those goods were imported in smaller vessels.

However, it was not too long before size did matter and St Katharine's was one of the first London docks to close in 1968. It still functions as a working marina offering berths to sleek-looking yachts, but it is also a floating museum, housing Thames sailing barges, a lightship and other historical craft that once were an integral part of life on the Thames. Although much of the dock's old quayside is now lined with more modern buildings, the old Ivory House of 1852 with its distinctive clock tower serves as a reminder of bygone days.

The comparatively straight reach that began near Blackfriars Bridge and continues on past the narrow entrance to St Katharine's Dock eventually ends when the Thames curves up past Wapping and Shadwell towards Limehouse. Wapping and Shadwell are typical of this stretch of the Thames, communities that became engulfed by the eastward expansion of London docks during the 1830s. For many it meant eviction without compensation, but for others, the docks provided a much-needed source of income. The Shadwell and Wapping complex covered some 30 acres and was made up of dock basins and interconnecting canals. The end came in 1969, when the docks suffered the same fate as St Katharine's, being prematurely closed because steam ships were by then simply too big to manoeuvre in and out of such enclosed areas.

Opposite Shadwell on the south bank lies Rotherhithe, arguably best known for its tunnels, and although motorists are familiar with the current road version, the older Thames Tunnel was built between 1825 and 1843 by Marc Brunel with help from his son, the legendary Isambard Kingdom Brunel. The engine house of that original tunnel, designed to be large enough to accommodate horse-drawn carriages, can be seen from the river and now houses the Brunel Museum. Rotherhithe was a renowned shipbuilding and dock area, whose many riverside wharves are now converted riverside apartments.

One of the most notable landmarks is the tower and spire of the early-eighteenth-century Georgian church of St Mary. Rotherhithe is very much a seaman's place, and lying somewhere in St Mary's churchyard in an unmarked grave is Christopher Jones, master of the Pilgrim Fathers' ship the *Mayflower*, which sailed from Rotherhithe in 1620 to collect supplies from Southampton before setting off on its historic voyage to the New World. The church also has more tangible links to the nation's maritime history through two bishop's chairs and an altar table fashioned from oak timbers salvaged from HMS *Temeraire*, a 98-gunship of the line that fought with Nelson's fleet at the Battle of Trafalgar in 1805. The vessel has been immortalized in Turner's poignant 1839 painting *The Fighting Temeraire*, which now hangs in the National Gallery. The ship is portrayed being towed by a steam-powered tug on its last voyage up the Thames to be broken up at Rotherhithe. The breaker's yard that had the contract happened to be owned by one of St Mary's churchwardens and it was he who donated the wood.

Another distinctive riverside landmark is St Anne, Limehouse, whose gleaming white Baroque lantern tower acted as a guide to shipping when it was built

around 1730. Despite encroachment by modern apartment blocks surrounding the Limehouse Canal basin, the thrice-restored church stands defiant amid the aesthetic mediocrity of its brick and concrete neighbours. St Anne was one of Nicholas Hawksmoor's three outstanding East End churches, and it is extraordinary to contemplate that there was little more than green fields and marshes when it was built to serve a community founded around the local lime kilns – the last of which disappeared in 1935. However, Limehouse will be forever associated with the sleazier side of London's dockland, an area where Chinese sailors settled and naturally set up a community that was home from home. The slums of nineteenth-century Limehouse became renowned as somewhere for middle class men to go and experience the darker side of life amid the brothels and opium dens. It was also a place often featured in contemporary novels and Sherlock Holmes was certainly no stranger to the area.

Above: A high-speed Thames Clipper passenger ferry carves a sharp turn round into Limehouse Reach, passing by the distinctive lantern tower of St Ann's Church and the entrance to Limehouse Basin and the Regent' Canal.

citi

Of course, that was a much more exciting spin to put upon the community than suggesting it was place that offered outstanding laundries and beneficial herbal medicines.

The towering buildings of Canary Wharf are visible from most parts of London but as one leaves Limehouse for the great U-shaped loop of the Thames that encompasses the Isle of Dogs, the architectural elephant in the room can no longer be ignored. Collectively known as Canary Wharf, the development that includes the 235-metre high skyscraper 1 Canada Square and other significant towers rose out of the vacuum created by the closure of the West India and Millwall Docks in the 1980s. They had fared better than some of their smaller counterparts further upstream in the Pool of London due to significantly better access; the Isle of Dogs really did become an island when a ship canal was cut across the peninsula shortly after the West India Docks were opened in the early nineteenth century. However, regardless of how hard the dock owners baled, the unstoppable torpedo of containerization had holed traditional methods below the waterline.

Lights burn brightly now on every floor of Canary Wharf, but it was not always so, and after the brash financial boom years of the late 1980s, the harsh realities of life after the early 1990s property crash hit the developers hard. However, Canary Wharf now thrives as a financial, shopping and business centre, serviced by the superb Docklands Light Railway. The Thames Path hugs the Millwall waterfront and the scene along the straightest section is significantly quieter today than it was at the end of January in 1858 when Isambard Kingdom Brunel's leviathan the SS *Great Eastern* was launched into the Thames. If she had been stood on her stern, the ship's bow would have been just 24 metres shorter than 1 Canada Square.

After a seemingly never ending succession of high-rise buildings, custom-built apartment blocks and converted warehouses, the Thames finally opens up towards the southern tip of the Isle of Dogs to give the first glorious sighting of Greenwich. We may currently be walking along the 'wrong' side of the river but the views of the Royal Naval College, Queen's House and Royal Observatory can only be fully appreciated from distance. The matter of regaining the southern shore can be addressed either by walking through the Greenwich Foot Tunnel leading under the river from the Island Gardens set directly across from the Royal Naval College, or from one of the DLR stations on the peninsula that connect to Greenwich. Regardless of how one plans to cross the Thames, it is worth making the pilgrimage to Island Gardens to pay homage to the vision of Wren, Hawksmoor, Vanbrugh and Inigo Jones, because only from that one spot can the pure symmetry of their work be seen as it was intended.

The Royal Naval College was originally commission by James II's daughter Mary during her joint rule with William of Orange. Appalled by the injuries to English sailors sustained in conflicts with the French, she wished to establish a hospital for disabled sailors similar to the Royal Military Hospital in Chelsea. Queen Mary's choice of site maintained the association between Greenwich and the navy that began with the Tudor monarchs. Inigo Jones had designed the perfectly proportioned Queen's House for Anne of Denmark in 1616, but the palace degenerated during the Commonwealth. Charles II had held ambitious plans for a new 'King's House' near by but luckily lack of funds brought work to a halt after the completion of just one wing.

Mary died from smallpox in 1694 aged just thirty-two, and despite being utterly devastated by

Above: When the West India Docks opened on the Isle of Dogs in 1802, they were considered the greatest civil engineering achievement of that era. The Canary Wharf estate that now stands on the site represents an equally impressive achievement, at the heart of which stands the giant pyramid-capped tower of 1 Canada Square.

Opposite: Although much of London's Docklands has been rebuilt or redeveloped, the creeks and inlets that once opened into bustling wharves and quays still punctuate the banks of the Thames.

Right: The Royal Hospital, Greenwich, was designed by Sir Christopher Wren and completed by Sir John Vanbrugh and Nicholas Hawksmoor. Although planned differently at the outset, the great hospital ended up as two perfect symmetrical sections because Queen Mary decreed that the view of the Thames from the Queen's House should not be obstructed.

her untimely death, William vowed to honour what she had described as 'the darling project of my life'. Sir Christopher Wren had been appointed to design the hospital, although his initial proposal to demolish everything on the site, including Inigo Jones' creation and the other Tudor buildings, had fortunately been rejected by the queen in 1694. Over the next fifty years, Hawksmoor and Vanbrugh were among the celebrated architects who continued the project. The final hospital building consisted of two equal segments, symmetrical masterpieces with the Queen's House as their axis. Although the latter building is architecturally inconsistent in scale, the view from it and the historical legacy of the site remain intact.

The Royal Naval College moved into the hospital in 1873 and remained until the late-twentieth century while the Queen's House is the present home of the National Maritime Museum. One of the hospital's triumphs is the Painted Hall, planned by Wren as the dining hall. It is remarkable for the glorious decoration by James Thornhill, which was began in 1707 and completed nineteen years later. The room became too small to accommodate the increasing number of pensioners and was unused until January 1806 when the ceiling painting (depicting Peace and Liberty triumphing over Tyranny) provided an appropriate canopy for the body of Admiral Lord Nelson. Having been brought back from Trafalgar, it lay in state there until it was taken up the Thames for burial at St Paul's Cathedral.

Set high above the classical buildings is Flamsteed House, the original Royal Observatory, commissioned by Charles II in the hope that the compilation of accurate astronomical charts and lunar tables might help to reduce the uncertainties of navigation. Of greatest urgency was the need to resolve the problem of how to accurately calculate longitude, essential in plotting a position at sea. The problem was eventually put out to a general competition ordered by the Longitude Act of 1714 and, much to the chagrin of the scientific community, a solution was found by a clockmaker rather than an astronomer. John Harrison's pendulum-free was impervious to extremes of temperature and the pitch and roll of a vessel at sea.

It accompanied Captain James Cook on his remarkable voyage of 1768–71, an expedition on which he drew on the chronometer's accuracy to produced detailed maps of the Pacific, Australia and New Zealand, claiming the eastern part of Australia for the Crown while he was there. The distinctive red time ball was set up on the roof of Flamsteed House in

Above: An ensemble view of Greenwich showing the Royal Hospital, Queen's House and the Royal Observatory set high upon the summit of Greenwich Park.

Left: The legendary tea clipper, *Cutty Sark*, photographed before the 2007 fire that almost destroyed it.

Above: After having appeared to be in terminal decline, the Millennium Dome has taken on a new lease of life as the O_2 Arena, and has suddenly become a world-famous concert venue and is also scheduled to host the gymnastics competition of the 2012 London Olympics.

Below: The giant cowls of the Thames Barrier at Woolwich.

1833 as a visual signal for mariners on the Thames by which to calibrate their chronometers. The ball was dropped at 1pm rather than noon, as the astronomers were engaged in their own duties of measuring the sun as it passed the local meridian at midday. Flamsteed House is just one part of an extensive visitor centre based upon the Royal Observatory and combines with the outstandingly well presented National Maritime Museum to create one of the most informative and worthwhile tourist destinations in Britain.

The majority of visitors start their visit to Greenwich down by the river, drawn by the rigging and spars and masts of the nineteenth-century tea clipper *Cutty Sark*. A disastrous fire during restoration work in 2007 could easily have resulted in the destruction of the historic vessel, but she is being saved, albeit at great cost. The tea clippers that brought the new season's harvest from China created considerable excitement in England and fortunes were staked on the outcome. One of the earliest entrepreneurs in the increasingly popular commodity of tea was Thomas Twining, who opened his first tea house on The Strand in 1706 and whose company logo is thought to be one of the oldest trademarks marks still in continuous use.

Because the north bank route of the Thames Path terminates in Island Gardens, there is just the southern option to follow onwards to Woolwich and the conclusion of the National Trail at the Thames Barrier. Unfortunately, that also involves a circumnavigation of North Greenwich, an upturned thumb-shaped spit of land around which the river charts an acute course before straightening out to pass through the Barrier. Opposite the tip of the thumb is the entrance to Bow Creek and the confluence of the River Lea, but perched on the very edge of the peninsula is the Millennium Dome, finally saved from further humiliation as the whitest of white elephants by being repackaged, re-branded and turned into the now hugely successful sporting and entertainment venue, the O_2 Arena. It was conceived in 1994 and intended to be something so spectacularly wonderful that a projected 12 million visitors would descend from all corners of the nation to visit the Ninth Wonder of the World. The design of Richard Rogers' structure was brilliantly innovative, and although a large area of toxic land was permanently cleaned up to accommodate the Dome, it still cost an awful lot of money.

For Thames Path walkers the end looms ever closer as the great stainless steel piers of the Barrier fill the river. The great cowls have two sections; the larger of the two houses machinery and the smaller carries a maintenance lift shaft. Their purpose is to control and operate ten massive gates positioned end to end for 520 metres across the river bed. In the event of a storm forecast or the likelihood of tidal surges, the gates pivot up through 90 degrees to effectively seal off the Thames and thereby potentially offering flood protection to 125 square kilometres of central London. The gates weigh a massive 3,300 tonnes and, when fully raised, stand as tall as a five-storey building and the good news is that it is possible to see them in action during routine maintenance closures without having to keep one eye open for the incoming tidal wave.

The Thames Barrier Park is the place to visit, as it not only gives great vantage point to see the structures but is also refreshing in its own right – a creatively designed space whose central feature, the Green Dock, is intended to reflect the river's ever-changing spectrum of tints, shades and shapes. From close to the river, there is a fascinating upstream panorama comprising the Barrier in the foreground, the Dome in the mid-distance and the ever-present Canary Wharf dominating the skyline. First-time visitors might be slightly alarmed to see planes sharply banking or descending just across the Thames but that is the site of another regeneration success story. The vast watery wastelands that were the Royal Docks now flank London City airport, and the whole area has been successfully regenerated. Due to their vast size, the Royals kept going longer than all the other London dock complexes further upstream, but they too eventually had to bow to the inevitable onset of irrevocable changes in the way that goods were shipped around the world.

Between the Barrier and Gravesend, the Thames is not the most appealing companion, as it is reduced to a blend of marshes, industrial sites, the Ford Motor Works at Dagenham and, of course, the famous Crossness Sewage Works, which were originally the culmination of Sir Joseph Bazalgette's master plan to clean the river and free London from the risk of disease caused by poor sanitation and an inadequate sewerage system. The works are now one of the largest and most modern in Europe but the original pumping station still stands, a Grade I Listed Industrial Building constructed in a Romanesque style with some spectacular ornamental cast ironwork. Another spectacular structure from a more recent era is the Queen Elizabeth II Bridge, opened in 1991 to double the capacity of the Dartford Crossing. Prior to its construction, all traffic used the Dartford Tunnel, but the bridge now carries the southbound flow and both bores of the tunnel take vehicles northwards.

The bridge was the largest cable-stayed bridge in Europe at the time it was built but that mantle has passed to others, including the Second Severn Crossing. Nevertheless, it is a spectacular sight and, for motorists driving over 55 metres above the Thames, keeping one's concentration can be difficult as the views are far-reaching. The only downside is that those vistas comprise mainly fuel storage depots. The central span of the bridge is 450 metres and its entire length

The Royal Docks may now be lined with hotels, apartment blocks and exhibition centres, but when only the gaunt silhouettes of the old cranes are discernable in the fading light, it is easy to imagine what an incredible sight the working docks must have presented.

Above: A traditional Thames Sailing Barge appears totally dwarfed by the massive chimneys of Tilbury Power Station.

Below: Gravesend Pier is the oldest remaining cast-iron pier in the world, by William Tierney Clark (who also designed Marlow suspension bridge).

including approach viaducts is almost 3 kilometres. Drivers will also be pleased to know that the concrete pier foundations have been designed to absorb impact from a dead-weight 65,000 tonnage vessel travelling at 10 knots. This is a toll bridge, and early predictions were that it would recoup its cost within a time span of between fourteen and twenty years, so we cannot have long to wait for free passage.

Around the next bend in the river, having left the crossing behind, the giant chimneys of Tilbury Power Station may visually dominate the scene, but almost unseen on the north bank lies the vast 800-acre estate of Tilbury Docks, now the official Port of London. Tilbury occupied a strategic position long before the docks arrived, a point emphasized by the presence of Tilbury Fort, a superb piece of seventeenth-century military engineering built to resist Dutch and French invasions. It was near here that Elizabeth I was alleged to have made her famous address to the troops in 1588 as the Spanish Armada advanced up the Channel.

Directly opposite Tilbury lies the town of Gravesend, whose waterfront still has the atmosphere of the Victorian resort to where people flocked in special excursion steamers to stroll along the gardens or just savour the sea air. Both Gravesend and Tilbury were regarded as front-line defences against sea-borne attack and were fortified accordingly. Henry VIII built a fort there in 1543, but the town is particularly noted for its later association with General Gordon (of Khartoum) who lived there while overseeing construction of several forts downstream from Gravesend. Some of his earthworks in the town were transformed into a public park and there is a Khartoum Place there. Although now not on the main tourist trail, Americans do still travel to Gravesend in search of Pocahontas (1595–1617) and will find a bronze statue of the Indian 'princess' in St George's churchyard. Stories and legends about her history are many and various, but what is known for sure is that she had been converted to Christianity, married a settler named John Rolfe and, accompanied by an entourage of other Indians, returned to England with him in 1616 as Lady Rebecca Rolfe and was presented at the court of James I. In March the following year, she was returning to the colony of Virginia

Right: The churchyard of St George's, Gravesend, contains a statue to the Native American 'princess' Pocahontas, who died while returning to Virginia and was buried at Gravesend in 1617.

Below: St Helen's, Cliffe, stands large and remote among trees above the marshes of the Thames estuary on the Hoo Peninsula. The cruciform church is predominately Early English, but has magnificent sedila, stalls and screen from the later Decorated period.

The tide goes out an awfully long way at Southend-on-Sea, and although the exposed mudflats beyond the seafront might be good for wading birds, they do not appear too inviting for those hoping to build sand castles.

in the governor's ship when she became seriously ill and was taken ashore at Gravesend. She was buried in the old church that once stood on the site now occupied by the present building.

Charles Dickens is very much associated with the landscape of the Thames estuary and spent the last years of his life in the village of Higham, set in an elevated location overlooking the river. He had apparently first seen and admired the house in childhood and was later in a position to purchase it, spending the last years of his life there from 1856–70. His son, Charles Dickens Junior, inherited the house but was not able to live there due to ill-health, and in 1924 the house became Gads Hill School and remains so to this day. The main road from Higham continues on to the Medway towns, but minor roads also fan out from the village down into the bleak expanses of the Hoo Peninsula. Both those roads and the few villages they serve gradually peter out before the high ground gives way to marshes and grazing land. Two of the last settlements encountered upon the edge of the low chalk escarpment are Cliffe and Cooling.

Cliffe is noted for its magnificent cruciform church, stylishly constructed from alternating layers of Kent ragstone and squared black flint. It stands on one of the very last vestiges of high ground, and from the edge of its graveyard, the ground just falls away onto the marshes. The parish church dedicated to St Helen is one of the largest in Kent and its size indicates that the village was a place of greater stature in the past. During the late-medieval period Cliffe supported a port, but a disastrous fire in 1520 stifled its growth but the village did return to greater prosperity with the development of a cement industry based upon the chalk cliffs from which the village derives its name. The road passing through the village continues to skirt around the edge of the marsh in a loop, on the farthest side of which is Cooling.

The village itself is unremarkable, but the thirteenth-century church of St James the Greater is famous as being the probable setting for the first chapter of Charles Dickens' novel *Great Expectations.* The churchyard is an appropriately sombre place and noted for its poignant collection of infant graves numbering thirteen, all clustered around the base of one adult headstone. The dead infants were not all from the same family and died in the eighteenth and nineteenth centuries aged from just one month to a little under two years. In the passage describing Pip's first encounter with the escaped convict, Magwitch, Dickens actually reduces their number, describing them as 'five little stone lozenges each about a foot and half long which were arranged in a neat row'.

From either Cooling or Cliffe, numerous farm tracks and paths lead across fields and marshes towards the estuary, crossing some of the narrow creeks and drainage channels via bridges of varying degrees of stability. One of best places to head for is Lower Hope Point, known as the starting point for the Thames Sailing Barge Match (see pages 143–4), but also a wonderful place to take stock of the Thames as it makes its way out to the sea. Despite the chimneys of Tilbury Power Station looming larger than seems appropriate in such a remote setting, the Thames has returned to a feeling of post-industrial tranquillity. The forts whose guns were seldom fired in anger are now clusters of masonry; wharves once used to load cement onto barges are but skeletal timber perches used by seagulls; and even the solid concrete sea wall does not really intrude upon the atmosphere of the salt marshes. One ancient stone monument set against the sea wall that does seem somewhat out of place is known as the Waterman's Stone, placed there to mark the official seaward limit of the licences granted to Thames Watermen.

The Kent coast continues on round towards Margate but to progress that far east takes one into the North Sea, and it would be far better to bid farewell to the southern shore of the Thames while one can still see the opposite shore. That northern bank of the widening river stands in total contrast – a heavily populated coastal strip culminating in the resort of Southend-on-Sea. If nothing else, Southend is famous for its pier, a remarkably durable structure extending out into the mudflats of the estuary for well over a mile. Since originally built in 1830 it has survived two wars, fires, boat crashes, economic decline and some pretty ferocious weather. It has been truncated yet again after a fire in 2005 destroyed the pier head and station, but the little trains still run out into the Thames estuary and anglers dangle rods over the side in hope rather than expectation.

At low tide, the Thames seems a world away, distinguished as a river only by the faint outlines of container ships making their way up the deep channel to Tilbury. The mudflats are filled with precariously perched yachts, waiting patiently for a high tide and their weekend sailors. But, as with its Kentish counterpart the Essex shore also soon leaves all traces of civilization behind and nature is once more in control. As one stares out over the vast expanses of sea and sky, it seems an awfully long way away from the tiny stream bubbling up from a field in rural Gloucestershire.

Below: Brightly painted beach huts at Southend offer respite from the biting estuary winds, and their owners can happily huddle around a flask of tea and watch the dinghies as they wobble around on the mud.

Overleaf: Journey's end!

Index

Page numbers in *italic* refer to captions

Useful contacts

Conservation

English Heritage
www.english-heritage.org.uk

National Trust
www.nationaltrust.org.uk

Society of Antiquaries
of London
www.sal.org.uk

Kelmscott Manor
www.kelmscottmanor.org.uk

Churches Conservation Trust
www.visitchurches.org.uk

Society for the Protection of
Ancient Buildings (SPAB)
www.spab.org.uk

River Thames

Environment Agency
www.visitthames.co.uk

Port of London Authority
www.pla.co.uk

The Boat Race
www.theboatrace.org

Thames Sailing Barge Match
www.thamesmatch.co.uk

Head of the River Races
www.horr.co.uk

Acknowledgments

Grateful thanks to my editor at Frances Lincoln, Michael Brunström, who has worked miracles on a manuscript that probably meandered significantly more than the many serpentine loops of the infant Thames.

I am also hugely grateful to the book's designer, Maria Charalambous, for making the book look so good by harmoniously blending text and images together to create an atmospheric and informative journey down England's most iconic waterway.

I would also like to offer my sincere thanks to English Heritage, the National Trust, the Society of Antiquaries of London and the Churches Conservation Trust for allowing to me to use photographs taken on the various properties in their care. Our priceless architectural heritage would be in a significantly more parlous state if it were not for the tireless efforts of all our conservation bodies, be they large national organizations or simply local volunteer groups.

Frances Lincoln Ltd
4 Torriano Mews
Torriano Avenue
London NW5 2RZ
www.franceslincoln.com

The River Thames

First Frances Lincoln edition 2010

A catalogue record for this book is available from the British Library.

ISBN 978-0-7112-2958-7

Printed and bound in China

2 4 6 8 9 7 5 3 1

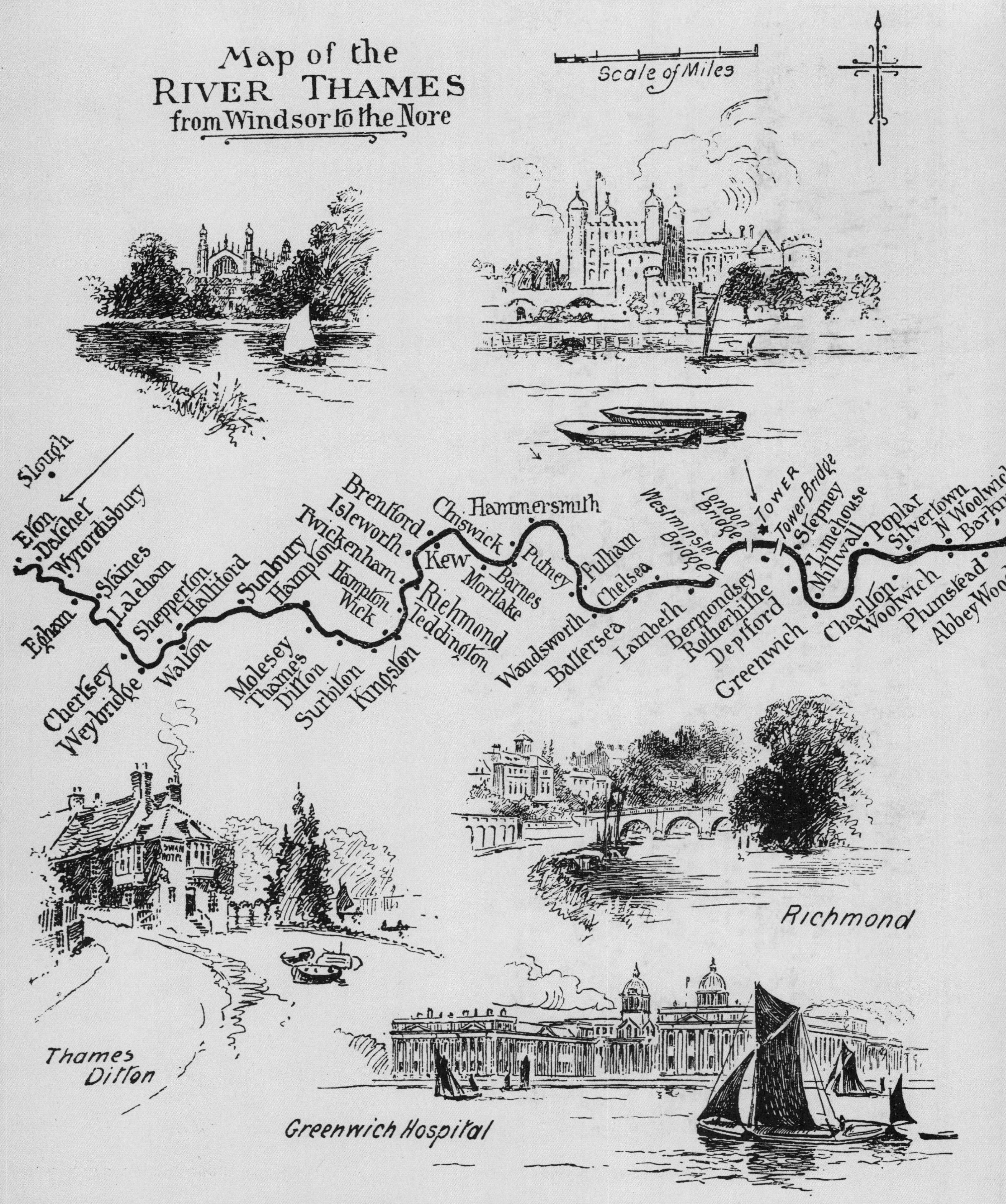
Map of the
RIVER THAMES
from Windsor to the Nore
Scale of Miles
Slough
Eton
Datchet
Wyrardisbury
Staines
Egham
Laleham
Chertsey
Weybridge
Shepperton
Halliford
Walton
Sunbury
Hampton
Molesey
Thames Ditton
Surbiton
Hampton Wick
Kingston
Twickenham
Isleworth
Brentford
Richmond
Teddington
Kew
Chiswick
Mortlake
Barnes
Hammersmith
Putney
Wandsworth
Fulham
Chelsea
Battersea
Lambeth
Westminster Bridge
London Bridge
TOWER
Tower Bridge
Bermondsey
Rotherhithe
Deptford
Greenwich
Stepney
Limehouse
Millwall
Poplar
Silvertown
Charlton
Woolwich
N Woolwich
Plumstead
Abbey Wood
Richmond
Thames Ditton
Greenwich Hospital